THE LAST EMPERORS OF VIETNAM

THE LAST EMPERORS OF VIETNAM

FROM TU DUC TO BAO DAI

Oscar Chapuis

CONTRIBUTIONS IN ASIAN STUDIES, NUMBER 7

GREENWOOD PRESS
WESTPORT, CONNECTICUT • LONDON

Library of Congress Cataloging-in-Publication Data

Chapuis, Oscar.
    The last emperors of Vietnam : from Tu Duc to Bao Dai / Oscar Chapuis.
        p.   cm.—(Contributions in Asian studies, ISSN 1053–1866 ; no. 7)
    Includes bibliographical references and index.
    ISBN 0–313–31170–6 (alk. paper)
        1. Vietnam—History—19th century.   2. Vietnam—History—20th century.   3.
    Vietnam—Kings and rulers.   I. Title.   II. Series.
    DS556.8.C4   2000
    959.7'03—dc21   99–047094

British Library Cataloguing in Publication Data is available.

Library of Congress Catalog Card Number: 99–047094
ISBN: 0–313–31170–6
ISSN: 1053–1866

First published in 2000

Greenwood Press, 88 Post Road West, Westport, CT 06881
An imprint of Greenwood Publishing Group, Inc.
www.greenwood.com

Printed in the United States of America

The paper used in this book complies with the
Permanent Paper Standard issued by the National
Information Standards Organization (Z39.48–1984).

10 9 8 7 6 5 4 3 2 1

TO MY DAUGHTER SOLANGE VALERIE CHAPUIS

CONTENTS

ACKNOWLEDGMENTS

I wish to thank David Totzke for his assistance in the field of word processing, Allan Dyer and Sarah Barnhart for their diligence in copying and printing, and Le Thien Thanh and Dr. Bui Dac Hum for their Vietnamese documentation. I am also grateful to the Library of the University of South Florida for its courteous hospitality.

Last but not least, I am deeply indebted to Greenwood Publishing Group, especially to Heather Staines, History Editor, for her continuous support, and Betty C. Pessagno, Production Editor, and her team, for helping to make this work a reality.

Map 1 The Yang Tze Kiang

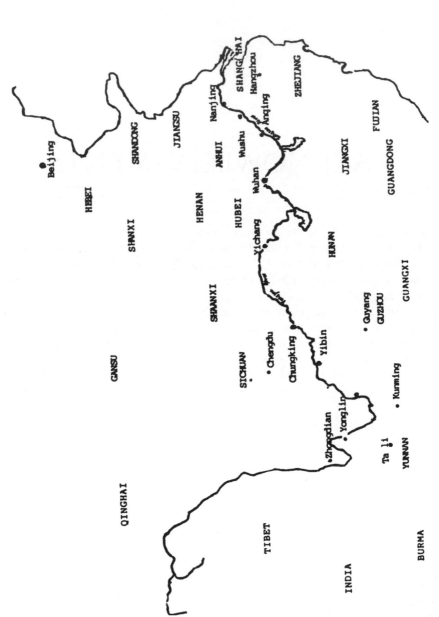

Map 2   The Mekong and the Red River

Map 3   RC4: Street without hope

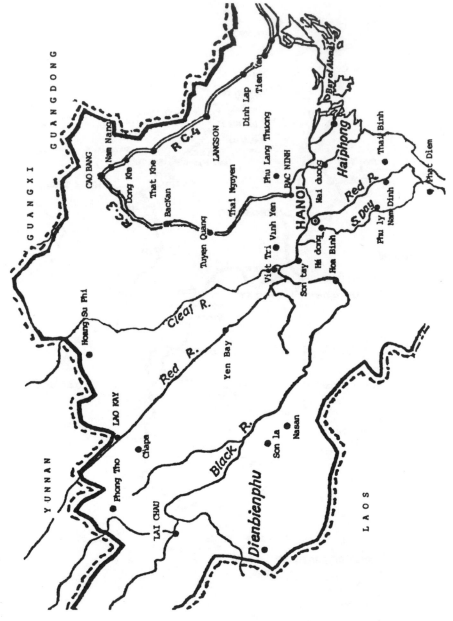

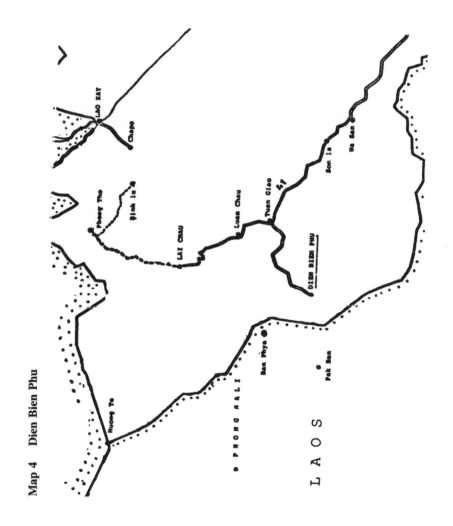

Map 4   Dien Bien Phu

INTRODUCTION

CHINA, VIETNAM, FRANCE: AN OVERVIEW

In the 19th century, the Sons of Heaven began to phase out of a world they had ruled for some 5,000 years. The long disintegration process began with the warring states (403–221 B.C.) and continued with successive dynastic usurpations. In 1388, the White Lotus general Chu Yuan Chang became the founder of the Ming Dynasty, which later was brought down by the Manchu Nurhachi (1559–1626) who began the Ch'ing Dynasty. From then on, the Ch'ing had to continually fight against the White Lotus millennarians in the north and the secret society Triads in the south. After having crushed these internal revolts, the Ch'ing had to deal with western aggression. As for the White Lotus, they spread to adjacent countries where, under various religious denominations, they become involved in emancipation struggles.

In 1840, instead of paying their trade in silver currency, the British East India Company compelled China to accept opium bread from India. In response, the Special Commissioner Li Hung Chang destroyed the British opium stock, which he later refused to indemnify. When a Chinese was murdered by British sailors, Li Hung Chang ordered the withholding of all foreign shipments. The British reacted by sending 20 gun ships with 4,000 troops to destroy Chinese coastal cities and Guangzhou. Their armed vessels were the advanced guard of a commercial fleet loaded with opium. This was the "Opium War" which British prime minister Gladstone described as "a war more unjust in its origin . . . I do not know and have not read of."[1] Two years later in 1842, an exhausted China had to sign the Treaty of Nanking, which opened five ports, including Shanghai, to international trade. In addition, Hong Kong became a British colony.

As for the French, taking advantage of a temporary lull (1830–1860) and with British approval, they also went on to create havoc in China. By the time of the Treaty of Whampoa in 1844, they had several Chinese ports opened to French trade and religion. That year, the United States obtained the same rights with the Treaty of Wanghsia.

In 1850, the impotence of the Chinese government and the influence of Protestant Christianity led to the outbreak of the Tai Pings, who seized half of the country and established the capital of Nanking. Their leader, a Christian mystic named Hong Xiu Quan, who claimed to be a brother of Jesus Christ, was supported by the West. But when his European allies sided with the imperial government and turned against him, he was defeated and committed suicide.

In 1856, hostilities resumed in Kwang Si after French missionary Chapdelaine was executed in Hsi Ling (Kwang Si) and a British ship was detained by the Chinese authorities. This was enough for France and Great Britain to dispatch several gunboats to seize Canton. This was known as the "gunboats diplomacy," which ended in 1858 by the treaty of Tien Tsin. China had to pay as war reparations 30 million pounds sterling to England and 15 million to France. Eleven Chinese ports were now opened to European trade.

The following year, 1859, Dowager Tzu Hsi, convinced that the Boxer rebels retained supernatural powers, allowed her troops to join the insurgents in a common assault against the foreign legations. In retaliation, 12,000 western soldiers stormed Peking and destroyed the Summer Palace. Tzu Hsi fled. She came back to sign the treaty of Peking on October 25, 1860. If it were not for the U.S. proposal of an Open Door policy, China could have become a western colony.

Treaties with China had ominous backlashes. Because westerners were allowed free trade, their first objective was to reach Yunnan, reputed to be the Chinese El Dorado. What was supposed to be the ideal road—the great Yang Tse Kiang River with its three splendid gorges—was nothing but a great disillusion. Thus, while the British went back to India to explore the Irrawady River, the French moved to Vietnam, determined to explore the Mekong. In the process, they secured control of Cochinchina (South Vietnam).

Actually, Vietnam policy was not explicitly formulated by the French government until Napoleon III. At the outset, the French presence was made possible by a quid pro quo among sailors, traders, and missionaries. The last-named provided political economic information on the Far East in exchange for transportation facilities on board merchant ships. The first missionaries even had to disguise themselves as traders, hence creating quite a confusion about their real activities.

In France, to win support for a conquest of Annam, they spread tales of a fabulous country where "gold was found everywhere even in ducks' feces." The French East India Company, created by Louis XIV's finance minister Colbert in 1664, took some initiative to establish in Asia. From 1732 to 1741, Thomas de St. Phalle relentlessly advocated the conquest of Vietnam. But before him, since 1720, Pierre Poivre had already been exploring Nam Ha (Cochinchina) as a missionary, and later he became a silk trader in China. In 1740, Dupleix, governor of the French East India Company, succeeded in ousting the British from Madras and Pondicherry. But six years later, the French were expelled from Madras and set about looking for more bases in the Far East.

In 1748, Pierre Poivre became an expert on Cochinchina politics. Having secured a position within the French East India Company, he succeeded in obtaining the direction of a trade mission for the account of the company. He had problems with a powerful ruler, Lord Nguyen Phuoc Khoat (Vu Vuong), who not only did not pay for his purchases, but was even less easy to deal with when Poivre, without his permission, left Vietnam with an attractive male interpreter, Michel Cuong, perhaps as collateral for imperial debt. This incident, which in our present culture is simply a fact of life, assumed unexpected proportions: Missionaries were banned from Nam Ha until Bishop Bennetat, under order from Dupleix, was able to locate Poivre with Cuong in the middle of Mauritius Island. Thus, relations resumed between France and Annam but not the way the French expected.

In 1758, Admiral d'Estaing sired the idea of dispatching an expedition just for the purpose of looting royal treasures in Phu Xuan (Hue). Perhaps, at that time, it was the way French businessmen recovered their losses. Anyway, his expedition ended in disaster.[2]

Ten years later, in 1768, de Choiseul, war minister under Louis XV, envisaged with the French East India Company an expedition against Nam Ha, but in 1770 he fell into disgrace and the French East India Company, after the recall of Dupleix, collapsed for lack of government support.

In Nam Ha,[3] rivalry developed among Jesuit, Lazarist, and Dominican missionaries, which resulted in the elimination of the Jesuit team in 1774. Whether a secret expedition ordered by French foreign minister Vergennes had any relation to this Jesuit problem was not clear. Yet, in 1787, an event of primordial importance occurred, which was to have a definite impact on Franco-Annamite[4] relations. In November 1787, the Treaty of Versailles was signed with Lord Nguyen Anh, the future Emperor Gia Long, by which King Louis XVI would provide Nguyen Anh with a contingent of troops in exchange for ownership of Poulo Condore Island and the port of Danang, and unrestricted rights to establish trade factories all over Nam Ha. Negotiated by Bishop Pigneau de Behaine for the account of Nguyen Anh, the treaty was conspicuously silent on missionaries' rights. It was probably a mistake in Pigneau's calculations, since he took for granted that later Nguyen would pay him back with money and religious privileges.

France never implemented the 1787 treaty. Although the 1789 Great Revolution was given as an excuse, history reveals that the Governor Count de Conway of Pondicherry had received discretionary power to implement the agreement. Because he chose not to cooperate with Pigneau, the bishop had to build up the expedition at his own expense. Nguyen Anh became Emperor Gia Long. In spite of his debt toward Pigneau, he had to protect his country's interests. Thus, at the first sign of French interference, he secretly instructed his successors to keep them at arms' length.

After the death of Gia Long, his son Minh Mang, who as a good Confucian did not like Catholic missionaries particularly after Le Van Khoi's revolt, began to show systematic hostility toward France. First he courteously rejected a friendship treaty offered by Jean Baptiste Chaigneau, who was acting then as the French consul in Hue. Later, he again refused audience to Captains Courson and de Bougainville when they came to Danang. In 1824, utterly disenchanted, Chaigneau definitively left Vietnam with Vannier. In 1826, France made the last effort for diplomatic resumption by appointing Eugene Chaigneau to succeed his uncle Jean Baptiste, a French consul. He was never able to obtain one audience with Minh Mang. After he left, France made no further attempts.

It was the beginning of a period of isolation in which the new emperor, following the 1637 Japanese example, closed his country to missionaries and official trade. By the end of his reign, the opium war was a dominant concern to Minh Mang. Professor Paul Mus reported that what happened in China "gave Minh Mang a new perspective on the dark dangers which came from the West."[5] The presence of the Spanish in the Philippines, the Dutch in Indonesia, and a French consulate in Manila, let alone the French Far East fleet cruising endlessly in the South China Sea, were his motivation for sending a friendship mission to France and other European nations. The resulting fiasco evidenced their alienation after the barbaric execution of Father Marchand. His death in 1841 prevented him from concluding an accord with America.[6]

Yet, as their purpose was to obtain a consensus in order to force Paris to intervene in Vietnam, the French missionaries succeeded in enlisting the navy commanders who were anxious to emulate the British by having their own colonial empire. Considering that communication with Paris, at that initial stage of submarine cables, was still problematic, it was a good pretext for French commanders to place Paris in face of the "fait accompli."

It is also doubtful that at the outset, the French government had any definite vision about Vietnam, for costly wars in Europe and interminable problems at home deprived Paris of any overseas ambition. Under pro-British king Louis Philippe, anticlerical prime minister Guizot, to avoid jeopardizing entente with Britain, would do nothing to help the missionaries, for he badly needed external peace to devote time to domestic problems. Hence, the protection of missionaries was not in his political agenda. According to him, they had to take responsibility for their own doing. But in the remote Far East, the collusion between the navy and the church was beyond his control.

In 1840, Captain Favin Leveque arrived in Danang to demand the liberation of five missionaries, including priest Miche, who would later play an important part in the orientation of Franco-Vietnamese relations. Not only did the new emperor Thieu Tri readily comply, but he was friendly enough to the French to expect a rapprochement. In fact, Thieu Tri revealed himself to be a ruler wise enough to avoid any open conflict with France. Thus, he refrained from ordering imprisonment or deportation of missionaries, although a death sentence might be pronounced to stay within traditions. When in 1845 the turbulent Bishop Lefebvre was sentenced to death, Admiral Cecille was dispatched by Guizot to obtain his release. Two years later, in 1847, Lefebvre was again captured when he returned to Vietnam. This time Cecille sent Captain Lapierre to Danang. Whether Lapierre was aware or not that Lefebvre had already been freed and on his way back to Singapore, the French first dismantled masts of some Vietnamese ships. Later, on April 14, 1847, in only one hour, the French sank the last five bronze-plated vessels in the bay of Danang. According to some accounts, this incident occurred after Vu Van Diem, a Catholic convert, had passed on military secrets to the French.

Finally, public pressure, manipulated by the Catholic church, forced Guizot to adopt an ambiguous line of conduct. Under the cover of assistance to the British in China, in 1843 he dispatched a fleet under the command of Admiral Cecille and Captain Charner, together with a diplomatic mission headed by Lagrene, who was to negotiate trading privileges with China. Because all of them were repeatedly instructed to keep away from the Vietnam coast for fear of British reaction, Lagrene went on to acquire the island of Basilan near the Philippines in order to build a base similar to Hong Kong. Unfortunately Spain strongly objected, claiming that Basilan was part of the Philippines. Thus, Guizot had to withdraw.

Later Cecille, at the instigation of his missionary friends, came back to Guizot with an even more daring project: France would restore the Le Dynasty in Tonkin and would obtain the possession of Danang as a reward. At this point, in the Pacific Ocean, Admiral Dupetit-Thouars, also with the advice of two missionaries, seized the island of Tahiti and proclaimed it a French protectorate. The British reaction was serious enough to compel Guizot to offer an appreciable indemnity. Afterward, a frustrated Guizot decided to shelve the question of Vietnam for an indefinite time.

In France, the fast-growing heavy industry—Le Creusot, Decazeville, Thionville—provoked the emergence of a worker class with social and political demands. Indeed, for 13 hours of daily work, men were paid 2 francs; women, 20 cents; and children, 10 cents.[7] Unanimously supported by republican intellectuals, progressive merchants, and liberal Catholics, the workers' movement organized banquets and demonstrations demanding reforms. They wanted, of course, higher wages. They also wanted voting rights, for out of a population of 30 million only 168,000 were able to vote, provided they paid a 200-franc special tax every year. In 1847, the famine came to exacerbate the general situation. The workers took to the streets joined by bourgeois intellectuals and the Catholics, who were against government monopoly over university education. Popular demonstrations turned to bloody confrontations when Guizot sent in the army under famous General Bugeaud. When he was finally dismissed by Louis Philippe, it was too late. The king himself had to go. His abdication to his grandson, the Count of Paris, was rejected: The people wanted no more of the Orleans or Bourbon dynasties; they wanted the republic. A provisory committee was formed with workers and intellectuals including Lamartine, Arago, and Louis Blanc.

In spite of popular inclination for a republic, Republicans were not ready. They preferred to stay in the opposition, which is a traditional politician's tactic. Furthermore, the Napoleon I myth was well alive. Hence, the people turned toward his nephew who had on his record two failed coups d'états. On December 10, 1848, Louis Napoleon was elected president. Obviously, it was not a good choice for, as one can expect, by atavistic instinct, he was obsessed with reestablishing the imperial regime. Indeed, three years later, on December 2, 1851, for the third time, he reenacted Napoleon I's coup d'état of 18 Brumaire (the second month of the Republican calendar, October 23–November 21). Then, capitalizing on popular illusion, on December 21, he made himself emperor by plebiscite. Now he could devote his time to restoring the two essential features of the imperial system: "internal authority and external prestige."[8]

For external prestige, Louis Napoleon was anxious to wipe out the shame imposed on his uncle by the Treaty of 1815. But Louis Napoleon was no military genius. The series of wars he prosecuted in Europe, except for a few minor victories, turned out to be disasters, as were some of his colonial enterprises. On June 19, 1867, Maximilian, his candidate to the imperial throne of Mexico, was executed by the Mexican revolutionaries.

At home, the opposition of the Republicans became a constant threat to the imperial regime. Indeed, Gambetta declared that "all regimes were honored with an anniversary except those of the 18 Brumaire and the December 2." Even inside the imperial cabinet, opposition developed. Since no official policy existed for Vietnam, on April 22, 1857, Napoleon III created the Committee of Cochinchina. The apparent reason was to find a market for French-built locomotives and ships, but it was more to restore French prestige after continuous failures. His ministers disagreed. Minister of foreign affairs Walewski conveyed to the emperor his colleagues' reluctance to bellicose action in Cochinchina. Finance minister Fould bluntly said he did not know where Cochinchina was and, anyway, he would not allocate 6 million francs for a military expedition. Another minister, Billaut, advised "not to trust priests and sailors," referring to the missionaries and admirals, and yet another accused the Jesuits of fabricating a deplorable situation in Annam. Finally, given a negative consensus, it was decided to leave imperial orders about Cochinchina to the discretion of the navy commanders on the field.

In China, Admiral Rigault de Genouilly received on November 25, 1857, the first instruction to move his fleet to Danang. One month later, December 20, 1867, the Anglo-French occupation of Canton released de Genouilly from the China field. On August 31, 1958, he took Danang with a contingent of 3,000 Franco-Spanish troops. Professor Cao Huy Thuan quoted Bishop Retord as declaring that the conquest of Danang was crucial, for it was located near Hue the capital and would consequently bring unbearable pressure on the Annamite government.[9] But de Genouilly, after experiencing more problems with the priest Pellerin than with the Vietnamese army, left Danang for Saigon. There were serious speculations that he was convinced that the conquest of Cochinchina would help to solve the problem of access to Yunnan through the Mekong River. He succeeded in taking Saigon but had to go back to France for health reasons.

The first to inaugurate the long dynasty of admiral governors was Admiral Bonard. By the Treaty of 1862, he obtained the three eastern provinces of Cochinchina. He was succeeded by Admiral de la Grandiere, who in turn annexed the west of Cochinchina. The fact that de la Grandiere set his first priority to be an immediate exploration of the Mekong was evidence of the mercantile concept of French colonization. In spite of heroic sacrifices, the Mekong expedition failed and ended with the tragic death of its commander, Doudart de Lagree.

In Europe, encouraged by his success in Annam and an entente with Britain, Napoleon III continued erratic diplomacy until he met with his nemesis in Bismarck. His outrageous flirtation with the Prussian led to a French defeat in 1870. He was made prisoner at the battle of Sedan.

In the aftermath of the fall of Napoleon III, Thiers was elected "chief of the executive power of the French republic." By the treaty of Frankfurt on May 10, 1871, France lost the entire Alsace and part of Lorraine. Paris revolted against the treaty. Under the influence of emerging communists, a revolutionary committee was formed to demand "power for the people, power for the Commune." Thiers managed to overpower the Commune. He became president and prime minister of the Third Republic, which was to last until World War I.

As mandated by Thiers, Admiral Dupre arrived in Saigon in 1871. The Mekong fiasco led him to turn toward the Red River in Tonkin. The conquest of Hanoi, with the loss of two exceptional officers, Garnier and Riviere, caused China to intervene with 200,000 troops.

The Chinese came to Tonkin because of a report from Emperor Tu Duc (1848–1883), which was not exactly a call for intervention. Anyway, it was a mistake, for he had provided the opportunity for French and Chinese to strike a deal at the expense of Vietnam. After two years of fighting, which resulted in a stalemate, the Chinese left Tonkin but not without recognizing French sovereignty in Vietnam.

The problem of Tu Duc was not only Vietnam's technological inferiority, but he was himself a victim of the Confucian tradition, which forbade his ministers to offer any sincere advice confining themselves to only approve whatever the emperor said.

At the end of Tu Duc's reign (1848–1883), the French were in control of Tonkin. Later they divided Vietnam into three Kys (states), making Bac Ky (Tonkin) and Trung Ky (Annam) their protectorates while keeping Nam Ky (Cochinchina) as their colony. This "divide and rule" policy led the Vietnamese into a long struggle for unity and independence. To begin with, in 1885, young Emperor Ham Nghi took to the hills to wage guerilla warfare, which was to last 20 years, as did Duy Tan, the son of Emperor Thanh Thai. Both emperor revolutionaries were captured and deported.

A succession of events brought irreparable damage to French international prestige, which culminated in 1900. Paris was then the capital of Europe. The Grande Exposition gathered 50 million visitors from all over the world, attracted by the newly built Eiffel Tower. France was also a pioneer of the automobile industry: Every year, 45,000 new cars were put into circulation. In the field of scientific research, Pierre and Marie Curie discovered radium. Abroad, France was the second colonial power after Great Britain. Her overseas empire spread over 10-million square kilometers with more than 60 million inhabitants. The "grande guerre" (1914–1918) allowed the French to recover Alsace-Lorraine and to occupy the Ruhr but at the expense 1.4 million dead and 3 million wounded.

The illusion of security behind a Maginot line led the French to return to "la joie de vivre" while Hitler trained his army behind his Siegfried line erected face to face.

During the Great Depression, medium and small enterprises disappeared, leaving national wealth to the "200 families" represented by banks and industry.[10] But as purchasing power dropped, automobile production fell to 75% from its previous 250,000 mark, the commodities index went down 30% for wheat and 20% for wine. Unemployment reached 400,000. Banks had to suspend their activities and transfer their assets abroad. The population rose up and threatened to "throw politicians into the Seine River."

Then came World War II, "la drole de guerre." On May 10, 1939, 145 German divisions attacked under the protection of 3,500 bombers and 1,500 fighters. One month later on June 14 they occupied Paris. Armistice was signed on June 22 and in July a collaborationist government was formed at Vichy under Marshall Petain. Charles de Gaulle had already left for Britain where, on June 28, the British officially recognized his government in exile.

In the Far East, the Japanese demanded on September 23, 1940, admission to Indochina for its troops. To force France into an agreement, on September 28, under Japanese instigation the Thai forces attacked the French. Yet after they had destroyed the Thai fleet at the naval battle of Koh Chang, the French still had to return two provinces, including Battambang, to Thailand. This incident was a warning for the Vichy government which the following year, 1941, accepted a Franco-Japanese accord for the "defense of Indochina."

Forced cohabitation with the Japanese was a long series of daily humiliations, which climaxed five years later. On March 9, 1945, the Japanese overthrew the French administration in Indochina.

The defeat of 1940 at the hands of Germany and the Japanese coup of March 9, 1945, wiped out all prestige the French had among the natives. In an effort to mend France's colonial pieces, in 1944 de Gaulle made his historic declaration at Brazzaville. But later, victory over Germany led him to shift away from it. In the name of "grandeur de la France," the first thing he would do was to reestablish France's shattered authority in Vietnam. The choice of priest Admiral Thierry d'Argenlieu as high commissioner in Indochina perhaps showed a reminiscence of the antique association between missionaries and admirals. Yet to be fair, d'Argenlieu's performance was purely political. His creation of a bogus Republic of Cochinchina destroyed the unity of the country and irremediably crippled the peace process in Vietnam.

The Franco-Viet Minh war began under Leon Blum's lame-duck cabinet. In 1947, Marius Moutet and General Leclerc were dispatched to Vietnam on a fact-finding mission over the December 19, 1945, incident. After his tour, Moutet rejected peace negotiations with Ho Chi Minh and opted for a solution of force. In fact, he had already made up his mind for he had given the go-ahead bombing of Haiphong, which triggered the hostilities.

After nine years of war in 1954, the French suffered a bitter defeat at Dien Bien Phu. In spite of their total withdrawal, it would take another ten year war with the United States (1964–1975) for Vietnam to be independent.

Vietnamese authors disagree on the original responsibility over French armed intervention in Vietnam. For example, Professor Cao Huy Thuan focused on the role of the missionaries by citing Bishop Guebriant, superior of the Catholic Foreign mission in Paris: "Propagation of Christianity will bring many benefits to colonization."[11]

As for historian Pham Van Son, he asserted: "If anything happened in the Far East, most of the time it is the fact of colonial military."[12] Indeed, there was a religious problem stemming from the basic opposition of Confucianism to Christianity. But the politico-economic question dominated Franco-Vietnamese relations from the onset. France demanded a commercial treaty, which deprived Vietnam of its rights to limit commerce to a few ports where inspection of goods and their taxation would be processed in accordance with Vietnam regulation. This was clearly explained by Minh Mang to Jean Baptiste Chaigneau, who after a vacation in France came back to Hue as a French consul with a friendship treaty.

To summarize, whatever the meaning of "French mission civilisatrice," the victory of North Vietnam showed definitively the total failure of Western religious and military efforts to subdue the country. In retrospect, one can see that missionaries were utterly unrealistic when they asked the Confucian king to protect Catholic religion. Furthermore, their dream to install a Catholic empire in a Confucian land was beyond reasonable expectation. As for the military, they relied exclusively on technological advantage, completely disregarding mass psychology. They would correct their view later in Algeria, but it was too late.

This book covers the history of French colonization, which began under Tu Duc and ended with the eviction of Bao Dai. It can be seen as part two of my work on Vietnam.[13]

NOTES

1. Arthur Cotterel, *China: A Cultural History*, p. 227.
2. Oscar Chapuis, *A History of Vietnam: From Hong Bang to Tu Duc*, p. 174.
3. Cochinchina.

    4. The word *Vietnam* has replaced Annam since the time of Gia Long. For convenience, both are used alternately.

    5. Paul Mus, *Ho Chi Minh, le Vietnam, l'Asie*, p. 66. Translated by author.

    6. Oscar Chapuis, *A History of Vietnam*, p. 195.

    7. Pierre Miquel, *Histoire de la France de Vercingetorix á de Gaulle*, p. 343.

    8. Georges Duby, *Histoire de la France des origines á nos jours*, p. 717.

    9. Cao Huy Thuan, *Dao Thien Chua va Chu Nghia Thuc dan tai Vietnam*, p. 99.

    10. For example, Credit Lyonnais, Societe Generale, Credit Industriel et Commercial, and the newly created Compagnie Francaise de Petrole.

    11. Cao Huy Thuan, *Dao Thien Chua va Chu Nghia Thuc dan tai Vietnam* (Christianity and Colonialism in Vietnam), p. 3, translation by author.

    12. Pham Van Son, *Viet Su Tan Bien*, Vol. 5, p. 228.

    13. Part one being *A History of Vietnam: From Hong Bang to Tu Duc.*

1

THE VIETNAMESE EMPERORS

If Emperor Gia Long had brought in the French to help him secure the throne of Annam, he probably believed he had paid them back with ranks, titles, and wealth. Indeed, when Pigneau died, he was honored with a national funeral, and Gia Long delivered a heart-rending eulogy. Chaigneau was made marquis and the other French volunteers were raised to peerage.

Yet, at the end of his life, Gia Long advised his successors to treat the French well but to refrain from giving them any influential posts in their government. For his descendants, who felt no moral obligation toward the French, Gia Long's will was quite welcome. As time passed, courtesy became indifference that ended in confrontation when Minh Mang ordered the execution of Father Marchand, who was involved in Le Van Khoi's revolt.

EMPEROR TU DUC (1829–1883)

The rule of Tu Duc was the turning point in the destiny of Vietnam. After Thieu Tri, the court did away with the principle of primogeniture and instead of his eldest son, Hong Bao, chose the youngest, Tu Duc, for succession.

Tu Duc was born on September 22, 1829. His mother was Pham Thi Hang, a native of Gia Dinh (Cochinchina), who was to become the famous Dowager Tu Du. Tu Duc was reputed to be the best-educated monarch of the Nguyen Dynasty. Through his written or verbal injunctions, he revealed himself as an outstanding scholar, but his literary endowment lost its significance in the context of westernization. He would be a perfect monarch in time of peace and prosperity in which Confucian filial piety would be seen as the foundation of social happiness, but against Western culture Confucianism was only a backward philosophy. Thus, the Vietnam of Tu Duc could only follow the steps of its role model, the decadent China of the Ch'ing. Worse, Vietnam kept going on where China had stopped: When in 1905 the Ch'ing put an end to the traditional examination system, Vietnam still carried it on for a few more years.

The dependence of Tu Duc on China stemmed first from the ambiguous conditions of his enthronement, which compelled him to seek legitimacy from the tradition of Chinese investiture. Thus, on September 10, 1849, a great amount of money was spent to greet the imperial delegate. From the port to the palace, streets were covered with precious carpets; adorned rest areas attended by graceful hostesses were built to allow the Chinese delegation to pause; several junks were decked with fresh flowers to serve as an alternative to land transportation. Bags of Chinese soil were constantly kept within the reach of the Chinese Ambassador, who should never feel far from his motherland. Pham Van Son, more patriot than historian, bitterly complained that in spite of such attentions, the Chinese affected an air of superiority no longer compatible with their conspicuous decline at European hands.

Yet, in spite of the Ch'ing's investiture, the legitimacy of Tu Duc remained a major problem. Indeed, at the outset of his reign, he was confronted with the rebellion of his eldest brother Hong Bao and later another coup d'etat perpetrated by a relative. There were also the periodical revolts of a population loyal to the Le Dynasty. In Tonkin, the Tai Ping remnants controlled the Red River. But the biggest challenge came from the defiant missionaries, and government persecution gave a pretext for French intervention.

The Hong Bao Coup

The role of Hong Bao seems to be a point of controversy among Vietnam historians. Pham Van Son declared that on learning of Tu Duc's enthronement, he vomited a basin of blood and went out to build a coalition with soldiers, peasants, traditionalist mandarins, Buddhists, and Catholics. But according to Trinh van Thanh, Hong Bao had never challenged Tu Duc's designation because he had announced that after all, it is better that the power be in his brother's hands than in a stranger's.[1]

Be that as it may, three years later, Hong Bao's party rose up. In spite of a blood oath for everyone to keep the utmost secrecy, a Bonze[2] revealed the details of the plot. The coup failed and Hong Bao was convicted. Under the intervention of the empress mother Tu Du, his capital sentence was commuted to life imprisonment. But Hong Bao chose to hang himself in prison with a bedsheet.

Giac Chia Voi Rebellion

Five years later, in 1866, taking advantage of a popular discontent caused by the construction of a mausoleum for Tu Duc, a man named Doan Trung fomented a coup in favor of Hong Bao's son.

The son-in-law of Prince Tung Thien Vuong, Tu Duc's uncle, Trung was a very articulate man. He first created a literary club as a facade for recruiting partisans. He chose as his headquarters the Phap Van pagoda, which was owned by Nguyen Van Qui, the abbot of the Long Quang temple.

On September 8, 1866, all the rebels met at the mausoleum, armed with mortar pestles.[3] There was also a blood oath to keep secrecy. But on the way to the palace, Bonze Nguyen Van Qui charted a bad horoscope and, to dissociate from the mutineers, went to inform the authorities.

In the meantime, the rebels had no difficulty in entering the palace and pillaging the arms depot. As a palace guard, named Thinh, held closed the door of the imperial quarters, the insurgents inserted a sword between the shutters and cut off his fingers.

When rescue arrived, Doan Trung and one of his brothers were captured while the third one ran to the kitchen where he committed suicide. All of them, including monk Nguyen Van Qui, were executed on the spot.

Under hot pincers' torture, Trung remained arrogant. Even when the red glowing pincers left nothing but bare bones on his thighs, he refused to confess, declaring only that he accepted his defeat as he would accept his victory, with serenity and determination. He and his entire family were beheaded, except for his estranged wife who, as a cousin of the emperor, had distanced herself from the plot.

With regard to Le loyalists who remained strong in Tonkin anytime someone claimed to be of Le descent, people would rise up to help him to dispute the throne. Indeed, in 1854, Prince Le Duy Cu, with the support of the celebrated poet Cao Ba Quat, rebelled in Son Tay. In 1861, in Quang Yen, Ta Van Phung an ex-enlisted soldier of the Charner expedition, proclaimed himself to be Prince Le Duy Minh. Then in 1862, Nguyen Van Thinh, known as Cai Tong Vang, also claimed to be a Le descendant and with the support of a few rebels set out to take Hai Duong. Emperor Tu Duc dispatched Nguyen Tri Phuong, who put an end to the anti-Nguyen movement by ultimately defeating the tenacious Ta Van Phung in 1864.

As for the missionaries, the few good intentions Tu Duc might have had for them vanished after priest Pellerin was involved in the Hong Bang coup.[4] This case illustrates a pattern of antigovernment policy: Under Minh Mang it was Father Marchand with the Le Van Khoi revolt, under Thieu Tri, Bishop Lefebvre openly defied religious prohibition and consequently was put behind bars.

In 1848, Tu Duc issued two decrees, one giving six-months' notice to Christian commoners to abjure their foreign faith. The recalcitrant ones were branded with the word "Ta Dao" (heretics); in addition, they lost the right to attend national examinations. The other decree concerned the converted dignitaries who had only one month to go back to their ancestral traditions; failure to comply entailed loss of all ranks and privileges with exile to pernicious regions. Finally, executions of Spanish and French missionaries provided the West with the pretext they needed to intervene in Vietnam.

In 1866, after the Tai Ping's defeat to the Ch'ing, their remnants crossed the Tonkin border and scattered in the Red River valley. The Black Flags settled at Lao Kay and the Yellow Flags settled farther downstream at Ha Giang. Unable to dislodge them, the Vietnamese governor Hoang Ke Viem resigned to let them levy a tax over a population that persisted to see them as Black Flags pirates (Giac Tau O).

In 1862, after losing the three eastern provinces of Cochinchina, Tu Duc decided to call for a military draft. Formal military training was initiated in 1865, and was to include a doctorate in military science (Vo Tien Si). But only 10 percent of the army were equipped and those with archaic flint muskets. Training occurred once a year, whereupon each soldier received only six bullets, and if he fired more than this assigned quota, he had to pay for the difference.

The peasant-soldiers system originated during the march to the south and was still in effect. For a detachment of 50 men, 30 were sent back to their native villages for rice cultivation. Thus, although records showed 119,000 men on duty, actually only 39,000 were present. When the French attacked Gia Dinh, the Vietnamese forces amounted to only 7,000 soldiers instead of the reported 12,000. There were no reserves on hand and in case of casualties, the army officers went to nearby villages to recruit replacements.

With regard to the imperial administration, while the central government appointed Huyen, Phu, and Thong Doc, respectively, for counties, districts, and provinces, villages remained independent under their own Councils of Notables, which were presided over by an elderly chairman (Huong Ca). The mayor (Ly Truong) was the chief operating officer presiding over agents in charge of tax and security. There were no records of vital statistics, and only male babies were registered at the Dinh, a small temple serving as both village administrative and religious center.

The claim that villages were the typical nucleus of democracy deserves a second look, for the Notables were traditionally elderly coming from the class of retired civil servants, scholars, or rich farmers. The electoral process was not among such traditions. Indeed, the Confucian society consisted of four classes: On the top were the Confucian scholars (Si), followed by the landlords (Nong), artisans (Cong), and merchants (Thuong). It is curious to find here a similarity with medieval Europe when each social stratum was given a distinct mode of clothing and lodging. While nobility, mandarins, and rich bourgeois wore silk attire and lived in decorated brick houses, the peasants wore sleeveless cotton blouses and loin clothes. Short pants were permitted only for trips outside the village. Generally the peasants dwelled in straw huts; under the best conditions, their houses were limited to an assembly of crude bricks or natural stones.

It is obvious that such a social stratification, which denied the importance of true economic forces (peasants, artisans, and merchants), could only have disastrous consequences. Some historians blame the court for failure to carry out reforms, but because the French ruled the roost outside the imperial palace, there was not much the government could do. This is not to say that the French were not interested in reforms. But these reforms were carried out within the context of a "mission civilisatrice," which Franklin D. Roosevelt referred to as the "milking of the Vietnamese." Thus historian Tran Trong Kim concludes: "Pov-

erty, deprivation, natural disasters, foreign aggression, government impotence
. . . at the end of Tu Duc's reign, were the reasons of Vietnam decline."[5]

"After Me, the Deluge"

Tu Duc breathed his last on July 17, 1883. In spite of fragile health and the
problems with the French conquest, he managed to live for 54 years. Given the
life expectancy at that time, it was quite an achievement, but the worst was yet
to come, and he could say, like King Louis XV of France: "Apres moi le
deluge."

Tu Duc had no sons to succeed him, but he had three adopted nephews: the
31-year-old Duc Duc (son of his fourth brother Kien Thoai Vuong), the 19-
year-old Chanh Mong (Dong Khanh), and the 14-year-old Duong Thien (Kien
Phuc), both sons of his twenty-sixth brother Kien Thai Vuong. Thus, Tu Duc
appointed three regents: Nguyen Van Tuong, Ton That Thuyet, and Tran Tien
Thanh.

As for Dowager Tu Du, she took advantage of the situation to form with the
two imperial consorts, Trang Y and Hoc Phi, the influential Tam Cung (Three
Harems). But besides palace intrigues, they had no other competence and had
to rely on Regents Ton That Thuyet and Nguyen Van Tuong, the latter sharing
more than political concerns with attractive widow Hoc Phi.

According to author Pham Van Son, Tu Duc had named the youngest prince,
Kien Phuc, as his successor, declaring that Duc Duc, because of his depravity,
was unfit to rule. But under pressure from the Tam Cung, the three regents
agreed to enthrone Duc Duc.

EMPEROR DUC DUC (JULY TO OCTOBER 1883)

According to Pham Van Son, on the eve of his coronation, Duc Duc asked
the three regents to delete from Tu Duc's will the incriminating part, and they
agreed. But instead of reforming himself, Duc Duc ignored court etiquette and
neglected mourning rules by inviting to the palace the dubious acquaintances
he had recruited among professional gamblers, cabaret singers, and popular ma-
gicians. Thus, at the enthronement ceremony, Ton That Thuyet retaliated by
having Tu Duc's testament read to the court in its entirety, creating a huge
commotion. The court decided to suspend the ceremony, and after a quick deliberation, Duc Duc was sentenced to death for failing to observe mourning rites
and having had intimate relations with his father's concubines. He was forced
to take poison. He was not even provided with a grave but was simply tossed
naked into a cavity.[6] Even by Asian standards, this punishment was out of
proportion to the crime.

Professor Trinh Van Thanh and historian Tran Trong Kim did not question
Duc Duc's enthronement and did not elaborate on his character. Moreover, ac-

cording to Thanh, Duc Duc was not forced to take poison but was left to die of hunger in confinement. Considering that Duc Duc died on October 6, 1883, four months after Hiep Hoa's enthronement on July 30, 1883, it seems that Trinh Van Thanh's account was closer to reality. In retrospect, the manner in which Duc Duc was treated might rather stem from personal vengeance, for he had interfered in the intimate liaison between Regent Tuong and Lady Hoc Phi. The treatment imposed on Duc Duc provoked a protest from mandarin Phan Dinh Phung who was banished by Ton That Thuyet.

EMPEROR HIEP HOA (1846–1883)

To replace Duc Duc, Thuyet and Tuong decided to enthrone 37-year-old Hiep Hoa. Mature enough to realize the regents' excesses, Hiep Hoa was reluctant to associate with them, but under Dowager Tu Du's pressure, he had to accept the crown. Aware of Hiep Hoa's animus, Thuyet and Tuong would consequently seize the first opportunity to destroy him.

On August 20, 1883, Hiep Hoa happened to see the sun colored in blue, and according to his seers, it was a bad omen. Indeed, Admiral Courbet's ships were blocking the mouth of the Thuan An River, which leads to Hue, the capital. After a heavy bombing, Admiral Courbet told Hiep Hoa, "We have no intention to annex your country but you must accept our protection. This is the only way your dynasty can survive."

On August 25, 1883, Hiep Hoa signed with Harmand a 27-article treaty.[7] Article one read: "Nam recognizes and accepts the protection of France. France controls all Nam's relations with foreign nations including China." Article two read: "The province of Binh Thuan is attached to Cochinchina." These were the two main clauses aiming to subject Vietnam to French control; the rest related to details of French implantation, such as location of French residents, their attribution, prerogatives and so on. The Nguyen Dynasty had just lost its Mandate of Heaven.

It is obvious that the treaty had destroyed whatever prestige Hiep Hoa could have at the court and among the population. It was also a good pretext for the regents to openly oppose his authority. In the presence of the entire court, Ton That Thuyet refused to kowtow and verbally abused the emperor. His increasing hostility led Hiep Hoa to fear for his life and to seek protection from the French Resident Champeaux with whom he discussed plans to dismiss the regents. Unfortunately, Thuyet got wind of the conversation and Hiep Hoa's fate was sealed.

On November 28, 1883, taking advantage of Champeaux's absence from Hue, Ton That Thuyet had Hiep Hoa arrested. In a closed session of the court, Thuyet accused the young emperor of having squandered the national treasury, ignored the regents' advice, and secretly plotted with the French by signing the Harmand treaty. Hiep Hoa was forced to abdicate. He was sentenced to death for which he had to choose between a sword, a three-meter-long scarf, or a mixture of opium and vinegar. He chose the last one and died at dusk on November 29, 1883. All his supporters were murdered. Because third regent Tran Tien Thanh protested against the treatment inflicted on Hiep Hoa's followers, he was killed by Thuyet's assassination squad.

EMPEROR KIEN PHUC (1868–1884)

On December 1, 1883, the regents presented the French with a fait accompli by having 15-year-old Kien Phuc hastily enthroned at five o'clock in the morning. Resident Champeaux sent a vigorous protest to the court invoking the Harmand treaty. Instead of affirming that the treaty did not give the French the right to interfere in matters of monarchic succession, Tuong argued that since Hiep Hoa was dead, the treaty had become obsolete. But as the French began a military action, the two regents claimed misunderstanding and presented a formal application for the nomination of Kien Phuc.

As emperor, Kien Phuc was a sickly young boy. The power was practically in the hands of his adoptive mother Hoc Phi and her lover Regent Nguyen Van Tuong. Yet he was not unaware of rumors about the couple. One night the ailing emperor caught the duo in the act and imprudently threatened, "When I get well, I will chop off your heads down to the third generation." He was never given this opportunity, for that same night, Hoc Phi put poison in his medication and Kien Phuc died at dawn on August 1, 1884.

Later the same year, Ton That Thuyet withdrew all bronze coins from the market to make guns for his Tan So secret fortress. This caused the rich to bury their cash, and the price of rice shot up, adding to the general discontent. The replacement currency did not meet either conventional weight or size—rumors had it floating on water like paper. To calm down the population, Thuyet shifted the blame to the Chinese team responsible for coinage. Their chief was promptly beheaded.

At the beginning of 1885, Prince Gia Hung, head of the Imperial family council, secretly opened an inquiry on Kien Phuc's death. In May, by order of Thuyet, he was stripped of all his titles and rank and sentenced to death. A timely intervention by Resident Rheinart had him released, but he was banished to Quang Tri. He mysteriously disappeared on his way to exile. By that time, the French realized that all the problems came from the two regents and decided to get rid of them.

EMPEROR HAM NGHI (1884–1885)

Through experience, the regents found that mature kings were only problems for them, so this time the regents chose to enthrone the 14-year-old Ham Nghi, younger brother of Kien Phuc. Because his mother was a commoner, he was not raised at the court and lived a miserable existence in the suburbs of Hue. When the officials came to take him for the enthronement ceremony, they found a street urchin in tattered rags.

Again, the French were presented with a fait accompli. Following Champeaux's steps, Resident Rheinart violently protested, demanding a written application for the succession. To show that he was deadly serious, Rheinart ordered a gunboat with 600 infantrymen and an artillery detachment to take position at the Mang Ca citadel under Colonel Guerrier. Then he let the court know that failure to comply with his demand by August 14 could have the most serious consequences. By the deadline, a subdued Ton That Thuyet appeared in person to humbly apologize for a "misunderstanding." Not being duped, Rheinart rejected the request written in Vietnamese script "nom" and demanded a document in good literary Chinese. Furthermore, when details of the enthronement ceremony were discussed, Rheinart adamantly demanded that the main gate (Ngo Mon) be opened to the French delegation. Shortly afterward, Rheinart, still a minor officer, was replaced by Lemaire, ex-consul of France in Shanghai.

As for Ham Nghi, although he had not received a noble education, he showed an atavistic concept of prestige and power: The first thing he did after his coronation was to sentence to life imprisonment his cousin Prince Ky Phong who not only opposed his enthronement but also called him a bastard. To be sure, it was his only display of power, for he rapidly fell under the regents' domination.

In May 1885, Thuyet managed to install an appreciable quantity of cannons around the imperial palace pointing directly to the French citadel. The French responded by having Colonel Pernot's troops continually patrol around the palace. Through diplomacy, Lemaire succeeded in having Thuyet remove all guns. But unbeknownst to the French, he transferred the weapons to his secret Tan So fortress.

Franco-Viet relations were then quite amicable thanks to the conciliatory attitude of Lemaire, who as a professional diplomat had a typical aversion for the military. He detested Hoang Ke Viem and Luu Vinh Phuoc as much as he disliked Briere de l'Isle and Pernot. To him, they were the major obstacles to a peaceful coexistence between France and Vietnam. But his philosophy was not to the taste of the Paris government, and soon Lemaire had to leave room for General Count de Courcy.

De Courcy and the Politics of Force

After the Tien Tsin treaty, the French government was determined to apply direct rule over Vietnam one way or another. General Count Roussel de Courcy was found to be the right choice for such a policy. Born into a noble family and graduated from the prestigious military academy Saint Cyr, he was arrogant and stubborn, a perfect example of the medieval warlord. To those who ever ventured to give him advice, he curtly declared that "In my entire career, there is only success. Wherever I go, my star is never dim."

On May 31, 1885, with the double title of Governor in Tonkin and Resident General in Annam, de Courcy arrived in Hanoi. After meeting with him, Resident General Lemaire resigned and went back to France without returning to Hue. Indeed, to be relegated to a subordinate position was an unbearable loss of face, particularly in Asia. To other civilian administrators, including Resident Champeaux in Annam and Sylvester, director of civilian affairs in Tonkin, de Courcy withdrew military power, which he reassigned to his chief of staff General Prudhomme.

It seems that de Courcy had more consideration for General Briere de l'Isle, who retained his post as commander in chief of the land forces. He also agreed with Briere that the two regent troublemakers must be eliminated. Indeed, at that time, Ton That Thuyet was openly working with Hoang Ke Viem against the French in Tonkin.

According to Captain Gosselin, de Courcy's biggest mistake was his complete ignorance of Annam. He was convinced that the court and the Vietnamese people were intimidated by French military might, and he recommended to Paris the use of force to solve political problems. As the Paris cabinet refused his agenda, de Courcy decided to ignore it and by means of provocation he went on to create incidents with Hue.

On July 3, 1885, to discuss the ceremony of the presentation of his credentials, de Courcy summoned to his residence princes and high mandarins led by Nguyen Van Tuong. He demanded that the central gate[8] be opened to him and his staff and that the emperor come down from his throne to greet him.

Then, noting Thuyet's absence, the general said, tongue in cheek, "Maybe he stays home to prepare an attack against me." As Tuong vehemently denied this, stating that Thuyet was really sick, de Courcy retorted, "If he is sick, he still ought to come even if he must be carried in his hammock. To make sure, I am going to arrest him."

De Courcy also refused the presents offered by Emperor Ham Nghi and told the audience: "If you do not want troubles for your country, you must pay within three days 200,000 gold ingots, 200,000 silver ingots, and 200,000 francs."[9]

The Mandarins Revolt

After the reception, Nguyen Van Tuong secretly met with Thuyet. Both agreed that de Courcy was out to destroy them and both decided to stake everything on a surprise attack that very night, not that they had any hope of defeating the French but they had no choice left. At 1 A.M. the Viet opened fire on the Mang Ca citadel and the French quarters. But the French managed to seize six Vietnamese cannons, which they turned against the Hue garrison.

Before dawn, the rebels began to disperse. Thuyet entered the palace with 5,000 soldiers. He forced Ham Nghi and the three empresses to follow him. The young emperor protested, "I did not fight against anybody, why should I run away?" In response, Thuyet swung his sword and shouted to the troops to carry the young monarch away. Their destination was Tan So, a fortress hidden in the Laotian mountains across Quang Tri Province.

When the French arrived at 9 A.M., they found an empty palace. At the armory, they discovered 812 cannons and 16,000 rifles. Inside Tu Du's quarters they also found such a large amount of silver ingots that it took five days and five soldiers to pack and ship them to France. These were the 700,000 taels balance left in the palace after Nguyen Van Tuong refused to transfer it to Tan So.

But the rebellion was doomed at the outset. On July 6, 1885, in the absence of Thuyet who was staying behind to protect the retreat, Tuong went back to Hue to negotiate with the French. He met first with Father Caspar at his Kim Long church. The next day Caspar took him to de Courcy, who against the advice of Bishop Puginier and de Champeaux, allowed him to reintegrate his post but gave him a period of two months to bring Ham Nghi and Tu Du back to Hue. Tuong begged Tu Du and Ham Nghi to come back to Hue. Thus, at Quang Tri, the Empress Dowager and the two consorts refused to proceed further. But Ton That Thuyet dragged Ham Nghi behind him and continued on his way to Tan So.

Three months later, Ton That Thuyet and Nguyen Van Tuong built a secret stronghold at Tan So with 2,000 peasants recruited from Quang Tri. It was a secluded fortress located in the mountains between Quang Tri Province and Laos. Inside the citadel, Thuyet had buried half of the imperial treasury, including 300,000 taels of gold and only Tuong's opposition prevented him from moving the rest. Their choice of Tan So was a mistake for they realized later that its isolation was an overwhelming obstacle to carrying out military recruitment.

At the Van Xa village where they stopped for rest, Thuyet had Ham Nghi issue a Can Vuong,[10] calling the people to support their emperor against the French.

To counteract, the French set in motion the process of replacing Ham Nghi by his elder brother Dong Khanh. Indeed, according to dynastic rules, "the nation cannot be one day without a king." Under Tuong's request, the dynastic council temporarily appointed as head of state (Giam Quoc) the 75-year-old prince Tho Xuan Vuong, head of the council. He was also Tu Duc's uncle. After the three empresses were back home, Dong Khanh was enthroned on September 19. This event destroyed any hope for Ham Nghi to return to power and again, prompted by Thuyet, he issued a second Can Vuong in which he accused Tu Du and Tuong of being French puppets. In a sense, it is not fair to accuse the dowager, for her decision was absolutely correct within the context of primogeniture, since Dong Khanh was in succession before Ham Nghi.

In 1885, after Can Vuong was finally subdued, Ham Nghi had to make an arduous retreat through the mountains of Laos and settled at Ham Thao among Muong tribes, well known for their hostility against the Hue Court. At that time, Ton That Thuyet realized that his end was near and that once captured he could in no way make a claim for mercy. Thus, he fled to China, allegedly to seek help. This was a fallacious pretext for two reasons; first, he had already dispatched Nguyen Quang Bich to Peking for this purpose, and second, as regent, he was well aware that by the Patenotre treaty, China had recognized the sovereignty of France over Vietnam, and there was no chance that the Chinese would lend a hand to help Ham Nghi.

After Thuyet's defection, left with a tiny escort under the command of Ton That Thiep, Thuyet's son, Ham Nghi stayed during the 1887 monsoon season at Ta Bau near a 40-meter-high waterfall. During alert, he was carried deep into the jungle on the back of a bodyguard. Another son of Thuyet, Ton That Dam, was holding a defense post some 30 miles away.

In November 1888, Ham Nghi lost contact with Ton That Dam, who had committed suicide. By that time, the king's resources were exhausted, and many of his entourage had already deserted. In early November, his chief bodyguard Truong Quang Ngoc secretly rallied the French. On the night of November 22, 1888, at 10 P.M. after killing Ton That Thiep, Ngoc entered the emperor's quarters and forced the emperor to come with him. Ham Nghi seized a sword and yelled: "You'd better kill me. Don't hand me to the enemy." He was promptly disarmed.

Brought in front of the French, Ham Nghi denied his identity, but his fate was sealed. Before he embarked for exile in Algeria, a French officer questioned him on Ton That Thuyet's whereabouts. He refused to betray his bad partner and said, "I don't know who is Ton That Thuyet. I don't know why you ask me." At that point, the officer pointed to a nearby ship and replied, "Because of Thuyet you are now going to be forever away from your country." Ham Nghi looked at the quiet lovely shore and silently wept. He was then 18 years old. In January 1889, he arrived in Algiers.

Ham Nghi's case should be studied in a better light. The fact that he was very young and immature should be taken into account. Although national prestige requires a myth with the young king leading anti-French resistance, it is more likely that Ham Nghi was only Ton That Thuyet's tool. Yet even if the Can Vuong no longer existed, Ham Nghi retained an element of uncertainty for the stability of the country. Therefore, for the French, his deportation was more a safety measure to preserve peace than an act of retribution. According to administrative reports, Ham Nghi was "sent to Algiers to recover from a long and exhausting journey in the mountains." What could be seen as a sarcastic comment, would later take another meaning: When the French were in the process of ousting Thanh Thai and Duy Tan, Ham Nghi's return to the throne was under serious consideration.

Nguyen Van Tuong

Tuong was born in 1810 in Quang Tri to a peasant family. Because his father was involved in some revolt, he was barred from the national examination.

Records do not reveal the nature of his relation with Tu Duc, but show that later under the emperor's protection, he was able to pass the national examination with the highest grades. In 1852, he was assigned to the ministry of justice. When his father died in 1862, in accordance with Confucian tradition, Tuong had to retire for a five-year mourning period. Afterward, he resumed his administrative career. In 1873, he was assigned to negotiate with the French. For all the accords he had signed with them, the French still considered him as the model of an Asian scoundrel. Thus, when de Courcy arrived, he had already made up his mind to dispose of Tuong and Thuyet.

After signing the Philastre treaty and recovering possession of Hanoi, Tuong was rewarded with the post of Minister of Domestic and Foreign Affairs. Later, in 1881, he became head of the imperial cabinet. When Tu Duc died, he was made regent together with Tran Van Thanh and Ton That Thuyet.

Now, as Thuyet was away hiding in China, Tuong remained the only one to bear the converging wrath of Dong Khanh and de Courcy. The French general, for all his shortcomings, was at least a man of his word. Since the two months of grace he had given Tuong for bringing Ham Nghi back to Hue had elapsed, on September 6, 1885, a phlegmatic de Courcy sent Tuong to Poulo Condore together with the 80-year-old father of Ton That Thuyet, Ton That Dinh. While on the high seas, Dinh died and his corpse was thrown overboard.

In prison at Poulo Condore, Tuong resumed his intrigues. He was caught red-handed sending secret instructions to call for more revolts. In retaliation, on October 26, 1885, the French resident superior seized his property and in the process discovered a hidden cache of 14.5 million piastres.

Then, on November 23, 1885, Tuong was deported to the isolated island of Tahiti where he died in February 1886. In July 1886, his body was sent back to his family in Hue.

Ton That Thuyet

Born in 1838, Thuyet was the eldest son of the ex-governor of Hai Duong, Ton That Dinh, who later died on his way to exile in Poulo Condore. He had earned notoriety during the early repression of three northern provinces: Lang Son, Cao Bang, and Thai Nguyen. At one time he was governor of Bac Ninh Province. In 1874, he was with Hoang Ta Viem, the two most influential leaders in Tonkin.

In 1881, Thuyet was back in Hue, assuming the position of minister of defense. But Tu Duc himself had serious misgivings about his character: "He [Ton That Thuyet] has great military ability but lacks honesty and sincerity. He also tends to avoid responsibility. Poorly educated, inconsistent, pusillanimous and suspicious, he is prone to offend people. He must learn more so that he might live as a Quan Tu."[11] And yet, before dying, the emperor made Thuyet coregent. Obviously, Tu Duc had not expected that Thuyet would kill his three successors, and if it were not for French intervention, regicide would have become a tradition in the Hue Court.

The truth about Thuyet lies in his pursuit of personal survival, which at the outset had led him to carry out a desperate attack against the French and, when he was defeated, to forcibly abduct Ham Nghi and the Tam Cung as hostages. But he was not keen enough to anticipate the possible replacement of Ham Nghi by his elder brother. Because of Thuyet's hatred for the French, some emotional Vietnamese exonerated him of all wrongdoings. They refused to identify the real nature of Thuyet. Yet by any standard, abducting a young boy and then leaving him behind in the jungle cannot be seen as a laudable behavior. Granted, he had left behind with Ham Nghi his two sons, Ton That Dam and Ton That Thiep, but this made no difference because in his political schemes, everyone except himself was expendable. Furthermore, no question was raised concerning the fact that instead of going to Peking, Thuyet remained in Kwang Tung doing nothing to pursue the fight for his country.

Under French pressure, the Chinese government put him under house arrest at Lung Chow. He received 60 taels for his monthly sustenance and reportedly used the allowance to smoke opium in order to calm down his twinges of conscience. The resulting mood swings caused his escort to leave and go back to Vietnam. Left alone, he married a Chinese widow in 1899, and at one time was involved in a legal suit over trivial matters, which did not add to his prestige, if he ever had any. During his last years, he went completely insane, striking rocks with his sword and uttering incoherent sounds.

He died at the age of 75. There is no evidence that his family or anyone else had claimed the return of his body. Thus ended the episodes of the two regents who, in spite of many errors, together were the last resistance opposed by the Hue Court to French direct rule.

EMPEROR DONG KHANH (1885–1889)

According to the rule of primogeniture, Dong Khanh was in direct line to succeed Tu Duc, being Ham Nghi's elder brother. But the two regents, Tuong and Thuyet, preferred Ham Nghi, who being younger was easier to manipulate. As for the Vietnamese people, they were not aware of these palace intrigues.

Dong Khanh's legitimacy, however, does not matter. The fact that his first move was to cross the River of Perfume and thank de Courcy for his support could only be seen by the people as a despicable act of allegiance. Then, with the French accord, he sentenced Thuyet and Tuong to death for having stirred up all the problems to which he now had to attend.

Added to Dong Khanh's unpopularity, was the fact that his father-in-law, General Nguyen Than, had largely contributed to put down the Can Vuong and Van Than revolts. When under French order, Dong Khanh toured the country to enlist popular support for a Franco-Vietnamese coexistence, it was a disaster.

Fearing for his life, he interrupted his journey and went back to Hue on armed junks.

Records on Dong Khanh are scarce; it seems that Viet authors prefer to remain silent over a period they consider a national shame. It goes without saying that the French had no problems with Dong Khanh, for he was the typical puppet, more preoccupied with his personal comfort than the plight of his country. To superficial observers, the situation did not seem so bad, since in 1887 the French returned to Vietnam the provinces of Binh Thuan and Khanh Hoa. Actually it was a Cochinchina territorial readjustment: Tonkin and Annam now depended on the newly created Department of the Navy and Colonies. Ensuing French determination to apply direct rule to the entire Indochina structure was revised to include a governor general at the top, residents and residents superieurs in Annam, Tonkin and Cambodia, and also a governor and province administrators for Cochinchina.

On January 28, 1889, three weeks after Ham Nghi was deported to Algiers, Dong Khanh died. There was a rumor about French refusal to enthrone Dong Khanh's descendant because of a history of mental illness in the family. Apparently, this led to the nomination of Thanh Thai on February 1, 1889. Ironically, soon Thanh Thai showed mental disturbances and became such a headache for everyone, French and Vietnamese alike, that he finally had to be discarded.

EMPEROR THANH THAI (1889–1907)

Born in 1879, Thanh Thai was the son of Duc Duc. After his father died, he had to spend his life in prison with his mother. When, on February 1, 1889, the court came to take him away for the throne, his mother feared for his life and begged for mercy.

According to some Vietnamese historians, at the age of ten, Thanh Thai appeared to be exceptionally intelligent and realized that the court now was taking orders from the French resident, who kept a network of informants inside the palace. It so happened that among the spies there was a mandarin named Truong Nhu Cuong, whose daughter was Thanh Thai's concubine. Thus, he had to feign insanity. Indeed, it was not the first time that a member of the Nguyen house chose to play the fool. At the onset of the dynasty, its founder, Nguyen Hoang, had to fake madness in order to preserve his own life. Yet Thanh Thai maintained peaceful relations with Resident Leveque. To lure the French, he even adopted Western customs, such as driving a car and having his hair cut short. But he obstinately refused to apply his imperial seal on decrees prepared by Leveque. Finally his scheme was put to the test when Leveque sentenced to death Prince Buu Thanh whom he accused of a murder attempt on his person. Thanh Thai opposed the French decision and demanded an an investigation team from Paris.

The above incident led Thanh Thai to consider that cohabitation with the French was too close for comfort. On July 30, 1905, he fled to China with the

intent of joining Cuong De's Dong Du movement. He was intercepted by the
French at Thanh Hoa. His escort was sent to Poulo Condore but, as far as he
was concerned, he was declared insane.

It is difficult to determine with accuracy Thanh Thai's mental condition. If
he had ever faked then he was probably carried away, for the French police
archives relate bizarre happenings between the palace walls where maids were
strangled to death at dawn after an overnight service to the emperor. One day,
he subjected a eunuch to near-death flogging for failure to provide him with
marbles. On still another day, he forced an old palace maid to drink alcohol and
afterward had her whipped for being drunk. Hence, a local French newspaper
called for his removal, accusing him of being "an uneducated and cruel youth."
Unruffled, he went to Danang and dismayed the public by parading in a car
escorted by 30 horsewomen. Soon his open oddities became a tourist attraction
and he was forced by the French resident to invite to his dinner table many
Westerners in search of gossip and scandals.

On September 15, 1893, under pressure from the court, he had to retire for
three months to the Lake of Meditation (Ho Tinh Tam), leaving the administration to Dowager Tu Du.

Perhaps the only one not duped by Thanh Thai's insanity was Governor General Doumer. In February 1897, upon his arrival in Hue, he met with the emperor, not because he was interested in his scandalous life, but because he
needed to define the conditions of his relationship with the native officials: Was
Thanh Thai able to take an active part in Doumer's vast colonization scheme,
or should Doumer leave him alone with his harem, dynastic rituals, and Confucian studies? Against public opinion, Governor General Doumer found Thanh
Thai "having a lively intelligence with a great self-possession although he appeared wilful, capricious and bizarre." Doumer had ready-made excuses for the
young monarch. First, at such a young age,[12] Thanh Thai had a large harem,
"which was not conducive to intellectual and moral stability. . . ." Second, "the
French books that were read to him and that dealt with the life of ancient kings
were not always edifying. They excited his imagination and pushed him toward
experiments that were dangerous for anyone who was their object."[13]

One month after Doumer went back to France at the end of his tenure, the
Danang police reported that on April 21, 1902, Thanh Thai had an incident with
two European ladies, while his fourth wife was molested by a French soldier.
This caused interim Governor General Bront to order the emperor immediately
back to Hue.

In retrospect, Thanh Thai's insanity, real or feigned, was of no real concern
to the French. Indeed, the deaths at dawn of a few palace maids were trivialities
compared with the lofty doctrine of French "mission civilisatrice." As long as
these incidents remained within the limits of the imperial palace, the French
could not ask for more. In a sense, it is even better, since Thanh Thai's political
absenteeism allowed them to take over some important privileges, such as presiding over the privy council (Co Mat) meetings. And had it not been for com-

plaints from the Vietnamese Court itself, life could go on forever. But to the mandarins, Thanh Thai's behavior was a national disgrace. Since none of them dared to openly criticize the emperor, they demanded that the French take appropriate action. Finally, a consensus was reached between the French and the court. On August 30, 1907, in spite of Ngo Dinh Kha's[14] opposition, Thanh Thai had to abdicate to his son Duy Tan. Relegated to the rank of duke, he was assigned to permanent house arrest at Vung Tau, in Cochinchina. In the process, he took with him 4 consorts, 10 children, and 20 female attendants. But he would not renounce his eccentricities. During World War I, he publicly hurt French pride by deriding the Legion of Honor or by ostensibly replacing French products with German ones on his shopping list. In private, he blackmailed Duy Tan's mother, his wife, for money. Having failed to pay back a 40,000 piastre debt, he was dragged before the French justice courts. To save face, the Hue mandarins had to pick up the tab.

Finally, Duy Tan's revolt provided an opportunity for everyone to get rid of Thanh Thai, once and for all. He was accused of collusion with his son. In 1916, both were deported to the island of La Reunion, in the Indian Ocean.

At La Reunion, in spite of repeated requests, Thanh Thai was barred from returning to Vietnam. In 1950, thanks to the intervention of his son-in-law, Education Minister Vuong Quang Nhuong, he was assigned house arrest in Saigon where he died on March 24, 1954.

EMPEROR DUY TAN (1907–1916)

Born on August 19, 1889, Duy Tan was the second child of Thanh Thai and Nguyen Thi Dinh. He ascended to the throne on September 5, 1907. In 1913, the opening of Tu Duc's tomb to search for gold was the first incident to arouse Duy Tan's hostility. As a member of the Nguyen Dynasty, Duy Tan could not be indifferent to the desecration of Tu Duc's tomb. As a Confucian son, his father's abdication was by no means welcome. That was the psychological field on which Tran Cao Van set to work for converting the young king to the revolutionary cause.

In August 1914, World War I broke out giving Vietnamese the opportunity to rise up again. On May 3, 1916, Duy Tan escaped from his palace at Hue to join Tran Cao Van. He took the direction of the operations and harangued the population from his junk. But in spite of the support of Vietnamese militia, the movement aborted and he had to take refuge in the Thien Mu pagoda. He was captured and incarcerated in the French Mang Ca citadel.

Unlike his uncle Ham Nghi, Duy Tan was not forcibly dragged into the quagmire against his will. Thus, the court and the Imperial family decided to remove him from the throne and to confine him to the rank of prince. But an influential mandarin, Ton That Han, insisted that he and his father Thanh Thai be banished from the court. This particularly fit into Governor General Charles's plans. On November 3, 1916, both father and son sailed toward La Reunion

Island. With them were Duy Tan's mother, his wife, Mai Thi Vang, and his sister, Princess Luong Nhan.

On January 11, 1917, upon their arrival at La Reunion, Duy Tan applied for the return of his wife to Vietnam, declaring that "she had accepted the advances of his father and that there was both adultery and incest." In Hue, the court agreed with Governor Albert Sarraut to keep the case away from the public. When, in the following August, Duy Tan applied for divorce, his request was simply ignored. Since life with Thanh Thai was unbearable, Duy Tan's mother and sister were allowed on April 24, 1920, to return to Vietnam for health reasons.

At the outbreak of World War II, Duy Tan tried in vain to enlist into the French army. Only in 1942 could he join the French free forces navy as a telecommunication officer. In December 1945, he met with de Gaulle and on his way back to La Reunion he died in an airplane accident on December 26, 1945.

Whatever was said between General de Gaulle and Duy Tan is of course off record but there exists some speculation on the possibility of his return to Hue to replace Bao Dai as the head of a constitutional monarchy.

EMPEROR KHAI DINH (1916–1925)

Khai Dinh, a younger brother of Ham Nghi, was born on October 8, 1885. He reigned from May 17, 1916, through November 6, 1925, leaving no more than the reputation of being a salaried employee of the French government. In 1922, during the Colonial Exposition in Marseilles, Phan Chu Trinh accused Khai Dinh of being corrupt and irresponsible. But it was said that under the influence of Pham Quynh, Khai Dinh had made a vain attempt to ask the French for more freedom for Vietnam.

One may say that Khai Dinh's rule, apparently peaceful, was in fact nine long years during which Vietnamese nationalism gradually crystallized.

BAO DAI, THE LAST EMPEROR

Prince Vinh Thuy, born in 1913 at Hue, "presumably the son of Khai Dinh and Hoang Thi Cuc,[15] became crown prince on April 28, 1922. At the age of nine, he was sent to study in France under the care of Governor Charles. He officially ascended to the throne on January 8, 1926, and then went back to resume school in France, leaving the administration of the country to the French resident superior and the council of ministers under Catholic Nguyen Huu Bai.

On September 6, 1932, Bao Dai returned to Vietnam to assume his imperial duty. His first move was to abolish the kowtow. Then on May 2, 1933, with Governor General Pasquier's blessing, he proceeded in what the Vietnamese called a "silent coup" by toppling Nguyen Huu Bai and his council. Young and progressive elements were then taken into his cabinet, the most remarkable being

Pham Quynh (Education), Ngo Dinh Diem (Interior) and Bui Bang Doan (Justice). As expected, all of them called for reforms with the difference that some, like Ngo Dinh Diem, tried to force the issues while others, like Pham Quynh, preferred patience. Siding with Pham Quynh, Bao Dai gave Diem the choice, "Se soumettre ou se demettre." He chose to go. As for Pham Quynh, now prime minister, he was probably sincere in preaching Franco-Vietnamese coexistence. But no matter how outstanding was his prose, which the French willingly compared with Maurras's and Barres's, there is no doubt that it failed to attract the Vietnamese people.

On September 3, 1939, France declared war on Germany. Ten days later, Bao Dai submitted a four-point reform: (1) Replace the Vietnamese viceroy with a mandarin acting as deputy to the Tonkin French Resident; (2) replace the Tonkin private council with a local government under the resident and his deputy; (3) restore the private imperial budget with contributions from Tonkin and Annam; and (4) have a representative of the Hue Court at the Ministry of Colonies.

All these propositions betrayed Bao Dai's clever intent to put a lid on French control. Not duped, the new Governor General Catroux pretexted the war situation in France to postpone the discussion. But as a consolation prize, he offered the young king a Morane 343 observation plane for his recreation. As for Pham Quynh, he dispatched to France the ONS laborers (Ouvriers non specialises) to help in war production. After the liberation, 25,000 of these ONS established a Delegation Generale des Indochinois in France to challenge the March 24 declaration on the status of Indochina.

In spite of his concern for reforms, Bao Dai was by no means a political leader or even a obstinate debater. When he presented his program, this time to Decoux, he was respectfully told that as in England, the Emperor reigns but does not govern. He did not waste time in protests. According to his supporters, contrary to his predecessors, Bao Dai did not hide his opposition under insanity: He chose the more comfortable role of a perfect playboy. It was quite easy given his Parisian background. Thus, when he heard about the young emperor's escapades, the governor general bitterly complained to Paris that the young king was not interested in politics and spent his time in frivolities. Later, Decoux would pay a high cost for these frivolities. When a jealous Empress Nam Phuong wanted to gun down her emperor husband, the admiral hurriedly dispatched his wife to reconcile the imperial couple. On her way to Dalat, she lost her life in a car accident.

The French demise in Indochina came suddenly on the night of March 9, 1945. With the help of Cao Daist paramilitary groups, the Japanese, after a short notice to Decoux in the afternoon, crushed French military defenses and seized all administrative services. Bao Dai, who was on a hunting party at Quang Tri, was forced to interrupt his amusement and go back to Hue. Quite surprised, he had these historic words to say, "I was wondering what had happened!" Yet, according to his supporters, he afterward tried to establish contact with de Gaulle through Bishop Antonin Drapier, apostolic vicar in Hue.[16]

But on March 11, after a meeting with Japanese Ambassador Yokoyama, Bao Dai publicly repealed the 1884 treaty with the French and declared the independence of Vietnam within the sphere of coprosperity of Great Asia.[17] He would later reveal that he had been given the choice to either accept independence from the Japanese or to see them take over his country. What he did not say was that Prince Cuong De had been brought to Hai Nan, awaiting to succeed him on the throne in case he rejected the Japanese offer.

On March 19, 1945, under pressure from the Japanese who hated pro-French Pham Quynh, Bao Dai had to let him go. A few weeks later, Pham Quynh was summarily executed by the Viet Minh. Bao Dai offered the prime minister post to Ngo Dinh Diem who never received his telegram. Hence, scholar Tran Trong Kim came in to fill the vacancy and, as one can expect, brought with him a host of intellectuals without any political experience. They set to work on a constitutional project and many reforms, before realizing that the decision-making power was in the hands of the Japanese who had replaced the French in every administrative function.

On August 8, 1945, Japan surrendered after the Hiroshima bombing. At that time, a famine erupted in Tonkin where hundreds of thousands died of hunger. Tran Trong Kim apologized that the Emperor and he were aware that the people were suffering. But there was nothing they could do. Thus they were ready to welcome the Viet Minh into the government if they asked for it. In response, the Viet Minh simply told Bao Dai to step down. Still under the shock of Pham Quynh's murder, Bao Dai promptly complied. On August 30, 1945, he officially remitted the powers to Viet Minh delegates, Tran Huy Licu and Cu Huy Can. Afterward, as simply citizen Vinh Thuy, he docilely followed them to Hanoi. On September 11, by decree No. 23 from President Ho Chi Minh, Vinh Thuy was appointed supreme counselor of the Democratic Republic of Vietnam.

After the March 6 accord allowing the French to come back to Tonkin, Ho Chi Minh began to fear a possible collusion between them and Bao Dai. Thus, he decided to send him on an indefinite mission to China. More than happy to comply, Bao Dai flew to Kun Ming and then to Hong Kong, where penniless, under the name of Wong Kunney, he rented a cheap room in the modest St Francis Hotel. Obviously, he decided that his political career had ended and he confided to some French journalists that his only ambition now was to be transferred to some country where he could enjoy hunting. But his imperial destiny did not stop there. The "Bao Dai solution," in which he had never believed, would contribute to a legacy of war and destruction involving another Western nation.

NOTES

1. Pham Van Son, *Viet Su Tan Bien*, Vol. V, p. 16.
2. A Buddhist monk.
3. Thus, the historic name of the Giac Chia Voi (Mortar Pestles rebels).

   4. See Oscar Chapuis, *A History of Vietnam*.
   5. Tran Trong Kim, *Vietnam Su Luoc*, Vol. 2, p. 252.
   6. Only under Thanh Thai was a modest mausoleum erected over his tomb.
   7. Harmand was the promoter of protectorate policy.
   8. The central gate was for the exclusive use of the Vietnamese emperor and Chinese ambassadors.
   9. Pham Van Son, *Viet Su Tan Bien*, Vol. VI, p. 31.
   10. An edict meaning "Save the King."
   11. In Chinese Chuan Tzu, Great Man.
   12. He was then 18 years old.
   13. Joseph Buttinger, *Vietnam: A Dragon Embattled*, Notes, p. 441.
   14. Ngo Dinh Diem's father.
   15. Chinh Dao, *Vietnam Nien Bieu Nhan Vat Chi*. p. 35.
   16. Again, according to his supporters.
   17. A Japanese invention.

2

THE GREAT EXPLORERS: PRELUDE TO THE CONQUEST

The industrial revolution had unexpected results for the relations between West and East. What was once promoted by Marco de Polo and other European merchants as a peaceful relationship between two different cultures now degenerated into wars of conquest and exploitation.

At that time, the French government had enough internal problems to deal with, and if it was not for preventing British hegemony in the Far East, it would not consent to costly adventures in China and Vietnam, no matter what politicians would say later in defense of the mission civilisatrice. But it turned out that China was so large a continent that everyone could find his profit without mutual bickerings. This explains how in one paradoxical instance, a Catholic France and a Protestant England joined together to punish China for the murder of a Catholic priest.

After compelling China to open her borders to their religion and commerce, including importation of opium from British India, the Western nations stumbled over access to the Western hinterland and especially Yunnan, a region reputed as the Chinese El Dorado. This led France and England to investigate the navigability of the three major waterways: the Yang Tze River, the Mekong, and the Red River.

A PRECURSOR: HENRI MOUHOT

Mouhot was the precursor to the French explorers de Lagree and Garnier. He had not secured a commission from any government for he was interested in entomology, not in overseas politics. Later, when he was on the verge of bankruptcy, he obtained personal help from the president of the Royal Geographic Society in London, owing to the intervention of his wife's family.

Alexandre Henri Mouhot was born on May 15, 1826, at Montbeliard in the Doubs department (France). At the age of 18, he taught French in a military academy in Russia. In 1854, fleeing the Crimean War, he returned to France and married Anne Park, the daughter of celebrated African explorer, Mungo Park.

In 1858, he sailed to Siam leaving his wife behind. Electing Bangkok as his base, he made several expeditions into Indochina by sea from Chantaboun to Kampot and by land from Bangkok to Udon (Cambodia). In January 1960, he visited the ruins of Angkor, which he would describe in poignant style. In 1861, he entered Laos by elephant. For three months he explored the Luang Prabang region. His health, so far excellent, finally ceded to the assault of the tropical climate: On October 19, 1861, he wrote in his diary. "Attacked by fever." On October 29, his last written words were: "Have pity on me, oh my God."[1] On November 10, 1861, he died at the village of Ban Naphao, away from family and civilization.

Mouhot left no systematic surveys but only emotional diaries in which man's achievements rivaled the beauty of nature. In fact, he was the one who "redis-covered" Angkor. His last words were a congruous surrender to the power of the Creator. Seven years later, his successors, de Lagree and Garnier, would endure the same torment: In 1868, Lagree would also die in a small place in China, after a long agony.

THE YANG TZE RIVER

The Yang Tze (Map 1) is the most important of the six major Chinese rivers.[2] With its length of 3,964 miles, it is also the world's third largest river after the Nile and the Amazon.

The origin of the Yang Tze was a historical controversy: From the time of the Ming, it was believed to be the Nin River in northern Sichuan. Only in 1976, a Chinese government expedition succeeded in locating its source in the KunLun Mountains in Ching Hai Province at an altitude of 21,700 feet. The Yang Tze runs east through Tibet, Yunnan, Sichuan, Hupeh, Hunan, Kiang Si, Anh Wei, and Kiang Su Provinces, to finally stop 14 miles before Shanghai where it discharges golden brown water into the South China Sea. The 6-billion cubic feet of sediment laid in Kiang Si Province made it a major region of rice cultivation.

Thus, the Yang Tze first appeared to be the ideal river road to western China, but its capricious course is similar in many ways to the Mekong River: alter-nating rapids, streams, and cataracts. Its three gorges are indeed world marvels.

With its intemperance, the Yang Tze shared with the Yellow River a major theme in Chinese history: By his efforts to build dikes and dams over the two rivers, the Great Yu (2205–2198 B.C.) won the title of Tamer of the Floods and by the same token the throne of China. Legge, comparing the European struggle against the St. Lawrence River with the realizations of the Great Yu, affirmed that it took the Westerners, with all their modern equipment, more than two centuries to bring the North American regions into cultivation, while it took only 20 years for the Chinese emperor to obtain the same results with the Yellow River.[3] But later under the Shang, the Yellow River surged again, threatening the An Yang capital and compelling Emperor Chung Ting (1562–1550 B.C.) to move to Lo Yang and to proclaim that the Yellow River was the "sorrow of China."

However, with the same tribulations, the Yang Tze turned out to be a natural defense against the invasion of the barbarians from the North. It was under the protection of this natural obstacle that the southern Sung Dynasty was able to peacefully develop a superior civilization.[4]

Navigation on the Yang Tze had to follow the whimsical course of the river. Since the 4th century, on 1,200 miles from Sichuan to Shanghai, dams had been erected on both sides of the river. But the strength of the flow coupled with the hardship of time thwarted human efforts. In 1788, dams and dikes broke, flooding the entire Hu Bei Province and killing more than 1 million people. Emperor Chien Lung ordered that nine cast-iron oxen be placed along the river.[5] Yet in the 20th century, floods alone claimed more than 300,000 lives.

Downstream toward Chung King, riverside cities offered a curious picture: Being built on a slope, their streets ran parallel to the river and were linked by stone stairways. After Chung King, the river leveled out. The last portion from Yibin up to the source was left to small junks and rafts. Toward the ocean, navigability gradually improved according to the following pattern: 500-ton vessels plied the river between Yibin (altitude 1,000 feet) to Chung King (630 feet); 1,500-ton vessels, from Chung King to Yi Chang; 3,000-ton vessels from Yi Chang (130 feet to Wu Han; 5,000-ton vessels from Wu Han to Nanking; and 15,000-ton vessels from Nanking to Shanghai.

Between Yi Chang (HuBei) and Chung King (Sichuan) the famous Three Gorges (Chu Tang gorge, Wu Hsia gorge, and Hsi Ling gorge) gave way to 12 confluents named after the Chinese zodiac. Myth had them built by the Great Yu, who with the help of dragons, moved mountains and valleys to provide fertile land for peasants.

According to recent exploration, the region of the Three Gorges is one of the true seats of Chinese civilization. As natural obstacles, they contributed to make the province of Sichuan a haven, first for the Shu kings during the period of the Three Kingdoms (A.D. 220–265), and later in 1937 for Chiang Kai-shek's army during the Japanese invasion.

The Chu Tang gorge is perhaps the most dangerous of the three. The current rushes at right angles into a narrow and misty five-mile gorge in which poor visibility is a matter of more death than life. The 25-mile-long Wu Hsia gorge runs among twelve 3,000-foot lime-stone ridges, with ferocious swirls and drafts. The third gorge, named Xi Ling, is the longest with 47 miles, but was considered the safest of the three.

Navigation on the Yang Tze has also relied on rope towing, recalling the same method used on the Mekong, with the only difference being that, in the riverside villages, there existed some 300 professional boatmen, who also worked as rescuers for the victims of the river. Traditionally, for each dead person retrieved from the river, they received a one-dollar reward. It was not necessarily a humanitarian occupation: If some survivors remained stingy, they were held under water until they become worth the one-dollar fee.

The Yang Tze and Red River run close in Heijang, which was renowned for its lychee crops. Under the T'ang, because Yang Kuei Fei was very fond of these fruits, Emperor Ming Huang had special daily relays of horsemen to bring them back to Chang An, 500 miles away.

In conclusion, given these adverse conditions, the British turned toward the Irrawady River in Burma, while the French set their mind on the Mekong in Cochinchina and the Red River in Tonkin. This partly explains why Admiral Rigault de Genouilly had preferred to sail down to the south and take Saigon, and why his successor, Admiral de la Grandiere, organized an expedition to the Mekong. It is obvious that the navy commanders who had involved themselves in costly wars with China were anxious to justify their action by some profitable fall out. The Mekong River was on the top of their agenda as an ideal road to Yunnan, the Chinese El Dorado. When this expectation failed to materialize, the French turned to the Red River and invaded Tonkin.

THE MEKONG RIVER

On July 20, 1641, long before the advent of the great French explorers—Mouhot, de Lagree, Garnier, and Pavie[6]—a Dutch merchant, Van Wuysthof, in search of gum resin and benzoin, sailed up the Mekong from his factory in Phnom Penh. After multiple difficulties, he arrived in Vientiane on November 3 and was quite welcomed by the new King Souligna Vongsa, who was seeking alliance with the West against his two foes Sisarath and Nokasat,[7] Thus, besides a sumptuous reception at the palace, which was still a pagoda, Wuysthof was promised all the gum resin and benzoin he wanted. But on his way back, he had second thoughts about the treacherous character of the Mekong River and decided against venturing further. The Mekong River (see Map 2) went into oblivion until two centuries later, when the French appeared in Vietnam.

Doudart de Lagree and Francis Garnier

Exploration of the Mekong was by itself an epic in the history of French conquest. The project was actually Francis Garnier's brainchild although he was not sure what was lying behind this 4,180-kilometer-long river, which runs through the Indochina peninsula to hurl into the South China Sea by a nine-dragon mouth (Cuu Long) in Cochinchina. It became a high priority in 1865, after Admiral de la Grandiere obtained from the minister of colonies the promise to dispatch an expedition for the Mekong. For that matter, there was a consensus within the government, since de la Grandiere's superior, the powerful navy minister Chasseloup Laubat, was also president of the French Geographic Society.

Anticipating diplomatic problems for the expeditions, de la Grandiere decided that the command of the expedition be given to a more seasoned politician. Thus, Garnier was put second to Doudart de Lagree, a 42-year-old graduate from the prestigious Ecole Polytechnique and 16 years his senior.

De Lagree was by no means a green horn: As an explorer, he had been with an archeological mission in Greece, and in the domain of diplomacy he had, as the representative of France in Cambodia, succeeded in securing the protectorate treaty for France three years before.

With regard to the Mekong, de Lagree had, during his tenure, explored the Mekong up to Sambor, where he discovered the first rapids, which seemed to him "uncrossable." Yet, he did entertain the hope that perhaps in high-water season, a powerful launch could overcome the force of the current or perhaps a deep channel could be located to permit navigation during March or April, before the river overflowed under the combined action of monsoon rains and melted snow descending from Tibet. But the existence of streams was not then anticipated.

Under these conditions, the party left Saigon on June 5, 1866, on a gunboat loaded with 150 cases of food, 700 liters of pinard,[8] 300 liters of brandy, and a cache of 25,000 francs in gold bars and various currency. There were also 15 cases of trade-goods for friendly exchange with natives along the river. Besides de Lagree, Garnier, and Delaporte, there were four staff members including two government delegates and two medical doctors. The party was under the protection of an armed escort of 16 with 3 native interpreters.

After one week's stay at Angkor, they arrived on July 6, 1866, in Phnom Penh, the new capital located 30 miles southeast of ancient Oudong. King Norodom, who was facing the Pu Kombo's[9] revolt in the east, legitimately expected some help from de Lagree, with whom he had negotiated the terms of protectorateship not so long ago. But in spite of a sumptuous dinner and interminable dances of the famous Royal Ballet, de Lagree left the following day, July 7, after refusing a gold bar generously offered to defray the expedition's expenses. Leaving Norodom to fend for himself, he proceeded toward Stung Treng some 170 miles northeast of the capital.

An incident occurred with the Khmer interpreter who, for fear of Pu Kombo, refused to come along. De Lagree had to lock him up on the ship. Then the first setback appeared on July 11 at the important town of Kratie where the Mekong was only a stream. They were compelled to transfer all provisions to pirogues[10] hastily carved out of forest trees. The gunboat, now useless, was returned to Saigon. Perhaps some of them could already see in this event the omen of a final fiasco.

After Kratie, on July 13, they moved to Sambor, already known to de Lagree.

This village, located some 100 miles northeast of Phnom Penh, was a famous site of a pilgrimage by Princess Nucheat Khatr Vorpheak, who was miraculously saved after being swallowcd by a crocodile, or so the tale went.

After Sambor, the rapids continued among small islands and multiple rocks surrounded by swirling water: As the banks disappeared under the roiling water, boatmen had to jump from rock to rock using ropes to haul the small crafts. But the idea that a powerful steam launch could overcome the fury of the current still prevailed.

Since the banks were under water, the hope to rest on dry land vanished. At night, the men had to sleeplessly remain on the overloaded pirogues, helplessly watching apocalyptic thunderstorms.

When they finally reached calm water, they were told of another rapid called Preatapang. Garnier went out for a vain exploration.

On July 23 they arrived at Stung Treng where they decided to split. De Lagree went to investigate the Sekong River, a tributary of the Mekong, hoping to find a navigable passage between Sambor and Stung Treng.

At the same time, Garnier went southward, determined to locate the Preata-pang rapids. When they heard the roar of powerful rapids, the boatmen refused to go farther. Under the threat of Garnier's revolver, they reluctantly moved toward the rapids. Garnier himself was taken aback at the spectacle. Now he saw the nature of the rapids. The muddy breakers savagely assailed the banks, unfurled into the forests, wrenching each tree and rock, smashing them into a thousand pieces. His frail craft was dragged at a speed of 10 or 11 miles an hour, in the middle of rocks and trees, beset by a deafening noise. All the boatmen could do was to use their paddles to fend off trees and rocks, to prevent them from being smashed.

On the afternoon of July 30, he went back to Stung Treng. Because of the violence of the downward current, it took him six long days instead of the 12 hours with the previous outgoing trip. As for de Lagree, his investigation of the Se Kong also turned out to be of no value.

The next destination was Luamg Prabang where Mouhot had died five years ago. As if destiny wanted to give them another warning, just before the departure, Garnier and Dr. Joubert were struck down by fever. While Joubert recovered in ten days, it took Garnier almost three weeks to be back on his feet. During his sickness, in a burst of delirium he rolled overboard and fell into the river. In the darkness of the night, his rescue took dramatic proportions. When he later recovered, his skin was peeled off, his hair gone, and he temporarily lost the use of his left leg. But he survived to find a more tragic end later.

Hardship became the expedition's way of life: The alternating rapids and streams forced them to resort either to strenuous hauling by ropes or to carrying their pirogues and their load on the banks, under the tropical sun and the stormy rains. Soon, their boots were in pieces and they went bare foot, their soles burning on overheated rocks. At Khone, they found seven miles of falls and cascades. Besides trees and rocks, dead fish and crocodile bodies, smashed by the violent current, floated in quantity on the river. They had to fight against dense vegetation, snakes, mosquitoes, and leeches. Leeches were a constant torture, but because stopping to remove them delayed their progress, they waited for the nightly rest to do this dreadful chore.

On September 11, 1866, they arrived at Bassac, an important center, where they decided to stay to await their passports for China. Garnier went back to Stung Treng to seek some information. He arrived at Stung Treng on November 8 only to find a Pu Kombo revolt in full swing: A few weeks earlier, the rebels had killed the governor of Sambor. Thus, Garnier was advised to turn back.

Upon his return to the camp site one week later, Garnier found the expedition in serious turmoil: During the absence of de Lagree, who was conducting another search on the Se Kong confluent, a man was put in irons by the commanding officer for a minor offense.

During his search, de Lagree stopped at Attopeu, a small industrial center east of Bassac. He was unaware that an epidemic was raging in that town, and there is where he probably contracted his liver disease of which he would die two years later.

On January 7, 1867, they reached Ubon, where they decided to separate again into three groups to meet later at Khemmarat. Garnier left first on January 10 for Cambodia, going southward on the Se Moun confluent. Delaporte, the third officer, left on January 15, following the same southward portion of the Se Moun but turned north after it joined the Mekong.

As for de Lagree, he left Ubon on January 20, 1867, travelling by land with an escort of elephants and ox carts. He reunited with Delaporte at Khemmarat on January 30, 1867. They spent the following 13 days in this region, finding out whether Vietnam had any influence with which France could avail herself of to build some trade by virtue of the 1862 treaty. On February 13, 1867, they left Khemmarat, again bound northward. The trip was hindered by a series of rapids, which ended before they were in view of Nakhon Phanom, famous for its stupa. On March 6, de Lagree conducted an investigation on a lead mine in the vicinity of Uthren.

As for Garnier, he first stopped at Sisaket where he exchanged the pirogues for ox carts. The lack of a Cambodian interpreter made his itinerary rather problematic. He was lost and at one point found himself at the edge of a cliff. He had the ox carts dismantled and carried down the cliff where they were reassembled. He continued on his way to arrive at Angkor on January 29. There Garnier was warned by the governor that the Pu Kombo rebellion was still going on and it was unwise to proceed to Phnom Penh. This time, Garnier disregarded the warning. He rented a Vietnamese fishing boat and arrived without incident at Phnom Penh on February 5. His perseverance was finally rewarded: The needed passports were awaiting him. He returned by land through the jungles where he had to deal with herds of elephants and other big game. On February 19, Garnier found himself at the foot of the same cliff he had been before. When he finally arrived at Ubon on February 26, de Lagree had already left. To overtake the party, Garnier walked 22 miles per day until he met up with de Lagree at Uthen on March 10, ending his two-month odyssey.

On March 13, the entire expedition left for Luang Prabang, and on April 2 they stopped at Vientiane for two days. After leaving Vientiane on April 4, the expedition paused at Chiang Khan, the southern limit of Luang Prabang, where they discussed their official entrance into the Laotian capital. They were still without shoes, and it is not clear why they did not get a supply in Vientiane. The best guess is they either were unable to find the appropriate sizes or they were having cash difficulties. Anyway, on April 29, 1867, they did put up quite a parade when they entered Luang Prabang barefooted but wearing their best clothes. They had their straw hats adorned with blue ribbons marked "Mekong."

The first thing de Lagree did was to request permission to erect a monument to Mouhot. But de Lagree's health, coupled with lingering hardships, led the leaders to consider for the first time the negative aspect of the expedition. Finally they decided to go on, and on May 25, 1867, they left. This time, given the long distance to China, heavy materials were sent away to Bangkok while each individual kept only a limited load.

On July 1, they arrived at Mong Lin where prices of rice and chicken were exorbitant. Thus, they had to reduce their meals at a time that their physical conditions required additional intake. To further limit expenses, the men undertook to carry the sick themselves instead of hiring native service. Delaporte's feet were infected because of leech bites, and another officer had dysentery. They would stay behind to recuperate. Later at Sop Yong, a small village, the party was reunited again. But, generally, health conditions were worsening. Garnier could barely walk because of his left knee pains, and de Lagree had a groin infection from extensive leech biting.

To gain time, they decided that alternatively a part would move ahead while the other would stay behind to rest. Thus, de Lagree, Joubert, and Delaporte remained behind, and Garnier volunteered to lead the expedition. He stopped at Mong Yawng in Burmese territory to await de Lagree. Reunited on August 14, they moved ahead toward Keng Tung, leaving Garnier behind.

On August 25, after covering 300 miles through mountainous trails, de Lagree entered Keng Tung. He began to feel the first symptoms of his disease. His exhaustion was so great that he forgot to date the letter he forwarded to Garnier, who would be reunited with him on September 13, 1867.

Leaving Keng Tung in September, they found some respite at Keng Khang. The navigability of the Mekong seemed a remote hazy idea, which only came back to mind when they decided to proceed to Keng Hung on September 17. They had to stop at Mong Long to wait for the Chinese entrance permit, for Keng Hung was under the control of not only Burma but also China.

Mong Long offered quite a glimpse of Chinese customs: Local beauties displayed typical tiny feet as a result of foot binding, which originated under the southern Sung. De Lagree sent his Laotian interpreter Alevy to arrange for the authorization, and the party entered Keng Hung on September 29. Soon it appeared that, in fact, Alevy had not obtained any permit, since, after a few days, de Lagree was told by a 12-member council that his passport did not include Keng Hung and, furthermore, it was delivered by an unknown authority. In response, de Lagree pulled out a document from his bag. It was a letter signed by Prince Kung, the powerful brother of the defunct Emperor Hsien Feng. It read that "The bearer of this letter is a man of high rank and all imperial subjects must give him profound respect and diligent service."

Later, on October 30, they reached Ssu Mao, where de Lagree and Garnier had their first significant disagreement. It seemed that de Lagree alone had decided to give up the Mekong project by suggesting to de la Grandiere an exploration of the Red River. In fact, he had been told long ago that missionaries used to travel on the Red River between China and Tonkin. As Garnier insisted that they should go to Ta Li and resume the exploration of the Mekong, de Lagree retorted that Ta Li was not safe, for it was in Chinese Muslim hands. Thus, he decided to proceed to Kun Ming but promised that if at P'uerh, their next stop, news on Ta Li was more optimistic, he would reconsider his plan. They arrived at P'uerh where the Chinese governor advised them against going to Ta Li.

From November 9 to November 16, on their way to Kun Ming, they stopped at Mo Chiang, where the city authorities provided them with abundant gifts of food. From Mo Chiang they followed the Red River and arrived the next day in Yuan Chiang, a city on the Red River bank. As the Red River appeared to be a quite comfortable ride, the two leaders agreed to separate on November 26, Garnier going down the Red River for some investigation, de Lagree making a reconnaissance of Chien Shui, a city he believed to be near Kun Ming.

THE RED RIVER

From its source in Yunnan near Kun Ming, under the name of Ma Lung River, the Red River runs for some 400 miles in China, then traverses the entire Tonkin, toward the east, parallel to the border of Kwang Si and empties in the South China Sea at Haiphong (see Map 2). From its source in Viet Tri in Tonkin, the Red River, also called Song Nhi or Song Thao, goes through many rapids and cataracts. From an altitude of 270 feet at Lao Cai, it decreases to 30 feet at Viet Tri. From here to the sea, the river twists and veers in successive curls, enough to make navigation an idyllic cruise.

The rich silt deposited by the river now spreads over a 5,792-square-mile delta, which, with the beginning of wet rice cultivation, was once the cradle of Vietnamese civilization.

Boarding commercial junks on November 27, 1867, Garnier soon faced the rapids with their familiar scene of unloading and reloading of the merchandise. Then hit by a terrible headache, Garnier had to spend the night in the customs house. He was promptly relieved with a few pipes of opium offered by the customs officer. The next day, the convoy arrived at another area of rapids and this time the boatmen refused to go farther. But they confirmed that the river was navigable again in Tonkin between Lao Kay and the South China Sea. Thus, with mixed feelings, Garnier went back to Chien Shui before de Lagree arrived.

It was difficult for de Lagree and Garnier to accept the failure of their expedition, because they had hoped for better results with the Red River. This frustration would haunt de Lagree until his last minutes: In his moments of lucidity, he repeated over and over that at least something should be brought back to France to justify so much sacrifice. As for Garnier, a victim of the same obsession, he would later leave France again to go back to China and ultimately lose his life in Tonkin.

At Kun Ming, they were contacted by two French priests, Fathers Prolleau and Fenouil. Then, to ease the tension with Garnier, de Lagree accepted to go to Ta Li where he found no help from the imperial governor. De Lagree had to contact the two Ma Muslim leaders. Because the expedition fund was exhausted, with the help of Father Fenouil, de Lagree was able to borrow 5,000 francs from Muslim General Ma Ju-Lung, but when he solicited an armed escort he was given an emphatic rebuttal. Thus, de Lagree turned toward the Muslim spiritual leader, Holy Man Ma Te Hsing, alias Lao Papa. Although he had rallied the imperial government, Ma Te Hsing's prestige among Muslim rebels remained unscathed, for in the entire empire he was the only one to have made a pilgrimage to Mecca. If his ambivalent personality did not always show compassion, he nevertheless was grateful to Garnier for having fixed a telescope he had acquired in Singapore when he went there to watch the equinox. The fact that the instrument refused to operate on his return to Ta Li was not only a personal frustration but also a serious blow to his religious prestige, for knowledge of astronomy was a criterion of Muslim religious leadership. Lao Papa readily provided Garnier with a commendation message for his followers in Yunnan.

The party left Kun Ming on January 8, 1868. On January 14, de Lagree's condition took a dramatic turn for the worse and he had to lie on a litter. On January 18, 1868, they arrived at Hui Tze, where de Lagree was put in bed. He still had the strength to sign orders and preside over meetings held at his bedside. Before Garnier's departure for Ta Li, on January 30, 1868, and knowing how much Garnier took the matter to heart, de Lagree gallantly gave him carte blanche to pursue the exploration of the Mekong whenever possible. It was the last time they saw each other.

De Lagree's illness was in its terminal stage: Besides amoebic dysentery, his liver was in a desperate condition. Dr. Joubert, left behind to take care of him, decided to operate. He removed an abscess in the liver, thereby bringing some relief to the sick man. Believing wine would help to strengthen de Lagree the doctor hurriedly sent for some communion wine from the Apostolic Vicar residence some 200 miles away. Afterward, de Lagree could walk a few steps and

Joubert clung to the hope that somehow his patient could recover. But on March 6, 1868, de Lagree suddenly collapsed. His end came a week later on March 12. The ensuing autopsy revealed another abscess in the liver. Joubert removed de Lagree's heart and sent it to his family in France. He buried de Lagree in a Chinese coffin at a corner of the Pagoda garden.

As for Garnier, after leaving Hui Tze, he set out toward the Yang Tze valley and reached the market town of Hui Li on February 5. For two days his party walked under compacted snow at an altitude of 10,000 feet. They found a Catholic mission under Father Lu, a Chinese priest who spoke Latin. Garnier learned from Father Lu that there was a French mission near Ta Li. On February 16, with Father Lu's servant as interpreter, the party crossed the Yang Tze to climb up to 6,000 feet. Then they stopped at a small hamlet where a curious incident almost put an end to the expedition. It began when a member of the escort tried to use a coffin left at a corner of the backyard as a manger for the horses. A woman yelled to alert the neighbours. Indeed, coffins in any culture are considered sacred things, but in this specific case her husband was taking a nap inside. It took all the eloquence of Father Lu's servant to calm down the maddened crowd. Needless to say, Garnier did not linger at the place.

On February 28, near Pin Ch'uan they finally found the French mission with Father Leguilcher. Under his guidance, they arrived at Ta Li on February 29. The presentation of Lao Papa's letter allowed them to enter Ta Li without a problem. But four days later, Father Leguilcher was summoned by the "sultan of Ta Li," Tu Wen-Hsiu, who declared that he had not killed them because of his respect for Lao Papa, but he might change his mind if they did not leave at once. It was probably the first time that they abandoned a place in such a hurry. In their haste the only gold bar left for their sustenance was irremediably lost.

As for Father Leguilcher, given the attitude of the sultan, he decided, for his personal safety, to stay with the expedition. By increasing their speed, they arrived in government territory 11 days later. Although his Mekong mission had failed, Garnier and his entire group were happy to be alive.

On his way back to Hui Tze, Garnier received contradictory news about de Lagree. But on April 2, Joubert's personal messenger confirmed de Lagree's death. The party rushed back to Hui Tze. There Garnier decided that they would not return to Saigon without their chief who deserved to rest in French soil. Thus, on April 5, 1868, the entire expedition ceremoniously gathered to disinter the corpse. The escort volunteered to carry the coffin to their destination. On April 5, they embarked on a boat going down the Yang Tze and they arrived in Hankow in June.

It was at Hankow that fate allowed Garnier to meet with Dupuis, who was then in his forties. He doned Chinese clothing and spoke Chinese. For more than eight years he sold arms and munitions to the belligerents. According to many authors, Dupuis's exploration of the Red River stemmed from the information provided at that time by Garnier, which Dupuis vehemently denied, claiming he knew of the river long before the Hankow meeting. Be that as it may, according to some records, Dupuis set sail on the Red River from Kun Ming to Yen Bay in January 1871.

The mourning expedition finally reached Shanghai where they proceeded toward Saigon. On June 19, 1868, led by Governor de la Grandiere and Bishop Miche, the entire Saigon administration with great pomp laid de Lagree to rest in the French cemetery. Although the Mekong expedition was a failure, more than 3,000 miles of Asian territory was carefully mapped by de Lagree's party.

PRELUDE TO THE CONQUEST OF TONKIN

Three men, Admiral Dupre, Jean Dupuis, and Francis Garnier, originated the conquest of Tonkin, a plot in which the French government was not apparently involved.

After the Mekong expedition, Garnier went back to France complaining about public indifference. Yet he was received by Emperor Napoleon III. In April 1869, he shared with the late de Lagree a Paris Geographical Society medal. But troubles loomed on the horizon. As he was preparing his report on the expedition, Admiral la Grandiere claimed to be the originator of the Mekong project. De Lagree's partisans also denied Garnier any part in the expedition's leadership. When Garnier was given a medal by the London Geographic Society, de Lagree's partisans loudly protested.

In the middle of these problems, Garnier took time not only to marry Claire Knight, the daughter of a wealthy Scottish merchant, but also to found the famed magazine *Le tour du monde* with the participation of Delaporte and Joubert.

The eruption of the Franco-Prussian War in July 1870 brought a change in the destiny of men. Garnier was recalled to active duty and was assigned to the command of a gunboat on the Rhine River. Afterward he served as an aid to the admiral commander of the Brest naval squadron. When the war ended, he was a navy commander, chief of staff to Admiral Mequet, commanding the southern defense sector of Paris. In 1871, Garnier shared with Livingston a special award from the Antwerp Geographical Congress.

Garnier became a fierce opponent to the terms of the cease fire imposed by a victorious Prussia. His political exuberance caused him to lose his rank of commander. Then began a series of setbacks: first, his failure to get elected to the senate, then the rejection of his candidacy to the venerable Institut de France. In 1872, as Dupuis was back in France with the aura of the Red River explorer, one can understand Garnier's state of mind: He persisted to believe that the Mekong was somehow accessible and decided to obtain a leave of absence from the navy to go back to the Far East.

He left Marseilles on October 1872 with his wife Claire, and on his way to Shanghai he made the fateful decision to stop in Saigon. By so doing he made Admiral Dupre aware of his whereabouts in China and paved the way to his tragic end in Tonkin.

In Shanghai, he left Claire behind and went to Peking in search of an affidavit to Tibet where he expected to find the source of the Mekong. Because he had to wait for the documents, he explored western China and particularly Chung King, which he chose as his base for future operations. Finally, since no papers were ready, he lost patience and went back to Shanghai. At home he found a summons from Admiral Dupre to come to Saigon to discuss "some serious matters." Believing in a possible nomination as France's representative in China, Garnier hurriedly sailed to Saigon on August 17, 1873, unaware it was the last time he would see his wife and Shanghai.

Admiral Dupre came to Cochinchina in 1871 as the first governor. He had three years' experience in the Antilles and had secured a commercial treaty with the king of Madagascar. He was the proponent of an intervention in Tonkin in 1872 and he began a series of recommendations to that purpose asking Paris to put an end to the ambiguity of policy in Tonkin, the "wealthiest province of Annam."[11] According to Dupre, his plan was twofold. On the one hand a victory would restore the prestige of France, utterly damaged by the defeat of 1870; on the other hand, it would put France at the Chinese gate to the southwest of China,[12] which is "a question of life and death for the future of our rule in the Far East. We must stay there either as an ally of emperor Tu Duc or as a military occupant."[13] At that time France had not entirely recovered from the 1870 disaster and could not afford any adventure while having to pay war indemnity to the Prussians. Dupre answered by affirming he needed no financial or military help from Paris. Yet foreign minister de Broglie and navy minister Admiral d'Horney rejected Dupre's project claiming that the situation in Europe did not enable any political problem. De Broglie wrote to Dupre reiterating his order to avoid any intervention in Tonkin at the present time. As one can see, he did not reject the principle of conquering Tonkin by force, but he feared a confrontation with the British who were already incensed by the treaty of protectorate with Cambodia not so long ago.

Dupre's position was strengthened by the support of missionaries in Tonkin. Bishop Gauthier told him that the Annamites only heard the calls of cannons. In fact, he counted on church funds to finance his war.[14] It was also at this time that he sired the idea of using Jean Dupuis to provoke hostilities with the Hue government.

In fact, Dupuis was an adventurer involved in illicit trade. He had acquired a profound knowledge of China, having travelled throughout it for more than a decade. He probably shared his knowledge with some French services. He obviously had some predilection for Yunnan where he suplied weapons to Muslim General Ma Ju-Lung who would later abandon his fellow rebels to side with the Ch'ing government. Anyway, the politics of Ma Ju-Lung might be the least of Dupuis's concerns for he was more interested in Ma's passion for firearms, which the turncoat general translated into shooting at anything including the furniture in his own house.

As for the French government, the Muslim revolt in Yunnan was a providential boon since it not only kept Peking busy enough to leave Vietnam alone, but also was a source of profit for French arms factories. Of course it was also a lucrative venture for Dupuis: Besides trading in weapons, he also sold rice and salt in Kun Ming at a price 30 times their cost in Hanoi. This common interest in the Red River seems to be the origin of a secret arrangement between the French government and Dupuis, leading some observers to believe he was a covert agent for France. For that matter, in 1872 during his stay in Paris, Pothiau, the minister of the navy, warned him that he was on his own[15] and should not expect any official help from the government. Thus, Dupuis went to secure a Chinese safe conduct from general Ma Ju-Lung. Thereafter he landed in Shang-hai to purchase two second-hand gunboats. Later in Hong Kong, he completed his flotilla with a steam launch, a large junk, and a staff of 25 Europeans and 150 Asians. Needless to say, this crew was a collection of international misfits recruited from the dregs of Shanghai.

On October 26, 1872, when the 30 cannons and 7,000 rifles he had ordered from France arrived, Dupuis sailed from Hong Kong to the coast of Tonkin. He met with a suspicious Justice Minister Le Tuan who declared that Chinese Gen-eral Ma was by no means qualified to deliver safe conduct for Vietnam and therefore advised Dupuis to go back to Hong Kong and wait for a decision from the Hue Court. Indeed the Vietnamese were not duped: The fact that Dupuis pretended to carry on commercial business with two gunboats and an escort of ruffians suggested that he did not have the best intentions. Moreover, if arms trade was more or less tolerated as a business with the Chinese government, private commerce in salt was definitely against Vietnamese law. Thus, the Vi-etnamese purposely delayed their authorization.

After waiting for a few days and in defiance to Le Tuan's opposition, Dupuis moved up the Red River to arrive at Hanoi on December 22, 1872. Notwith-standing a champagne reception offered by Dupuis to the local authorities, they still refused to deliver the necessary travel permit. As his patience was wearing out, on January 18, 1873, Dupuis again took to the river bound to the north.

It is surprising that during this trip, Dupuis made the fatal mistake of stopping and visiting the Yellow Flags, for being familiar with the delta, he should have been aware of their discord with the Black Flags. Later, as he reached Lao Kay, the safe haven of the Black Flags, their chief Liu Yung Fu (Luu Vinh Phuoc) refused to meet with him. This hostility would later develop into armed conflict, with Liu Yung Fu inflicting severe casualties on the French.

During the first week of March 1873, Dupuis's convoy arrived at Mang Chao, his final destination in China. Detaining the official evidence that the Red River was indeed navigable, Admiral Dupre hurriedly cabled Paris, again urging an immediate occupation of Tonkin. But as we have seen, he would not wait for the French government's answer. As if bureaucratic insubordination was the appanage of admiral governors, he would, like Admiral d'Argenlieu later in 1946, confront their government with politics of the fait accompli.

NOTES

1. Christopher Pym, *Henri Mouhat: Diary*, p. 156.

2. China has six major rivers: the Yang Tze, the Yellow, the Heilung, the Pearl, the Hai Ho, and the Huai.

3. Friedrich Hirth, *The Ancient History of China*, p. 37.

4. See Oscar Chapuis, *A History of Vietnam*, p. 77.

5. This was an application of the principle of mutual conquest from the five-element theory. Here, metal conquers water through wood and earth.

6. August Pavie, born in 1847 at Dinan, was the last of the great French explorers, following Doudart and Garnier. He was a functionary at Kampot when Governor Le Myre de Vilers assigned him the task of mapping Cambodia and Laos. For 20 years, from 1875 to 1895, he roamed Indochina with a party of 40, and as a result, succeeded in making the first intelligible map of the peninsula. He was later appointed as French consul at Bangkok and commissioner in boundaries settlement to deal with Siam and England. He also specialized in the study of the Black River, which joined Tonkin and Laos. The part he had taken in helping the king to escape Luang Prabang and taking refuge at Vientiane paved the way for a French protectorate in Laos.

7. Oscar Chapuis, *A History of Vietnam*, p. 66.

8. Military term for red wine.

9. A self-proclaimed pretender to the Cambodian throne.

10. Small crafts resembling American Indian canoes.

11. Annam was already separated from Cochinchina but still had Tonkin as a province.

12. Yunnan.

13. His September 11, 1873 letter to the minister of Navy and colonies. Archives Nationales Outre Mer, 30. Cited by Cao Huy Thuan.

14. Later he told Garnier to call on the missionaries in case of financial problems.

15. Henry McAleavy, *Black Flags in Vietnam*, p. 114.

3

THE CONQUEST OF VIETNAM

In spite of many traders' and missionaries' reports, it is doubtful that at the onset the French government had any definite vision about her mission civilisatrice in Indochina. In fact, the word came long after with the rule of socialist governors from the beginning of the 20th century. But costly wars in Europe had first deprived the French of any ambition other than to put a spoke in the English wheel in Asia.

In retrospect, given the difficulties of communicating with Paris, even by newly installed submarine cables, the French expedition commanders had to rely more on their personal intuition than on any policy dictated by the government. This was a traditional excuse for a continual insubordination.

Yet, contrary to common belief, the first foreign armed intervention in Vietnam was not a French initiative, but came from American John Percival. He arrived in 1845 at Danang on the USS *Constitution* with the purpose of freeing French bishop Lefebvre who had been sentenced to death by the Thieu Tri government. He kept all local mandarins as hostages against the release of the French priest. Because the Vietnamese refused to bow at his unorthodox diplomacy, Percival found himself caught in a kind of dilemma. Finally, he released his prisoners and left but not without first firing a few rounds at the city port. Five years later, in 1850, Joseph Balestier, head of an American mission, came to Danang to apologize for Percival's past action. Because the Vietnamese refused to transmit his message to Tu Duc, he left it on the beach and sailed away.

In 1856, French Captain Leheur de Ville sur Arc, also came to bombard Danang and left. Later, de Montigny, the French consul in Siam, arrived in Danang asking for freedom of religion and commerce. All his requests were rejected on the grounds that the religious freedom the Catholics asked for themselves, had been denied to others. Indeed, in 1774, a papal bull forbade Vietnamese Catholics to worship their own ancestors.

The objective of the French missionaries was not entirely centered on faith propagation among the masses. Having a Catholic king in Vietnam, as they had vainly hoped likewise for Siam, was their ultimate goal. Thus, they would support or foment any popular revolt against an unfriendly monarch. When they incurred royal reprisals, they demanded protection from the French forces.

But missionaries' pleas only served as a pretext for French navy commanders to build their own empire like their British, Dutch, Spanish, and Portuguese counterparts had in Asia. Thus, in 1858, after the fall of Tien Tsin at the hands of the Anglo-French, the French Far East fleet was made available for the conquest of Cochinchina.

COCHINCHINA

On September 1, 1858. Admiral Rigault de Genouilly, with the assurance given by Father Pellerin, one of the promoters of the Annam conquest, that 600,000 Catholic converts were awaiting to join him in Danang, moved his 14 ships with 3,000 Franco-Spanish troops[1] from China down to the coast of Vietnam. Unfortunately, not only did no Catholic adepts show up to cooperate, but some of them were found in the local resistance. De Genouilly also discovered that contrary to Bishop Retord's[2] assertion, the river of Hue was in no way accessible to his ships. Nevertheless, after shelling the city port of Danang, he went on to engage the battle with the 2,000 troops of the mandarin Le Dinh Ly. Ly was mortally wounded at Cam Le, and the An Hai and Ton Hai citadels fell to the French. Then Marshall Nguyen Tri Phuong arrived with 10,000 soldiers. Instead of directly challenging de Genouilly, he first built a fortress at Lien Tri and a rampart from Hai Chau to Phuc Ninh, behind which his troops were well protected. Danang quickly became a quagmire, and during a few months, the admiral fought an elusive war, unable to extend his control to the countryside. Then an outbreak of tropical diseases threatened to decimate his troops. It was far from the idyllic promenade painted by the wilful Pellerin. The ensuing "explication" between de Genouilly and Pellerin almost reached physical confrontation.

On February 2, 1859, after advising Pellerin he had no use for Catholic interpreters including Pellerin himself, de Genouilly sent the priest back to Macao in spite of his vehement protest. Then de Genouilly put Danang under the command of Colonel Toyon and weighed anchor off toward Saigon.

On February 17, 1859, de Genouilly took the deserted city of Saigon in Gia Dinh Province. Here the French made a startling discovery: They found 200 cannons, 160,000 pounds of powder, and 180,000 francs in perfect condition. After having the Gia Dinh fortress razed, he went back to Danang where he managed to evict Nguyen Tri Phuong. In April 1859, for health reasons, de Genouilly had to transfer his command to Admiral François Page and he went back to France to run for the senate the following year. As for a humiliated Pellerin, he took temporary refuge at the Penang French mission in Malaya.

In February 1860, as the French were again at war with China following the

Boxer revolt, Admiral Page had to divert almost all his forces to reinforce Admiral Charner's contingent in China. At the same time, Page tried to negotiate with Hue for freedom of trade and religion, as Montigny had done before. Since it was against the territorial design of his chief, the navy minister Chasseloup Laubat, Page was abruptly recalled. In April 1860, he transferred his command to a naval captain named d'Aries with only a 1,000 man garrison.

Nguyen Tri Phuong, after his semivictory at Danang, found himself in Gia Dinh with 10,000 fresh troops. Against the Vietnamese superior numbers, d'Aries was fighting a losing battle and had to call for help.

In October 1860, the Anglo-French defeated the Chinese at Palikao and the ensuing treaty of Peking enabled Charner to go to d'Aries's rescue with the 70 warships of the Far East fleet and 3,500 Franco-Spanish troops under General Vassoigne. On February 7, 1861, Vassoigne stormed Gia Dinh. After two days of fierce resistance, the Ky Hoa fortress, six kilometers from Saigon, fell to his troops. The French had 300 dead, and both General Vassoigne and his Spanish counterpart Colonel Palanca were wounded. At Ky Hoa, the French were surprised to discover 500 heavy guns and 2,000 French Saint Etienne–manufactured rifles. They also destroyed an amount of rice large enough to feed 8,000 people for a period of two years. While Nguyen Tri Phuong retreated to Bien Hoa, the French went on to occupy My Tho.

With the loss of Gia Dinh, Emperor Tu Duc[3] realized it was time for a truce and appointed mandarin Nguyen Ba Nghi to negotiate with Admiral Charner. But in November 1961, Charner went back to France, transferring his command to Admiral Bonard, who in the process became the first governor of Cochinchina. As Nguyen Ba Nghi beat about the bush, refusing to cede one ounce of land, Bonard seized Bien Hoa and Vinh Long.

At that time in Tonkin, Nguyen Van Thinh (Cai Tong Vang), claiming vague ties with the Le Dynasty, was controlling Quang Yen, Hai Duong, and Bac Ninh and was about to take the entire delta. A Catholic convert, Pedro Le Duy Phung,[4] calling himself emperor of Tonkin, was claiming the Le succession. He began to rally support from both missionaries and Le partisans. Obviously, it was more than Tu Duc could handle at one time. Preferring to lose a few Cochinchina provinces to the French rather than all of Tonkin to the Le, he decided to go back to the bargaining table.

The Three Eastern Provinces and the 1862 Treaty

On June 6, 1862, with navy captain Aubaret as interpreter, Phan Thanh Gian agreed to cede Gia Dinh, My Tho, Bien Hoa, and the Poulo Condore Island, and to pay for war reparations of 400,000 silver dollars over 10 years.[5] It was called the Treaty of Saigon, or the 1862 Treaty.

Afterward, Tu Duc rewarded Gian with the post of governor of Vinh Long. But the emperor's troubles were only beginning. To Queen Mother Tu Du—a native of Cochinchina—to the entire Court, and to the people, the 1862 Treaty was a national disgrace. Thus, Emperor Tu Duc ordered Gian to rescind the treaty and take back the three provinces.

In Cochinchina, it was too late. The emperor was accused of "selling away" the southern population in exchange for his personal safety. The population organize their own protection: The movement of People Self-defense (Dan Chung Tu Ve) was founded by scholar Nguyen Van Huan (Thu Khoa Huan)[6] in My Tho, and by fisherman-farmer Nguyen Trung Truc in Tan An. Thieu Ho Dang, a landowner, and Truong Cong Dinh, a veteran of the Ky Hoa battle, raised their own private army. To Governor Phan Than Gian's call for peace, Truong Cong Dinh replied: As long as you speak of peace and surrender, we are determined not to obey the Court's orders.[7]

Phan Thanh Gian

Like Le Van Duyet, Phan Thanh Gian was one of the few Cochinchinese holding a high position at the Hue Court. But his roller-coaster career suggests the existence of some latent ethnic conflict inside the imperial entourage.[8] Obviously, without the protection of Queen Mother Tu Du, Phan Thanh Gian would not last.

Graduated Tien Si[9] through the national competitive examination, he was every now and then academician, minister, ambassador, province governor, and also petty librarian. In 1838, under Emperor Minh Mang, because he had neglected to impress his seal on an imperial edict,[10] he was declared a rebel and stripped of his cabinet rank. Thereafter, he was dispatched to Tonkin to serve as a minor inspector in the gold mines.

Because none of the French present would return to the provinces, with Captain Aubaret[11] as interpreter, the 70-man Phan Thanh Gian mission set out for France where they arrived in November 1963. Phan Thanh Gian was received in audience at the Tuileries by Emperor Napoleon III and Empress Eugenie. It seems that he had deliberately adopted a psychological approach by posing as a defenseless victim of French aggression. Looking old and fragile in his mandarin garb, he joined his hands to his forehead and humbly kowtowed three times, unlike French envoys who had refused to prostrate themselves before their own emperor. Then he wept and moaned while pleading his case. The spectacle was so pathetic that Empress Eugenie was moved to tears. As for the French emperor, he was not comfortable with the idea that his powerful nation gained no prestige in humiliating such an insignificant country. Thus, an uneasy Napoleon III promised to return these strange provinces that he would not even consider for his summer vacation. To be fair, it should be said that Phan Thanh Gian had also offered to pay cash for the war indemnity. Although some officials doubted Annam's financial capability, the French minister of finance would not turn up his nose. Finally, Aubaret was instructed to revise the treaty with Gian upon their return to Hue.

The Annamite mission went home in March 1864. On July 15, 1864, Aubaret signed a draft treaty with Phan Thanh Gian returning the three provinces Gia Dinh, My Tho, and Bien Hoa to Vietnam, but allowing the French to keep troops in Saigon, My Tho, and Thu Dau Mot for the protection of ports and trades. Furthermore, Vietnam must accept French protection and pay 2 million silver dollars as war indemnity every year for 40 years.

At this time, a sergeant Duval, secretly dispatched by Laubat to watch the negotiations, managed to send a copy of the draft to his minister. In a cover letter, he convinced Laubat that Tu Duc had no intention of ratifying the treaty: All the king wanted was to temporize. This was a good pretext for Laubat and his admirals to strongly oppose the new treaty. Knowing the faltering nature of Napoleon III, Laubat took a powerful approach. On the one hand, he asserted that the treaty would leave the Catholic population without protection—a situation of primary concern to the empress—and on the other hand Cochinchina was an economically sound investment: The colony revenues were 947,000 francs in 1862, 2.8 million in 1863, a projected 3 million for 1864 and 4 million for 1865. On the contrary, expenditures went on decreasing from 22,600,000 in 1862 to 19,000,000 in 1863, 14 million in 1864 and 8 million in 1865. As a conclusion, he simply threatened the emperor with resignation of the entire cabinet. Thus, Napoleon III gave in and Aubaret was told on June 8, 1864, to cancel the new treaty. Later, on more than one occasion, the court of Hue was told to refer to the original 1862 treaty.

Laubat had a vision of another Annam. He did not see it as simply a colony, for with its natural resources—sugar, silk, rice, and gold—it would be absurd to transform it into a nation of slaves under foreign authoritarian rule. In fact, like his missionary allies, he wanted Annam to be a French Catholic empire in the Far East.

After the conquest of Saigon-Gia Dinh, Admiral Charner placed French officers at every echelon of the administration partly because of his own policy and partly because the native cadres had fled. As Charner failed to fill the vacuum, a chaotic situation ensued. This led his successor, Admiral Bonard, to opt for a form of association: He undertook to convince the Annamites that the French would respect their law and customs, that French religion would not force any conversion, and that the natives could safely pursue the cult of their ancestors and other faiths of their own choice. They would be free to cultivate their own lands and trade and transport the produce to Saigon. In a nutshell, Bonard was inclined toward some form of protectorate leaving Annamites to govern their own people but under the ultimate control of the French. Bonard's liberalism was based on the assumption that the Annamites were not true believers, for their religious knowledge was very limited; their faith was based on superstitions and would quickly pass away in contact with Christian evangelization. Hence, with Laubat's blessing, Bonard began to implement his policy and surrounded himself with a handful of young and talented officers, among which were Aubaret and Philastre. As we were not yet to the Republican era with separation of church and state, cooperation between the administration and the foreign mission was necessary and profitable for both: The admirals used the missionaries for political purposes, and the missionaries used the admirals for religious benefits.

When Bonard returned to France in May 1863, Admiral de la Grandiere took the succession and began a series of conquests, which led him to also occupy West Cochinchina and extend the French protectorate over Cambodia. He gave the command of the Mekong exploration to Doudart de Lagree, although the project was the brainchild of Garnier. de Lagree had represented Bonard at Oudong, the Cambodian capital, where he succeeded in arranging the Franco-Cambodian treaty of protectorate.

Protectorate Treaty with Cambodia

At that time, Cambodia was under the dual suzerainty of both Siam and Vietnam. Because the 1862 treaty allowed French free trade on the "big river of Cambodia" (Mekong), Bonard was determined to enforce the clause. For this, he must have the Annam protectorateship over Cambodia transferred to France. He went to Oudong to meet with King Norodom and found the Cambodian king experiencing, like Tu Duc, serious dynastic problems with a pretender named Pu Kombo, who was wreaking havoc at the Vietnamese border. Since Vietnam was of no help, Norodom would rather accept French protection. Yet his only fear was that the French would leave some day and that Cambodia would have to suffer Vietnamese retaliation. So, he dragged his feet, and impatient Bonard went back to Saigon, but not without leaving at Oudong Doudart de Lagree, a naval lieutenant, as his representative. When Norodom headed out to Bangkok to be officially enthroned by his Siamese suzerain, de Lagree went on to occupy his Silver Palace[12] compelling the king to interrupt his journey. Back home, Norodom readily signed the protectorate treaty with France on August 11, 1863. Siam reacted by forcing Cambodia to also sign a treaty according to which Siam recognized Norodom as the viceroy and governor general of Cambodia.

All parties agreed to carry out his investiture at Oudong. The Siamese delegate handed the crown to his French counterpart who in turn gave it to Norodom who finally placed it on his head. This parody resulted in 100 years of Franco-Siamese peace until 1944, when, at the instigation of Japan, Thailand opened hostilities with France. It was not a good idea, for its entire fleet was sunk by the French in the battle of Koh Chang.

The Three Western Provinces of Cochinchina

As expected, diplomatic rivalry surfaced when drunken French sailors violated the residence of a Cambodian prince. Notwithstanding, de Lagree's official apologies and punishment of the delinquents, Siam pressured Norodom to expel all French, including de Lagree. This was, for the newly arrived Admiral de la Grandiere, a warning of future problems with Siam and led him to realize the strategic importance of the three western provinces in case of a conflict with

Siam. Hence, in 1864, he went back to France to confer with Laubat. When he returned to Saigon in 1866, de la Grandiere worked toward an annexation of the rest of Cochinchina.

In 1866, a French delegation arrived in Hue to officially complain about the insecurity in Cochinchina. They offered to reestablish peace if the court consented to place West Cochinchina under French control. The French would even forsake the 4-million franc war reparations if the court agreed. Again Tu Duc applied his dilatory tactics. Anticipating more trouble from him, Phan Thanh Gian, then governor of Vinh Long, put up a formal resignation, which was rejected by the court.

On June 19, 1867, de la Grandiere arrived in My Tho with an armada of eight warships, dozens of transport vessels, 1,000 European troops, and 400 local recruits. On June 20, as Hue was still loath, he served an ultimatum for the delivery of Vinh Long, Ha Tien, and Chau Doc. Tu Duc appointed Phan Thanh Gian viceroy in charge of the negotiations. At My Tho, while Phan was busy discussing with de la Grandiere the terms of the accord on the French flagship, the French went on to occupy[13] the three provinces (see Map 3). Later, an outraged Phan wrote to de la Grandiere: I have relied upon your good faith but you attacked me behind my back. Since your forces are too mighty, I would be a fool to resist. Thus I agree to your demand but I strongly protest.

On July 7, 1867, after completing a lengthy report to his emperor and kowtowing five times to the north, Phan Thanh Gian went on a 17-day fast, expecting to die at the end. But it was to no avail. On August 7, 1867, he took a lethal mixture of opium and vinegar.

Phan Thanh Gian's case unveiled a very unpleasant aspect of Tu Duc's character: Forgetting that he had forced the mandarin into such a predicament, he proclaimed in an edict that the loss of the six provinces was due to the failure of Nguyen Tri Phuong, Ton That Cap, Pham The Hien, and Nguyen Ba Nghi to build up adequate defenses as well as the incapacity of Phan Thanh Gian, Lam Duy Hiep, Nguyen Huu Co, and Truong Van Uyen to convince the French. And he posthumously stripped Phan of all ranks and titles, even removing his name from the Tien Si stele. Later, Phan was rehabilitated by Emperor Dong Khanh but it was too late: According to some Vietnamese accounts, immediately after his suicide, his two sons, Phan Thanh Liem and Phan Thanh Ton, revolted. On the night of November 9, 1867, they took Huong Diem, ten kilometers from Ben Tre. On November 12, three French gunboats shelled Huong Diem, forcing the rebels to retreat to nearby Giong Gach Canh where both were killed. Yet according to French archives, the two were forced into exile in France.

TONKIN

After the setback of the Mekong expedition, the French, still haunted by Yunnan and its numerous resources, decided to extend the exploration of the Red River in Tonkin. As one can expect, the commercial exploitation of the

Red River required a peaceful environment, and Tonkin was far from giving such a warranty. Besides the periodic uprisings fomented by the Le pretenders, legitimate or not, there was also the growing hostility of a Buddhist population toward the expansion of Catholic influence.

As for the ex–Tai Ping, Ngo Con took Cao Bang in 1868 causing Tu Duc to call for Ching's help. Chinese general Ta Ke Qui came down to direct Tonkin pacification. In 1869, the Kwang Si general Phung Tu Tai with Vietnamese Vo Trong Binh took back Cao Bang. In 1870, Ngo Con was shot to death but his constituents split into various "flags" among which were the Yellow Flags under Hoang Sung Anh, and the Black Flags, under Liu Yung-Fu (Luu Vinh Phuoc).

Liu Yung-Fu (Luu Vinh Phuoc)

Liu Yung-Fu was born in 1837 in Ch'in Chou (western Kwang Tung) where his father Liu I-Lai was a petty bootlegger. At the age of 13, Liu Yung-Fu served as an occasional pilot on the local rivers. After the death of his parents, at 17 Liu moved with his half-brother to the adjacent village of Kao Feng where they spent their days on the hills cutting wood to make charcoal. At night, both slept in a pig sty. One day, according to his biography, Liu had a dream: An old man asked him: Why did the Black Tiger General still hide in these cogs? Why did he not go down the hill?

Indeed, Liu's life turned around when he later met with the Cheng pirates. Wu Yuan Chung, the Cheng leader, was no ordinary cutthroat: He came from a rich family ruined by rapacious Ch'ing mandarins. In 1862, Chung lost his life in an encounter with mandarin Feng Tzu T'sai, a Tai Ping turncoat. His son, Wu Ya Cheng, crossed the Tonkin border with Liu Yung-Fu, but three years later was killed at Lang Son by the same Feng Tzu T'sai.

Left alone, Liu Yung-Fu organized his own band under the name of Black Flags, in remembrance of his old dream. He was then 42 years old and one of the best warriors in South China. To justify his early cutthroat career, Liu said that he could not continue to eat rice gruel to alleviate his hunger. His unique strategy was to put his military skill to the service of both Vietnamese and Chinese, following the example of Feng Tzu T'sai. He would later exterminate his partner and rival Yellow Flag. In 1871, when Prince Hoang Ke Viem was appointed governor of Lang Son, Thai Binh, and Ninh Binh, his first move was to seek Liu Yung-Fu's cooperation against the French.

Jean Dupuis

When Jean Dupuis was back in Hanoi, after reaching Yunnan by the Red River, the local authorities had already jailed his Cantonese partners, Banh Hoi Ky and Quan Ta Dinh, who had provided him with rice and salt for sale in Yunnan. In response, with elements of the Yellow Flags he had hired, Dupuis went on to build his defense base in Hanoi. Then, in an blatant act of provocation, he seized the chief of the Hanoi police as hostage and demanded the release of the Chinese duo. At this point, the Hue Court filed a complaint with the governor of Cochinchina, Admiral Dupre, who knew the tacit arrangement between the Paris administration and Dupuis. Apparently legality was on Dupuis's side: As he detained travel documents from the Chinese government, it was up to Vietnam to deal directly with China. But to prevent a Sino-Viet collusion, Admiral Dupre ostensibly agreed with the Vietnamese to order Dupuis out of Tonkin. He then commenced a cat and mouse game: A defiant Dupuis declared that nobody had the right to kick him out, for he was legally holding a Chinese passport and therefore he was subject only to Chinese law. At one point he apparently indulged in pure blackmail: He advised Dupre that he was running out of funds, and unless he received some assistance he could look forward to a cooperation with the British or even to turn over the Red River operation to the Chinese themselves. Dupre's promptness to comply was once again evidence of some secret quid pro quo. Indeed, Dupre immediately delivered 30,000 piastres to Dupuis. The clear consequence was that the fund allowed Dupuis to reinforce his forces by hiring 500 Kwang Si army deserters. If Dupre wished to provide military support to Dupuis, he would not do otherwise.

By that time, 77-year-old Marshall Nguyen Tri Phuong arrived in Hanoi, well remembered by the French for all the troubles they had with him in Gia Dinh at the time of D'Aries. In the pure Chinese tradition, the old marshall began to issue his proclamations: Anyone who provided the French with rice and salt would be sentenced to death. In response, Dupuis had his men tear down Phuong's announcement and carry it in a procession around the town. Then from words they passed to clashes between Dupuis's men and Phuong's forces, which erupted more and more frequently. It was then that the court of Hue asked Bishop Puginier, who was residing at Ke So, to intervene to restore peace. But Puginier in a pure display of hypocrisy—to say the least—replied that he was only liable for spiritual matters and had no authority to intervene in politics. In fact, the role he endlessly played in "providing advice" to Dupre and his associates showed that he was deeply involved in the French design over North Vietnam.

Admiral Dupre

Dupre's responsibility in the conquest of Tonkin was undeniable. Given French government fears of arousing British hostility, he probably left France with an ambiguous agenda. But the fact that he possessed an extensive experience in colonial affairs (Madagascar, La Reunion, China) suggests a definite context to his mission. He arrived in Saigon in April 1871 as the fifth governor of Cochinchina, ten years after Bonard inaugurated the line of admiral governors. The prudence he displayed justified his nomination: By contrast, with the annexation of Cochinchina before assessing the capability of the Mekong, Dupre waited for the Red River exploration before he recommended the occupation of

Tonkin. Since 1872, he carefully mapped his approach. First, he acknowledged Tonkin as the richest province of Annam. Then he expressed fear of losing it to interference from Prussia claiming that many German traders expected their government to establish a colony in Tonkin. He revealed that Tu Duc was trying to acquire an old English warship from the Prussians as a first step to secure an alliance against the French. But the French foreign minister, Remusat, declared that "no matter the interest in an occupation of Tonkin, no matter the commercial importance of its vicinity to the South West of China[14] I do not believe that, given our present condition, we can envisage such an action which does not seem absolutely necessary to protect our current interest."[15] As for the minister of the navy and colonies, Admiral Pothuau, he sided with Remusat with a second thought because he would later help Dupuis acquire arms and munitions in France.

Given Paris opposition, Admiral Dupre cleverly changed his belligerent policy into a friendly association with Annam. Through the intelligence provided by the Tonkin missionaries,[16] he was well aware of Tu Duc troubles in that province. Thus, as a first step toward protectionism, he would induce the Annamites to ask for his cooperation to restore order. This time, Pothuau could not reject such an astute scheme but strongly recommended extreme prudence and discretion. Furthermore, Dupre assured him he needed no help from Paris and guaranteed final success.

The pacification problem in Tonkin was an Annamite internal affair in which France had no grounds for intervention except upon the Annamites' request. At that time, Jean Dupuis was operating his ambiguous commerce of arms between Tonkin and Yunnan. As he was dealing with Muslims who rallied to the Chinese imperial court, and as Annam was still China's vassal, such commerce was not considered illicit. But by adding salt and rice to his trade, Dupuis acted against Vietnam prohibition. A series of incidents ensued leading the Tu Duc government to complain to Dupre. As Dupre used dilatory tactics, the court decided to dispatch a mission to Paris. Since they had to embark in Saigon, the mission was intercepted by Dupre who offered to send 3,000 troops to get Dupuis out. As this was tantamount to a threat of invasion, the Annamite delegation took the hint and asked for only a few soldiers. Now Dupre was ready to implement his project by calling back into service Francis Garnier.

Francis Garnier

There was no evidence that Dupre was sincere when he promised the Hue Court to expel Dupuis: In fact, after Dupuis's success in establishing the navigability of the Red River, the governor immediately cabled Paris to urge the occupation of Tonkin.

Furthermore, using an officer of Garnier's caliber just for the purpose of removing a simple civilian like Dupuis did not seem quite rational. Anyway,

Dupre gave Garnier written instructions to kick Dupuis out of Tonkin, and he made sure that the Hue Court was well aware of these official instructions.

As for Garnier, before leaving Saigon, he informed Dupuis in a letter that Admiral Dupre intended to continue business as usual and that he was very pleased with Dupuis's performance. He added that he counted on Dupuis's experience to help him carry out his mission. He also wrote to his family to boast that he had carte blanche to conduct this mission and also the capacity to call, if necessary, for additional troops from an escort ship. Be that as it may, Garnier's appointment was not to the liking of the Paris cabinet.

Upon his arrival, Garnier delivered a letter from Dupre to the Tonkin Catholic missionaries in which the governor asked for assistance in case Garnier met with any financial difficulties. Thus, we now know why Dupre needed no help from the Paris government.

On October 11, 1873, Garnier left Saigon with 83 marines, to be followed two weeks later by a second group of 88. He arrived in Hai Duong on October 23 to find Dupuis warmly greeting him in public. The old China hand even had his launch tow Garnier's contingent up to Hanoi where they arrived on November 5. This time Dupuis had his ragtag troops present full military honors to the naval officer. This display of friendship did not go unnoticed by old Marshall Nguyen Tri Phuong who began to doubt French sincerity. Thus, he conspicuously stayed aloof inside his citadel and assigned Garnier to billet in a poorly equipped inn. Either it was under Dupuis's suggestion, or seizing this opportunity for himself to open the hostilities, Garnier marched directly into the Hanoi citadel. There he bluntly told Phuong that he decided to share the place with him.

The next day the game of proclamations began. Garnier took the lead by announcing to the Vietnamese population that he, "the Great mandarin of France," had come to defend them against pirates and to restore peace to the country. In response, Phuong proclaimed that Garnier had come to remove Dupuis at the request of the court of Hue. In turn, Garnier denied any obedience to the Hue Court; he had been simply instructed by the French governor to settle the dispute but there was no question of expelling anybody. He also added that his role was to safeguard trade by opening the country and its rivers to all nations, under the protection of France.[17]

Then, according to historian Pham Van Son, Garnier and Dupuis entered into secret negotiations with a Le pretender but had to abandon the project on the advice of Bishop Puginier. Nevertheless, many Le partisans stayed with Garnier as suppletive forces.

The situation created by Garnier was a cause of discord between Spanish and French missionaries. While Puginier, French vicar apostolic of Ke So (Hanoi), openly supported war, the Spanish vicar apostolic of North Tonkin, Colomer, wrote to Admiral Dupre that the primary reason for the missionaries' presence in Annam was to propagate Christianity separately from politics.

In Hanoi, the proclamations contest ended but war preparations began. While governor Nguyen Tri Phuong was awaiting Hue permission to attack the French, Garnier decided to take action as soon as the second half of his contingent arrived. In view of the showdown, Garnier quietly wrote his last will. The next day, November 18, 1873, he delivered an ultimatum to Phuong to surrender by 6 P.M. The following dawn, the French attacked Hanoi. Nguyen Tri Phuong commanded in person on the field, displaying his rank with four large yellow sunshades. As an ideal target, he was soon hit in the abdomen and thigh and was made prisoner. After one hour of violent combat, the 7,000-Vietnamese citadel fell to the 200 French troops.

Garnier came to Phuong's bedside to say pointedly how much he was honored to be his opponent even for such a short time. Refusing the dialogue, Phuong kept a haughty silence. But when Bishop Puginier arrived for the extreme unction rites, the Buddhist warrior exploded: "Shut up. You missionaries have helped the French to rob Annam of Cochinchina and Tonkin. I do not want to see you. All I want is to die." Then he ripped away his dressing and bled to death. In the following 20 days, Garnier took three additional provinces: Ninh Binh, Nam Dinh, and Hai Duong.

As for the Hue Court, on the one hand it appointed Le Tuan as governor of Tonkin to replace Phuong, on the other, it dispatched mandarin Nguyen Van Tuong to Saigon to negotiate with Dupre. From Hue another delegation, with Bishop Bohier and Father Dangelzer as interpreters, sailed to Hanoi to talk with Garnier. But Prince Hoang Ke Viem, the Son Tay commander, was instructed to take all defensive measures. Thus, Hoang called in Black Flag's Liu Yung-Fu (Luu Vinh Phuoc), promising considerable reward for each French head; slices of enemy flesh had a lower prize.

Liu Yung-Fu attacked on December 21, 1873, during a mass celebrated by Bishop Puginier. Repelled by Garnier's guns, he retreated, but in the ensuing hot pursuit, Garnier accidently stumbled on a rock and fell to the ground to be repeatedly stabbed by the Black Flag soldiers. All French dead had their heads severed, including Garnier. According to Dupuis, "Garnier's clothes are in ribbons: his body is covered with wounds made by swords and spears. His chest has been cut open and his heart removed."[18]

The situation created by Garnier compelled the French government to officially disavow his action. Paris felt justified to do so for moral and political reasons. First, Garnier was not commissioned by the metropole[19] but by Dupre alone. Second, Paris could not afford to acknowledge any involvement, for fear of further complications. Indeed, at that time, the Prussians were still occupying part of France after their 1870 victory, and France had not yet recovered her full strength to envisage any significant military action. As for Dupre, he could only join the official rejection by gutlessly putting all the blame on the defunct Garnier. But he was honest enough to recommend that Garnier be posthumously promoted to the rank of navy commander; it was of course rejected. In its scheme to keep secrecy, the Paris cabinet played dumb and even forbade a subscription for a statue to Garnier. In 1875, when Garnier's entire body[20] arrived in Saigon, not only did the city arsenal refuse to supply a lead sheet for his coffin, but the new Governor Duperre himself refused to attend the funeral. Only friends and family were allowed at the ceremony.

Philastre Accord (January 5, 1874)

Although Dupre apologized to the Hue Court, he also realized that he had to rebuild a trust shattered by his personal protege Garnier. He needed a third party to whom Vietnamese would lend a friendly ear. And he was lucky enough to find such a rare bird in the person of Captain Philastre.

With Aubaret, Philastre was one of two most distinguished sinologists in the entire Saigon administration. Perhaps his marriage to a Vietnamese lady had fueled his opposition to colonial policy: "Vietnamese do not need any of our good services and it is a crime against humanity to pursue the suppression of such an old and venerable civilization,"[21] he wrote to Garnier. With that, it was quite probable that he was on Dupre's black list of "unwanted" and ready for immediate "rapatriation."[22] But probably the admiral had been held back by Philastre's international fame. He was awarded the Stanislas Julien prize for his French translation of the Gia Long Code.

Given full power to negotiate with the Vietnamese, Philastre arrived in Hue to find an atmosphere of emergency as Tu Duc was actively preparing for war. Tu Duc assigned mandarin Nguyen Van Tuong to negotiate with Philastre. He insisted that Philastre accompany Tuong to Tonkin to reestablish order. Both left on December 20 and arrived at Hanoi on December 26. The first news Philastre learned was of the tragic death of Garnier. The 300 soldiers he left behind were in an extremely precarious condition. They lacked money, food, medication, and munitions. No rescue was in sight.

As for mandarin Tuong, he found a chaotic situation due to the desertion of all Tonkin officials and consequently an increase in insurrection in the delta. It was impossible for the Hue government to immediately reestablish an administration. The idea of using officials dispatched from Hue would surely be opposed by the Tonkin population, which had come in the past to appreciate their relative autonomy. Thus, it did not take long for Tuong and Philastre to reach an accord on January 5, 1874, by which French troops regrouped in Haiphong after returning all positions they had captured including Hai Duong, Ninh Binh, and Nam Dinh. Within the context of this agreement, Philastre gave Dupuis the choice to either resettle in Haiphong, or wait in Yunnan until the Red River officially opened for trade. Dupuis argued that he had the right to be in Hanoi like any Frenchman had the right to be in Saigon, to which Philastre tartly replied that they came to Saigon as pirates and bandits. Thus having lost his commerce as a result of the Philastre treaty, Dupuis filed a claim for one-million francs damages. Rejected at first, he kept roaming Paris ministries for years until he obtained satisfaction.

On February 2, 1874, the Philastre agreement was finalized: All hostilities between France and Vietnam in Tonkin end now with the return to Vietnam of all positions seized by the French. The French must leave Hanoi to regroup at Haiphong, while in Hanoi the Vietnamese garrison must be reduced to a simple police force. Amnesty must be granted to all former French collaborators.

Back in Hue, Emperor Tu Duc promoted Nguyen Van Tuong to a higher rank and sent official compliments to Philastre for his "magnificent cooperation." Afterward, as war indemnity had still to be paid, in order to raise enough funds, a Chinese resident, Hau Loi Trinh, was commissioned to sell opium for the court account. But the proceeds only amounted to 302,200 piastres, thus the court decided to distribute honoric titles: 1,000 piastres for a ninth-degree mandarin, 10,000 for a sixth-degree.

Dupre-Tuong Treaty (March 15, 1874)

As for Admiral Dupre whose career almost came to an end with the Garnier incident, he was quite happy to ratify on March 13, 1874, a final revision of the Philastre accord: France recognized Vietnam as an independent nation, under the protection of France for its internal and external security. In return, Vietnam agreed to embrace French foreign policy and to refrain from accord with a third country without consulting with France. Nevertheless, Vietnam kept its current ties with some neighbors. The emperor of Dai Nam recognized French sovereignty over the six Cochinchinese provinces. France donated to Dai Nam, five 500-HP steamships with 100 cannons and 1,000 rifles with 5,000 bullets. All war indemnities owed to France were forsaken. As for the one million silver dollars Vietnam owed to Spain for war reparations[23] France would undertake to pay and replace Spain as a Vietnam creditor. Vietnam opened the Red River and the ports of Thi Nai and Ninh Hai for trade. Religions and trade were also allowed in the entire Dai Nam territory.

This treaty intended to bring peace back to Tonkin, began to record its first casualty: While Nguyen Van Tuong was relishing his success, Le Tuan committed suicide.

Furthermore, Article 9, protecting Catholic subjects, would become the source of multiple confrontations between the non-Catholics and the missionary adepts. Such was the Xuan Hoa case. This village was under the despotic rule of a rich man named Liem who was related to a high mandarin at the Hue Court. As many inhabitants left to seek protection under the Annamite priest An, the latter advised them to demonstrate. According to Annam law, demonstrations were grave offenses and incitation to demonstrate bore the same penalty: caning. The situation was exacerbated by the fact that Catholic converts went to gather harvest in the Xuan Hoa village, on a land they had not cultivated. The landowners reacted by taking back the harvest by force. Priest An was sentenced to death, but by virtue of Article 9, the death sentence was commuted to caning. Under violent protest from the missionaries together with the French administration, emperor Tu Duc decided that caning could be replaced by a fine. As for Philastre, he openly criticized Catholic abuses and consequently incurred the missionaries' wrath. Puginier declared he was a traitor to French national interests and opposed adamantly Philastre's nomination suggested by the Hue Court.

As for Dupre, having succeeded in securing French sovereignty over all Cochinchina, he went home in triumph. His first move was to win the Legion of Honor medal for Philastre and to have him confirmed as a French representative at Hue. But under ceaseless complaints from the Church, the Paris government was finally convinced that Philastre had stayed too long in Annam and that his posture as a scholar prevented him from implementing a stronger policy. Subsequently he was recalled.

The departure of Philastre marked the beginning of deterioration of Franco-Vietnamese relations. Yet, since 1874, France tried to maintain a peaceful coexistence with Annam. Krantz, Dupre's successor, spent much time in keeping the missionaries and their associate, Rheinart France, charge d'affaires in Tonkin, from creating and supporting sedition against the Hue regime. On one occasion in 1874 he went a step further by ordering Major Dujardin to put down a rebellion in Hai Duong. In fact, since France and Annam were more or less allied, it is difficult to assert against which one the popular revolt was directed.

Obviously, Philastre's successor Rheinart had chosen to carry his hawkish policy upon the advice of Bishop Puginier. His attitude led Tu Duc to seek external protection by resuming Vietnamese traditional ties with foreign powers. Vietnamese historians agree that Tu Duc at no time had any intent to abide by any treaty he had to accept under duress. He had bitterly declared that it was because of the impossibility to enlarge their foreign relations that they were now meeting so many difficulties. Thus, taking advantage of a loophole in the 1874 treaty allowing Vietnam to keep the status quo in foreign relations, he first undertook to strengthen his relations with China. So far, there was no need to go to Peking, for tributes were remitted directly to the governor of the two Kwang[24] but in 1876, two years after the Dupre-Tuong treaty, Tu Duc dispatched a three-man embassy to Peking. In 1880, another mission went to pay homage to the Ch'ing. In 1881, China sent a mission to Hue to negotiate commercial trade. On November 10, 1880, the Chinese ambassador in Paris declared that Dai Nam[25] was still a vassal of China and rejected the Franco-Vietnamese treaty of 1874.

In 1878, Vietnam renewed relations with Siam. In 1880, Tu Duc welcomed an Italian commercial mission. In 1881, a Viet mission went to Hong Kong to purchase ships. But the French deplored two incidents: In 1881, a German exporter demanded indemnification for the damages caused to his rice shipment by a delay in a Hai Phong custom inspection. The French in Saigon had to disburse 5,000 piastres to prevent the situation from worsening. In 1882, a Chinese British citizen named Ang Chi Lock terrorized the Hai Duong population with his fire arms. He was arrested and executed by the Vietnamese authorities. While the British consul in Saigon worked with the French on the indemnification, Tu Duc undercut the negotiations by sending a mission to Hong Kong to deal separately with the British; yet Governor Le Myre De Vilers had to pay 20,000 piastres from his Cochinchinese customs budget. Actually, the French avoided giving any pretext to other European powers to intervene in Vietnam as they had done in China. It is quite probable that the Hue government deliberatedly took these inopportune initiatives in order to embarrass the French.

Such Franco-Vietnamese animosity reached personal proportions as Tu Duc began to shut his doors to Rheinart, Philastre's successor. The Vietnamese spared no unfriendly act to express their antagonism. One day as Tu Duc was fishing on the River of Perfume, Rheinart arrived by junk in the vicinity. The imperial guard forced him to disembark and to continue his trip on foot. All these humiliations led the French to seek more and more opportunities to "give a good lesson" to a recalcitrant ally. In 1877, Rheinart retaliated by refusing to let Vietnam take part in the Paris International Fair. He again opposed sending a Vietnamese delegation to Paris for the inauguration of French President Grevy.[26]

In the aftermath of the Dupre-Tuong treaty, the provinces of Nghe An and Ha Tinh rose up against both their emperor and the French. Tu Duc's army had to carry on a bloody repression, which added to the popular contempt for a monarchy "only capable of persecuting its own subjects."

Jules Ferry

In 1880, six years after the 1874 treaty, England, Germany, and Spain still debated over their rights to deal directly with Annam. Tu Duc gradually showed signs of independence although his problems in Tonkin were far from being resolved. As for Paris, they adopted patience and ingenuity in their protectionist objective for two reasons: Ultimately, either Tu Duc would ask for their help against the insurgents or the insurgents would request their help against Tu Duc Anyway, they bet on a certainty.

In 1880, Jules Ferry was elected prime minister under president Jules Grevy. He was a proponent of Leroy Beaulieu's doctrine of colonization, which, published in 1874, had now become the bible of a group of intellectuals, bourgeois, and republicans concerned with national pride or international prestige. Indeed, Beaulieu wrote: "Besides Russia, Germany, and England, France is a power dying a slow death. We can avoid this fate by carrying out colonization overseas. For France, this is a matter of life and death."[27]

Ferry was seen by Vietnamese historians as a colonialist devil when he declared: "Export is a basic factor of public prosperity and the success of investing together capital and labor is measured by the magnitude of overseas markets." His first move was to decide on a revision of the 1874 treaty, which he found ambiguous in many respects. The problem was to find a way to compel the court of Hue to accept such a revision. Jaureguiberry, the navy minister, first proposed a solution of force, which required at least 12 warships and 6,000 troops. His colleague, Freycinet, the foreign minister, argued that France should avoid any action that could be seen as an aggression against Vietnam. According to him, France must try to have the terms of the treaty clarified in another treaty; particularly, the word "protectorate" must be clearly spelled out. To support the negotiations, a show of force could be carried out without necessarily taking the aspect of an armed intervention. Because Cochinchina governor Le Myre de Vilers was currently in France for a vacation, the government assigned him to devise plans for Tonkin. De Vilers in turn dispatched Colonel Riviere to Tonkin under the pretext of helping French forces against the Black Flags. Before leaving Paris, Riviere was clearly told to avoid alerting international opinion and to refrain from any conflict with China. Only with prudent politics, sustained peace, and intelligent administration could France expand and maintain her presence in Tonkin and Annam.

Henri Riviere

Riviere came to the French navy with a redolence of Parisian literary salons. Because his ambition was to obtain a seat at the French Academy some day one can understand that at the age of 56, he had by military standards, a rather conventional career. This mission was to be his last assignment before retirement.

Like Garnier, Riviere received contradictory orders: On the one hand, Governor de Vilers insisted on only a show of force, but on the other hand, he asked Riviere to "display both force and altruism" with war prisoners who were not to be killed but were to be dispatched to the Poulo Condore concentration camps. Anyway, given the way the Black Flags had treated Francis Garnier, it was probable that no governor expected the military to take his vacillating orders seriously.

Whatever way the French chose—either war or only threats—they did not have to create incidents. Soon, two French explorers, Courtin and Villeroi, were kidnapped by the Yellow Flags while two others—Fuchs and Stadin—had to flee before the Black Flags. On March 13, 1882, French resident superior Champeaux was arrested by the Black Pavillions who were being commissioned by Annam governor Hoang Ke Viem. For the French, it was exactly the last straw they were waiting for: On the same day, de Vilers sent a firm protest to Tu Duc threatening to take "appropriate action." Two weeks later, on March 26, 1882, Colonel Henri Riviere sailed to Hanoi with two warships and 300 troops.

On his arrival in Hanoi, Riviere began to pay courtesy visits to Governor General Hoang Dieu. But the wary mandarin ostensibly reinforced his citadel and called in his regional troops. However, if Riviere had any concern for peace, he would then have taken steps to appease the Vietnamese, but he remained silent. And when his second contingent of 250 men arrived on April 25, 1882, Riviere immediately ordered Hoang Dieu to surrender by 5 A.M. the next morning. That day at 8.15 A.M., the French attacked. At 9.15 A.M., judging the situation untenable, Hoang Dieu disbanded his forces, then wrote a long report to his emperor and hanged himself from a tree at a nearby pagoda. Nguyen Cao, the provincial judge of Hai Duong and Bac Ninh, made harakiri after cutting off his tongue. At 10.45 A.M., all Hanoi was in the hands of the French.

Emperor Tu Duc reported the fall of Hanoi to the Kwangtung governor, and in September 1882, the Chinese sent down 17 divisions totaling 200,000 men to occupy Lang Son, Cao Bang, Bac Ninh, and Thai Nguyen.[28]

On March 12, 1883, on receipt of a 750-man reinforcement, Riviere went on to occupy the Hon Gay coalfield, not only to prevent a commercial takeover by the British, but also to use the mine as security for further settlement of war indemnity with Vietnam.

As Prince Hoang Ke Viem was feverishly preparing the defense of Nam Dinh with volunteers from the Kwang Si army (the Black Flags were still sitting on the fence), Riviere decided to move first. With eight gunboats and 800 troops, he laid siege to Nam Dinh. Meeting an unexpected resistance, a maddened Riviere let all hell break loose: According to French captain Gosselin, fifty Chinese mercenaries were hanged from the grand masts of French warships; a very large number of Vietnamese prisoners were shot or beheaded on the field. Gosselin insisted that Riviere had deliberately ignored Saigon orders to spare the enemy's lives. As for some Vietnamese observers, they candidly believed that Riviere was possessed by Garnier's spirit calling for revenge. But it is more realistic to think that he was either subjected to Jean Dupuis's crafty brain-washing or he had been given counterorders by the French governor in the utmost secrecy.

Dupuis also reported the curious case of a Catholic convert found among the prisoners. Providing him with a priest for his last sacrament, the French were genuinely happy to have "opened the gates of Heaven to a criminal who would certainly never have found such a chance again."[29]

With regard to China, setbacks encountered so far showed that it was difficult to wage war without the cooperation of the Black Flags. As Liu Yung-Fu persisted to stay in his Lao Kay stronghold, claiming that his troops had not been fairly treated by Hoang Ke Viem on previous occasions, the Peking government sent minister T'ang Ching Sung to romance him. T'ang then suggested that instead of letting Tonkin fall into French hands, Liu Yu-Fung should seize the country and proclaim himself king. Whether Liu took the hint or not was not clear, but he later moved his troops to Phu Hoai in the vicinity of Hanoi. There he issued a public challenge to Riviere and his men: "I, the invincible general Luu Vinh Phuoc, declare that I consider you Frenchmen only petty bandits. You said that you come here only to protect your religion but it is all lies. You are just hungry foreign beasts who come to destroy our country. . . . Your sins are like hair on the head, impossible to count. Being such evil you must die. Since I don't want to harm the Hanoi population and if you are such good fighters, come to meet me at Phu Hoai. But if you are afraid then just send me the heads of your chiefs and I will let you go back home to reunite with your wives and children. Otherwise you are going to die. Think it over."[30] And to show that he was deadly serious, Liu Yu-Fung shelled and destroyed a nearby Catholic mission.

In response, on May 19, 1883, Riviere took his 450 troops to Phu Hoai. At the Paper Bridge (Cau Giay) north of Hanoi, they were pinned down by heavy enemy fire. Just as a cannon caught in the mud was about to fall to the adversary, Riviere went to the rescue with no other protection than his walking cane. He was repeatedly hit by bullets and fell to the ground. Those who came to his rescue were also killed and his troops had to retreat leaving him behind. French prisoners and the dead were beheaded and their heads were preserved in brine as war trophies. What was left of Riviere was a mass of bones, for as with Garnier, the Black Flags had sliced him to pieces in order to claim the rewards promised by Governor Hoang Ke Viem. As an ultimate vengeance, Riviere would not be allowed to rest in peace. He was purposely buried in the middle of a road to allow passers-by to trample on his carcass.

In this disaster, besides Riviere, the French lost 50 dead, including 20 officers and 76 wounded. In Paris the news of Riviere's death triggered mass demonstrations. On February 26, 1883, almost unanimously, the National Assembly voted approximately 6 million francs for the pursuit of the war and forwarded 3,000 more troops to Tonkin. On May 27, the Paris government cabled to the governor of Cochinchina: "France shall revenge her brave children."

Accord Li-Bouree (1882)

This was the second time Hanoi fell into French hands; the first time having occurred under Garnier. Bouree, the French ambassador in Peking, received a formal protest from the Chinese government. He retorted that by the 1874 treaty, Vietnam had become an independent nation. The same year, the Chinese ambassador to Russia was instructed to demand French withdrawal from Tonkin.

For Ambassador Bouree, the presence of 200,000 Chinese troops in Tonkin was an event of extreme gravity and needed an urgent solution: thus, without consulting Paris, he signed an accord with Minister Li Hung Chang, giving China the northern part of Tonkin with Lao Kay as the main port, while the French would keep southern Tonkin. They would be also permitted to use the Red River for trade with Yunnan. Perhaps this accord fulfilled the old concept of Yunnan as a French commercial objective. But Paris policy had evolved with Jules Ferry making Tonkin and Annam a protectorate. Thus, Bouree was accused of disobedience and had to transfer his post to Ambassador Tricou. Since his treaty was officially rejected by Prime Minister Jules Ferry and Foreign Minister Lacour, the so called Li-Bouree accord was no longer heard of.

The Harmand Treaty (1883)

Dr. François-Jules Harmand was a Navy medical doctor transferred at his request to the foreign service as a consul at Bangkok. He arrived in Hanoi in

June 1883 with the title of general commissioner. To a friend he confided: "Do you believe we are here to wage a religious war? No. We are here with an objective purely commercial . . . and if we protect the missionaries it is because of the national interest."[31]

Harmand installed a de facto triumvirate, with him at the top assisted by General Bouet, commander of the Tonkin land troops, and Admiral Courbet, commander in chief of the naval forces. There would be a two-fold strategy: On the one hand, General Bouet would remain in Tonkin to fight the Black Flags and the Sino-Vietnamese combined forces. On the other hand, Harmand and Courbet would move to the south to force Hue to formally accept French protection over Tonkin and Annam. They were very far from the principle of show of force.

Left in Tonkin, Bouet took Hai Duong on August 16, 1883, and forced the Black Flags to retreat to the Paper Bridge, but torrential rains and ensuing floods precluded further operations. Thus, Bouet went back to Hanoi to ask for more troops from France.

As for Harmand, on July 17, 1883, he arrived with Admiral Courbet at the mouth of the Thuan An River, which led to Hue, the capital. Immediately he sent words to the court to surrender all defensive positions in the area. He advised Hue that failure to comply with his demand would result in the destruction of these positions on the afternoon of August 18. That day, a duel of artillery began between the French and Vietnamese. On August 20, Courbet landed under the protection of his warships. At dawn, the Vietnamese abandoned their positions. On August 21, at 9 A.M., all Hue defenses were in French hands. Emperor Hiep Hoa dispatched mandarin Nguyen Thuong Bac to negotiate. Harmand handed him a letter for the king, accusing Annam of creating troubles in Cochinchina, refusing a borders definition between Cochinchina and Annam, slowing down traffic on the Red River, supporting the Black Flags, and plotting with Siam and China against France.[32] He also told them: "You have to choose between war and peace. If you choose war, it will be total destruction of your country. If you choose peace, we are ready to be generous. We do not intend to take your country, but you must accept our protection. This will bring security, peace, and prosperity to Vietnamese people, and it is also the only chance for your monarchy to survive."[33]

Under these conditions young Emperor Hiep Hoa could not do better than his predecessor Tu Duc. On September 25, 1883, mandarins Tran Dinh Tuc and Nguyen Trong Hop signed with Harmand and Champeaux a 27-article treaty known since as the Harmand Treaty. As a result, the province of Binh Thuan was added to Cochinchina as a war reparation. All the cadres who had fled Tonkin to seek refuge in Hue had to be sent back to work in Hanoi. The emperor continued to govern Annam without interference from France except in matters of customs. Qui Nhon, Danang, Xuan Dai opened for trade. Annam and France shared the expense of building a road from Hanoi to Saigon. Telegraphic cables were installed by the French, and France guaranteed protection of Annam and undertook the expulsion of the Black Flags.

The Vietnamese regents Ton That Thuyet and Nguyen Van Tuong marked their opposition by executing Emperor Hiep Hoa. They also began national resistance. Regional Governors Hoang Ke Viem at Son Tay and Truong Quang Dan at Bac Ninh were secretly instructed to close their ranks with the Chinese. Phan Van Hoe at Kiou Liou and Nguyen Quang Binh at Hung Hoa also joined the Kwang Si army. As for the field commanders, Admiral Ta Hien in Nam Dinh took an admiral commission from China and General Nguyen Thien Thuat from Son Tay moved to attack Hai Duong.

At this time, the French in Tonkin began to face internal problems. Once in the drivers seat, Harmand had done away with professional courtesy and self-control. After his diplomatic success in Hue, he went back to Hanoi where he severely blamed General Bouet for his lack of aggressiveness. During a heated exchange, Bouet in turn charged Harmand with military incompetence, having ordered operations under adverse conditions. Then the general curtly left for Paris. But an exalted Harmand pursued his smear campaign. He publicly declared Dupuis responsible for the entire situation in Tonkin and threatened to take action against the old hand if he did not show more restraint in his relations with the Chinese in Hanoi: "The fact is, Monsieur Dupuis, you are a good deal too Chinese yourself. It is you who caused all this trouble China is stirring up for us about her suzerainty."[34] This is, after all, very true.

But if it was easy for Harmand to get rid of Bouet, it was another story when he crossed swords with Courbet. Not only had Bouet's complaints not fallen on deaf ears in Paris, but Courbet had become "untouchable" after his occupation of Hue. Without further ado, Harmand was recalled. On September 25, 1883, Courbet became commander in chief in Tonkin over land and sea forces.

While Courbet was preoccupied with his new installation as commander in chief, Ton That Thuyet ordered Hoang Ke Viem to attack Hai Duong, causing severe damage to the city. On October 11, 1883, after having received a reinforcement of 9,000 men, Courbet went on a three-day fray to dislodge Hoang Ke Viem and Luu Vinh Phuoc and occupy Son Tay. As more and more Chinese troops arrived in the area, Courbet paused to wait for fresh troops.

On November 12, 1883, the Chinese laid siege to Bac Ninh but French resistance forced them to retreat. In Paris, Chinese ambassador Marquis Tseng (Tang Ky Trach) protested against the Harmand treaty and proclaimed China's support for the Black Flags and Hoang Ke Viem whose combined forces had reached some 14,000. Furthermore, while 20,000 Chinese troops were poised on the Tonkin border, another 14,000 were closing in on Son Tay, Bac Ninh, and Hung Hoa.

At the end of 1883, one French brigade arrived in Tonkin bringing French forces to some 16,000. At that point, drawing experience from the Harmand case, it was decided in Paris that the overall command should be assumed by an army man. Thus, on January 16, 1884, General Millot was appointed commander in chief of the expeditionary corps in Tonkin, while Courbet received one additional star, but had to step down to only be navy commander in Tonkin.

Millot divided his forces into two brigades under General Briere de l'Isle at Hanoi and General Negrier at Hai Duong. From then on, the French would record a series of successes to allow the signing of the so called Treaty of Tien Tsin between Fournier and Ly Hung Chang. From February 11 to February 16, 1884, Briere de l'Isle took Bac Ninh, forcing the Chinese to retreat to Thai Nguyen. On February 23, he took Yen The and Thai Nguyen. On March 17, with General Negrier, he overran Hung Hoa, chasing Chinese and Black Flags into the mountains. As for the Vietnamese, it was the final defeat. Deprived of his allies, Hoang Ke Viem fled to Hue. On May 8, 1884, in only one hour, Colonel Duchesne took Tuyen Quang, forcing the Black Flags to retreat. At that time, the Chinese still held Lang Son, Cao Bang, and Lao Kay.

The Li-Fournier Agreement (1884)

While French victories in Tonkin caused China major concerns, a minor affair developed into a major event. In March 1884, a man named Detring, a German employee of the Chinese customs, was appointed customs commissioner in Canton. At Hong Kong he boarded on a ship under the command of Captain Fournier. During the trip, both talked about the situation in Tonkin and both agreed that China had no chance to stand a war against the West. Furthermore, counting on the Black Flags' cooperation was by no means a sound policy: Despite their military performance, the Black Flags remained unreliable partners ready to sell to the highest bidder. To compound China's tribulations, France could send Algerian troops to help the Muslim rebels in Kansu and Yunnan and wage a holy war in the rest of the empire. On top of that, France had the potential to seize any important port until China came to terms.

Thus, upon his arrival in Canton, Detring reported to Minister Li Hung Chang his conversation with Fournier. In the ensuing meeting at Tien Tsin, Li Hung Chang agreed to withdraw Chinese troops from Tonkin, to renounce Chinese suzerainty over Vietnam, and, to save Chinese face instead of an indemnity to France, the Chinese would open the Sino-Vietnamese frontier to French commerce. On May 11, 1884, duly mandated by France, Captain Fournier signed an accord with Li Hung Chang, which is incorrectly called by Vietnamese historians the Tien Tsin treaty.[35] Besides the written terms agreed to above, a verbal accord fixed the total withdrawal of Chinese troops by June 26, 1884.

In Tonkin, General Millot began to implement the Li-Fournier treaty: on June 15, 1884, Colonel Dugenne was ordered to symbolically take 800 men to reoccupy Lang Son. At Bac Le, 30 miles before Lang Son, the French received a message from the Chinese garrison claiming they had no instructions to leave Lang Son and asked the French to "be kind enough to urge the Chinese Command to send necessary orders"; they also insisted that there was no need for fighting since there was a treaty. In reply, Dugenne gave the Chinese one hour to pack up. As time went by, the French moved forward and realized Chinese duplicity when they were pinned down by overwhelming gunfire. Surprised, the French fought desperately overnight, only to withdraw at dawn with 20 dead and 60 wounded. Needless to say, in Paris, government and population cried vengeance. On June 28, 1884 Tricou, the French chargé d'affaires in Peking, strongly protested, to be told that there was no date for Chinese evacuation in the Li-Fournier treaty (which was true).

Peking's refusal to implement the Li-Fournier agreement led Paris to appoint career diplomat Patenotre to China to mend the broken pieces. On his way, he stopped at Hue to sign a revised Harmand treaty.

In Hue, as news of the Li-Fournier accord confirmed the French rights over Vietnam, the hope for further Chinese support vanished and the court gave up dilatory tactics. On June 6, 1884, the Patenotre treaty was signed between plenipotentiary mandarin Pham Than Duat and Ambassador Patenotre. Then a ceremony took place to mark the repudiation of kinship between Vietnam and China. In presence of the Hue Court and the French delegation, the traditional symbol of Chinese suzerainty, a gold and silver seal weighing 13-pounds, was melted in a clay stove.

The Tien Tsin Treaty (1885)

On July 1, Patenotre left Hue for Shanghai and was joined by Admiral Courbet a few days later. After deliberation, both decided to send an ultimatum to China asking for the implementation of the Li-Fournier treaty, immediate evacuation of Tonkin payment of 250-million francs as war indemnity, and putting Foochow and Nanking arsenals into French hands as security. By any standard, the amount asked by the French was disproportionate to the damages they had actually suffered at Bac Le, but unfortunately for the Chinese, in his report, the governor of Kwang Si himself had boasted over the death of several thousand French troops. As the period of three days elapsed without a Chinese reply, on Aug 1, 1884, Courbet took his fleet to the Strait of Formosa.

At Foochow (Fu Kien), on August 22, 1884, Courbet served an ultimatum to the director of the arsenal. After deliberation with the military commanders, and in a perfect Chuan Tzu fashion, the director replied that he was not ready yet and would appreciate Courbet's courtesy to postpone his attack until the next day. But for some reason, the message did not get through and Courbet began shelling the port at 2 P.M. At 2.30 P.M. the dock was destroyed. At 3 P.M. all Chinese ships burned or sank. Chinese officers ran for their lives and took refuge in pagodas.

The loss of Foochow caused the Peking government to formally declare war on France. In Canton, a bounty was placed on French heads and even in Singapore, Chinese were ordered to poison French residents. This prompted a violent protest from the British government. In Tonkin, Liu Yung-Fu was named general by Peking with the mission to take Tonkin back.

After Foochow, Courbet proposed to occupy Port Arthur with 2,000 men, but Paris disagreed, fearing a quagmire war on the continent. As a result, Courbet was ordered to take Keelung instead. On October 2, Courbet's chief of staff, Admiral Lespes, began to silence the coastal batteries of Tam Sui, which defended the entrance to Keelung. Then 600 French landed to discover 2,400 Chinese well entrenched and equipped with sophisticated rifles. They hurriedly retreated to their ships and from then on confined to a blockade of Keelung.

On October 30, 1884, Courbet gave foreign ships three days notice to move out of Keelung port, but the year ended with the arrival of 20,000 fresh Chinese troops. Obviously, the blockade was not quite effective. Courbet realized that this Keelung stalemate could be seen as a French defeat unless he won another victory. Thus, he went to the Pescadores Islands and seized the important post of Makung on March 31. His idea was to make the Pescadores a French Hong Kong. In fact, Courbet also had in mind to occupy Shantung and Manchuria.

If war can be seen as extension of diplomacy, in some circumstances diplomacy reflects more clearly the conditions of the war. Thus, the Keelung operation remained what it really was: a French failure, which forced Ambassador Patenotre to lower his tone in a second ultimatum on August 21. This time the indemnity was reduced to 80 million francs. Empress Tzu Hsi, who decidedly was no longer the young and timid bride of decades ago, responded by ordering the shutdown of Chinese embassies, and so did the French for their legations in China.

In Tonkin, more Chinese troops arrived from Kwang Tung-Kwang Si while after the Bac Le incident, Millot's health forced him to go back to France leaving the supreme command of the army to General Briere de l'Isle. After receiving a new contingent of 6,000 men, which brought the total of French to 20,000 de l'Isle launched on August 20 an attack forcing the Chinese to abandon the two posts of Chu and Kep. Later, French forces again dislodged the Black Flags from Tuyen Quang and moved to occupy Thai Nguyen. At Yen Bac, the Chinese had 600 casualties against 19 French dead and 65 wounded. At the beginning of 1885, General Negrier took a series of posts before occupying Lang Son. A few days later, he reached Dong Dang throwing the Chinese back to the border. At the end of January, he arrived at Chennankuan (Nam Quan), the Gate of China, threatening Kwang Si and Yunnan.

While Negrier was chasing the Chinese, the Black Flags and other Chinese elements sneaked back to besiege Tuyen Quang. The situation was so desperate that the French had to let the river carry their calls for help in bamboo tubes. De l'Isle went to the rescue. After three days of fighting, the Chinese and Black Flags retreated. This victory became the highlight of de l'Isle's career, as French chansonniers celebrated his triumph in every cafe in Paris.

But once again the tide turned. While the festivities were going on in France, Kwang Si Admiral Phung Tu Tai attacked Dong Dang. Sent to the rescue, Negrier lost 200 men at Long Chau and had to retreat to Lang Son. Later at Ky Lua, he was seriously wounded and passed the command to a Colonel Herbinger: More and more Chinese and Black Flags were rushing in for the spoils of Lang Son. In spite of his 35,000-man force, Herbinger ceded to panic and abandoned Lang Son in a hurry: All arms, baggages, munitions, and anything apt to delay the retreat had to be thrown into the river. This included 600,000 francs of regimental cash, which was recovered in remarkable condition 50 years later by Admiral Decoux's services. Yet it was reported that no enemy was seen in the vicinity of Lang Son at the time of withdrawal.[36]

The loss of Lang Son caused the fall of Jules Ferry's cabinet, but also made possible another round of talks with China. On April 4, 1885, a ceasefire was signed between Campbell, representing China, and Billot, representing France: While France agreed to lift Courbet's blockade in the Formosa Strait, China must evacuate Tonkin and open her ports to French ships. As for the Black Flags, Campbell also agreed to relocate them in China. Finally on June 11, 1885, Li Hung Chang and Patenotre signed a treaty in Tien Tsin, which was in fact the confirmation of the Li-Fournier accord. That same day, Courbet died on his flagship anchored in the Makung harbor. This put an end to his dreams of conquering China. In June 1885, the Chinese went home after recognizing French protectorateship over Tonkin and Annam. They also opened Yun Nan and the southern provinces to French trade.

In Vietnam, the French expected that the so called Tien Tsin treaty would coax Vietnamese to lay down their arms. But, instead, there were more and more revolts, fueled by the hostility of the two regents. By appointing on May 31, 1885, the rude General de Courcy to the overall command in Vietnam, France clearly demonstrated that the era of the carrot and stick policy had ended and that only the stick remained in French hands.

NOTES

1. Fortunately for the French, the Spanish had no imperialistic objective in Vietnam; their actions stemmed from the execution of Spanish priests.

2. Another prominent Catholic priest.

3. He was the second son of Emperor Thieu Tri and Empress Tu Du and took the succession in 1848 as Emperor Duc Ton Anh. Although reputed for his quiet demeanor, his filial piety, his benevolence and intelligence, he soon became involved in religious persecution against the Catholic missions.

4. His true name was Ta Van Phung. He was a Catholic adept.

5. The silver standard was the medium of exchange in the Far East, so the piastres used in Vietnam were also called silver piastres. In Indochina, the French used gold francs within their administration (for budget, salaries of government employees, etc.). To regulate the exchange, in 1875 the French obtained the monopoly of coinage, and

the Bank of Indochina was created for this purpose. Eighty years later the rate of exchange would have a fatal impact on the prosecution of the Indochinese war. When the piastre was valued at 10 francs instead of 17, Indochina was no longer worthy of French colons' efforts.

6. First laureate at national competitive examinations.

7. Truong Buu Lam, *Patterns of Vietnamese Response*, p. 74.

8. Also realizing this, Ngo Dinh Diem later told one of his generals, Nguyen Chanh Thi: "After all, we are on Southern land and it is not worth having problems with them (the Southern people)." See Nguyen Chanh Thi, *Vietnam: Mot troi tam su*.

9. Doctor or Ph.D.

10. Failure to print the mandarin seal on an imperial edict was seen as a disagreement with the emperor.

11. Aubaret had been French consul in Bangkok. He and Philastre were of two most prominent sinologists of the French administration. An Asian old-hand, he served as a political advisor to Admiral Bonard.

12. Norodom's residence.

13. Trinh Van Thanh, *Thanh Ngu Dien Tich danh Nhan Tu-Dien* (Dictionary of Vietnamese Celebrities), Vol. 2, p. 995.

14. Yunnan.

15. *AOM* (Archives Nationales outremer), A 30 (18).

16. The Catholic priests reported to the French administration secrets obtained during confession seances. These practices were also carried out during the World War II, according to a private conversation of the author with a member of the French 2nd Bureau in Kunming.

17. Henry McAleavy, *Black Flags in Vietnam*, pp. 130–131.

18. Ibid., p. 139.

19. A French term designating France compared with her overseas posessions.

20. Garnier's head was returned by the Black Flags a few days earlier.

21. Pham Van Son, *History of Vietnam*, citing A. Delvaux, *La legation francaise á Hue*, Vol. 4, p. 339.

22. Recall to France.

23. At the rate of US$1 = 0.62 tael.

24. Kwang Si and Kwang Tung.

25. Dai Nam was the name used in diplomatic language for Annam, since Annam for the Vietnamese had an offensive connotation meaning Pacified South.

26. Pham Van Son, *History of Vietnam*, p. 339.

27. Leroy Beaulieu, *De la colonization chez les peuples modernes* (Paris: Guillemin, 1st ed., 1874).

28. Pham Van Son, *Viet Su Tan Bien*, Vol. V, p. 360.

29. McAleavy, *Black Flags in Vietnam*, pp. 200–201. Quoting Dupuis.

30. Pham Van Son, *History of Vietnam*, Vol. V, pp. 369–370.

31. AOM AOO (10) I.

32. Pham Van Son, *History of Vietnam*, Vol. V, p. 394.

33. Ibid.

34. McAleavy, *Black Flags in Vietnam*, p. 218.

35. The Tien Tsin treaty signed by the British and China in 1858, ended the Anglo-Chinese war, which began in 1856.

36. McAleavy, *Black Flags in Vietnam*, p. 274.

4

FRENCH ADMINISTRATION

At the outset, wars with China associated with permanent revolts in Vietnam prevented the French from having any definite policy, but since they were there to stay, they genuinely endeavored to make Vietnam a profitable venture for themselves, if not also for others. Indeed, Albert Sarraut president of the French Union, candidly wrote: "Colonization is a selfish act of force. The people who seek to establish colonies in remote continents think only for themselves, work only for their supremacy, conquer only for their profit" (*Grandeur et servitudes coloniales*). Even the connotation of the words "mission civilisatrice" denotes an ethnocentrism that remained for a long time a characteristic of Western culture.

THE FRENCH CONCEPT OF ADMINISTRATION

The French administration of Indochina acquired a push-pull outlook, stemming from the competing influence between the Catholic mission and the civil administration, the mutual hatred between the church and the anticlerical groups, the conflicting concepts of association and assimilation, and above all the powerful opposition of the colons to any change that could free the natives from their domination.

In Paris, many parties rejected the assimilation principle as "a utopia, because a colonial policy which ignores the values, the deep roots, and the vitality of primitive culture was foolish and doomed to fail."[1] It was obvious that such a policy would have to be supported by the use of force that, promoted by General de Courcy, turned out to be a disaster. Consequently, for the first time since Gia Long, Emperor Ham Nghi took to the hills and called for an anti-French struggle, which was to last some 20 years.

Granted that 2,000 years ago, the Han had also carried out an assimilation policy. But it was possible because Vietnam was then a virgin land and the

Chinese did not have to tear down any permanent structures, political or cultural. Furthermore, the fact that the Han pursued a conquest of cultural prestige rather than of economic exploitation also made the difference. But in the 19th century, the French had to deal with a totally different situation. They had to fight against millenarian Confucianism and a nationalism well represented by a long established monarchic dynasty, which was strong enough to defeat invasion, including the Mongolian attacks in the 13th century.

On the contrary, the concept of association that invited natives to share with the West a new world order of mutual respect and equality was worth enough to rally even some professional militaries such as Gallieni and Lyautey. As for political parties, the democratic groups—liberals, anticlericals, radicals—were also in favor of association. Indeed, they had realized that the defeat of Russia by Japan in 1905 had destroyed the myth of white supremacy entertained by the colonial powers themselves and that only association theory could keep Vietnam away from the pervasive influence of a militaristic Japan. Thus, after many debates, the principle of association was adopted by the French parliament. In a significant gesture, the ministry of navy and colonies was relieved from its control of Indochina and was replaced by the ministry of foreign affairs. In addition, General Count de Courcy was recalled. In defiance, he abruptly left Vietnam in February 1886 without transferring the powers to his successor, Paul Bert.

Paul Bert (February–November 1886)

Bert was a physician teaching in Bordeaux and Paris universities. After the 1849 revolution, he entered government service as a prefect. Later, as a deputy at the national assembly, his views on association with Tonkin and Annam led to his nomination as the first resident general with full power. He was to remedy the impasse caused by de Courcy's hawkish policy. On his arrival in Hanoi in 1886, he reassured the natives: "Nothing will be changed in your rites and your customs. Your traditions will be respected. You will continue to have your laws and regulations. Cantons and villages will be administered as yore. You will select your own notables and they will be charged to arrange the taxes and supervise the administration of your territory."[2]

Paul Bert restored the post of viceroy (Kinh Luoc) to represent the Hue emperor in Tonkin. Unfortunately, his education and industrialization programs were compromised by his faltering health, and he had to plan with Paris for his replacement. He died before his work could be achieved. His tenure lasted only nine months, from February to November 1886. A series of insignificant functionaries succeeded, only to be preoccupied with their petty rivalries until de Lanessan took the command five years later.

De Lanessan (1891)

De Lanessan, another physician, professor, and explorer, had been dispatched by Paris to study colonial problems in various parts of the world and, particularly in 1886, in Cochinchina where he was able to observe the work of Paul Bert. Obviously, he was so impressed that when he was assigned as governor general in June 1891, he followed Paul Bert's footsteps and gave back direct administration to the Vietnamese, reserving for the French only top supervision. Hostile to his liberal policy, the colons also criticized him for a 12-million franc deficit in the budget of Tonkin. Later, under the willful pretext that he had divulged state secrets, they obtained his recall. Commenting on the attitude of the Paris government about his case, de Lanessan wrote in his memoirs. "It is not enough that the government formulates a fixed policy. What is also needed is that it choose for the implementation of this policy men who are capable of understanding and determined to follow it."

After de Lanessan, under the influence of the colons, each governor came back to the old policy before the association period.

Paul Doumer (1897–1902)

Doumer had been a journalist of the opposition. He was considered dangerous enough for the French government to keep him at arms length with an assignment as governor general of Indochina. For better or for worse, he was an exceptional administrator because he had succeeded in creating a local government independent from Paris and, thus, from the dictates of the powerful colons clique in France.

Yet, under Doumer, the association principle was submerged under a series of reforms showing more and more the aspect of direct rule. In Tonkin, the Vietnamese viceroy was replaced by a French resident superieur.[3] In Annam, the privy council (Co Mat) was supplanted by a council of ministers presided over by the French resident superieur who took orders from Doumer himself. In the provinces, the Tong Doc (provincial governor) and Tuan Phu (county governor) disappeared to leave room for French provincial residents. In Cochinchina, in addition to its 20 members, the colonial council had to accept four additional delegates representing the colonial administration. This brought the total of French members to 14 against ten Vietnamese, out of which seven were still French citizens.

A standardized administrative system allowed for the creation of an Indochinese Union in 1898. Under the denomination, all five states—Annam, Tonkin, Cochinchina, Laos, and Cambodia—became interdependent at the expense of Cochinchina, which provided 40 percent of the federal budget. Indeed, there had always been a tremendous economic discrepancy between colonies and protectorates. For example, on the eve of the World War II, only 74,000 acres were under cultivation in Tonkin in contrast to 247,000 in Cochinchina. This overwhelming Cochinchinese contribution to federal welfare met with opposition by the French colons led by Paul Blanchy, the mayor of Saigon. This also explains the southern people's aversion toward a unification with the two other Kys. Later, this ethnocentrism came to support the concept and creation of the Republic of Cochinchina.

It also became obvious that Doumer's public works program took an oriental despotism coloration when, to build up labor forces, villagers were forced out of their dwellings and shoved to constructions sites. Those who fled were shot by military squads. The working conditions in rubber plantations were no better: Disguised slavery was practiced in the middle of jungles.

Industrialization was stepped up with the construction of textile and cement plants in Haiphong, and the expansion of coal mines in the Bay of Along. In Cochinchina, to boost rice cultivation, a large network of canals was developed by the Societe des Dragages.

By a series of new taxes, Doumer intended to make Indochina self-sufficient. In less than two years after the foundation of the Indochinese Union, he succeeded in balancing the budget. But he was shrewd enough to also address the problem of military expenditure, which was a nightmare in Paris. He managed to bring in an additional 14,000,000 francs to significantly reduce the military burden of the Metropole. He capitalized on this exploit to obtain a 200-million franc bonus from a euphoric government in order to satisfy his "folie des grandeurs": the Yunnan Fu railroad (from Hai Phong to Yunnan), the Trans-Indochinese railroad (from Hanoi to Saigon), and the famous Paul Doumer bridge in Hanoi (reputed to be the biggest one in Southeast Asia) But where his works could really be seen as "folly" was when, instead of building an essential sewage system for Hanoi, he chose to erect an opera house.

It is in the cultural field that he won general esteem: He created the world-renowned Ecole Française d'Extreme Orient staffed with prominent scholars such as the Masperos brothers, Coedes, Groslier, and Maybon, to cite the best. When he left Vietnam, the federal services of geography, meteorology, and archaeology were in full expansion.

Yet his realization of a railroad would not significantly improve the Indochinese situation: In Tonkin where the Yunnan line had to compete with emerging air transport. The Trans-Indochinese had problems with floods and became costly. In Cochinchina, importation of trucks and cars relegated the Saigon-Mytho train to a marginal importance. Finally, it served to carry only Saigon students back to their native villages during the holidays and weekends.

Although Doumer's memoirs over a happy and prosperous Vietnam became dogma for his supporters, the truth according to famous author Colonel Fernand Bernard was that after 40 years of French presence, there was "no real agricultural prosperity, no commerce, no industry." If this revelation was a terrible blow to Doumer's prestige, it would not stop him to later become president of France. But the term "folie des grandeurs" remains attached to his performance in Asia.

Perhaps some other governors also had the same ambitions, but none had the power and talent to subdue the Colons party. After a long and bitter political fight, Doumer defeated Paul Blanchy, who died in Saigon of a broken heart. This allowed Doumer to cynically declare in his memoirs that "a man having power and dedicated to public service should certainly be trash if he could not overcome Blanchy."

At no time did Doumer have doubts about his mission in the Far East. He sincerely believed he had labored for France and Indochina. Actually he was well served by a series of good harvests, which led the population to be more lenient over his errors, for his government was not flawless: He lacked the fundamental cognizance that mutual consent is the basic factor in human relations. This concept would be the ideal of his successor, Paul Beau, during his entire tenure.

Paul Beau (1902–1908)

Beau was a professional lawyer before he entered the world of diplomacy. He was third embassy secretary in Rome and later, in 1901, was named envoy extraordinaire to Peking. The following year, he was appointed governor general of Indochina.

On his arrival in 1902, Beau addressed the human issue, which had not been exactly Doumer's concern. In this respect, he would later be emulated by Sarraut, as the French finally realized they were dealing with human beings. "France will respect human rights and will not injure the soul of the people of which she has accepted the guardianship." But the time of good harvest under Doumer and the related euphoria was over. Taxes became a less acceptable burden, for the natives saw them as a blatant contradiction of Beau's promises.

Beau's failure had another cause: To run the country with him, he had chosen people incapable of offering any sincere opinion, preferring to agree with him rather than disagree. This mentality had been the mandarinate tradition under monarchic regimes. Yet there existed a few good men. Phan Chu Trinh, for example, wrote to Beau: "If you give any value to my words, let's meet together and I will show you how to make the Vietnamese people happy." But if Beau had any impulse to listen to Trinh, he was inhibited by his entourage who was, to be sure, closely associated with mandarins and colons, the former having sentenced Trinh to death for antimonarchist views, the latter opposing any measure that could endanger their domination over the natives.

The promotion of Vietnamese representation in government assemblies was put in check either by a majority of French members or a potential alliance between elected colons and the bureaucracy. Aware of such setbacks, Beau tried to obtain some help from activist Phan Chu Trinh and, in so doing, triggered more antagonism from the opposition.

Since the lack of partisan support prevented Beau from pursuing Doumer's "politique de grandeur," he confined himself to recruiting more natives for subservient positions. He focused only on human issues by organizing little medical assistance and abolishing traditional punishments, such as body dissection or public exposure of severed heads.

On the economic side, railroad exploitation began to be in the red, following poor harvests. Yet Beau had no courage to stop these expensive programs. He found some solace in the improvement of education. There was practically no basic education: The village teachers responsible for the peasants' instruction had fled during the French conquest. In Cochinchina, which had over 1.5 million inhabitants, only 5,000 were in primary classes.

In Hanoi, Beau laid the groundwork for a university, but again met with colons' opposition. For them, a higher education could only provide the natives with the tools for rebellion. But Beau knew that the natives would seek education in any way, and it was not in the French interest that they addressed anti-French educators. But the colons would not relent in their opposition to Beau's humanitarian program: In 1908, the poisoning of the French garrison in Hanoi provided them with the pretext for Beau's removal. In spite of his good intent, Beau had to leave.

Albert Sarraut (1911–1914; 1917–1919)

According to Vietnamese historians, Albert Sarraut was superior to Doumer. He was a leader of the Radical Socialist Party. He was occupying a senate seat at the time he was nominated governor general. Later, for his rare knowledge of overseas politics, he would be made minister of the colonies before World War II. After World War II, he became president of the French Union. His prestige among the Vietnamese was immense and perhaps served later as a favorable background to his son-in-law, Sainteny, in his negotiations with Ho Chi Minh.

Sarraut devoted many efforts, not only to admit more natives into representative bodies, but also to improve the number and qualifications of the Vietnamese cadres by opening more training centers. He also surrounded himself with the Grand Conseil Economique, the Conseil Colonial, and the Chambre de Commerce et d'Agriculture. To curtail the influence of colons and industrialists,[4] Sarraut reduced these organizations to a consultative role, fit to discuss only problems submitted by the governor himself.

In Cochinchina, provinces were under a French administrator assisted by French trained Phus[5] and Doc Phus.[6] It is among the Doc Phus that the French governor of Cochinchina recruited his cabinet aides. At lower levels, the Phus governed counties (Quan), the Huyens administered districts (Huyen) and the Cai Tongs controlled cantons (Tong). Only elected councils of notables ran villages (Lang) and hamlets (Thon).

Sarraut appeared to be the most liberal proconsul France had ever sent to Vietnam. Under him, the term "mission civilisatrice" probably took some significance with creation of schools and hospitals. Between 1921 and 1925, 144,300 natives attended 17,000 primary and secondary schools. Parallel with vernacular institutions, such as the Chu Van Chuong high school in Hanoi, the Quoc Hoc college in Hue, the Petrus Ky Lyceum in Saigon, he opened colleges for the French residents: Albert Sarraut in Hanoi, the Yersin in DaLat, and Chasseloup Laubat in Saigon. Many Vietnamese were also selected to attend French schools based on their scholarly performances.

Later, the University of Hanoi was opened to produce medical doctors, lawyers, and superior civil servants. Although qualitatively comparable to metro-politan degrees, their diplomas had no academic equivalence. Thus, only those exceptionally gifted or coming from affluent classes were allowed to go to France to receive their metropolitan degrees. This would later be the well-known class of "retour de France."

In 1914, on the eve of World War I, Sarraut timely reminded French officials that "the natives are human beings just like us and should be treated like human beings."[7] This liberal policy bore long-term benefits: During World War II, France was able to import Vietnamese ONS (*ouvriers non specialises*[8]) to bolster her war production in exchange for a vague promise of freedom after the war. Thus, when she did away with such a promise, the ONS turned to nationalist agitation.

In retrospect, Sarraut's politics had a serious drawback for the French: In teaching Western democratic ideals, he willy-nilly sowed the seeds of revolu-tionary militancy. He would later personally witness these consequences during the Franco-Viet Minh war.

Economy

By and large, there is no evidence that the Vietnamese had any significant share of the colonial wealth. In 1931, the median income of a European civilian was 5,000 piastres as compared with 49 piastres of the poorest native. For that matter, a Pondicherian[9] janitor, considered European, earned an "expatriation bonus" that, added to his basic salary, brought along a figure at least three times higher than the salary of a native Doc Phu[10] or "a retour de France"[11] university professor. But in response to Paul Bernard, Philippe Devillers writes that the discrepancy "was not so much due to the excessive advantages enjoyed by the privileged class but to the fact that the poor class's living standard was excep-tionally low.[12] Because this low living standard was the result of imports limited only to the rich (Europeans, Chinese, and wealthy Vietnamese), "this leaves little to the middle class and nothing to the poor class."[13] Later, when Vietnam-ese rice was put on the list of international commodities, the stock market fluc-tuations only worsened the peasant's condition.

Usury

It is fair to remember that the French had tried to eradicate a time-immemorial practice that plagued not only Vietnam but also the entire Far East: usury. While in Annam and Tonkin usury was a common practice for landlords, in Cochin-china it marked the first steps of a rising capitalism. In this field, the Chinese were outwitted by the Indian Chetty, who since 1900 earned "no less than 182,000,000 piastres of which 42,000,000 were exported to India and 40,000,000 reinvested in new loans in the colony."[14]

These Indian traffickers, who ganged up in the notorious Ohier Street of

Saigon, usually loan-sharked at 120 percent interest. As such a rate was beyond the reach of the peasant tenant, only landlords had access to such loans, which they later shifted to their tenants at a higher percentage. To counteract these Indian activities, the French decided to establish "mutuelle credit agricoles" (rural credit offices). But they failed to reach the tenants, since loans still required collateral. As a result, the mutuelle employees were the first to borrow the cash and reloan it at higher rate to landlords, making the loan process much worse for the peasants. Then the French sired another idea: They created credits populaires (popular credit) to distribute seeds and fertilizers to farmers who would later pay back in kind. But the systematic opposition of landlords on the one hand, and the inability on the peasants to properly use recommended seeds and fertilizers on the other, kept the project at an experimental stage. Finally, as time went by, the rural society took more and more the aspect of "an upper class of landlords with an agricultural proletariat."[15]

Moreover, the collusion between French banks and Chinese businessmen gave way to an intermediary class of "compradores" who manipulated prices by securing their monopoly in the transportation of rice. Thus, Phan Boi Chau claimed that "day and night, year by year, the French took hundreds of measures, used thousands of stratagems to strip the Vietnamese people of their properties and their energy, to suck their blood and marrow until nothing remained for them to eat or to wear.[16] But Chau was too intelligent to really believe all of what he said. Indeed such genocidal schemes were neither a French ideology nor a particular ambition of any French governor, given the high expectation they had placed on colonial exploitation.

Taxation

Taxation was an unjust system. As Bernard puts it: "Nobody had the least idea of what was taxable—we knew nothing specific, neither the size of population nor the extent of the cultivated land nor their yield." Thus, a curious tax, called "thue than" (corporal tax), was applied indiscriminately. It would become the theme of Nguyen An Ninh and other reformers fully supported by the population, and it was that which made the difference with the Constitutionalists. Seen as a slavery in disguise, this corporal tax would last to the final days of colonialization.

In his *Vietnam Vong Quoc Su* (History of the Loss of Vietnam), Phan Boi Chau cited, besides the corporal tax, at least 14 other taxes: land, habitation, ferry transportation, private junk and sampans, sales, market stands, pagoda revenues, birth and death registration, home festivities, handicraft, forest produce, and tobacco. Taxation was incoherent for there were no land survey or organized vital statistics that could enable a fair distribution of wealth and an equitable levy of tax. Be that as it may, given the cultural development at that time, the Vietnamese population was unable to comprehend the political and economic importance of government taxation. And even if they had acquired correct knowledge, the irrationality of the system could only let them side with Phan and consider taxes as a French measure of oppression.

Public Health

Having realized that peasant health was a foremost economic asset, the French set out to build a medical system for which they scored worldwide praise. Two major hospitals were built that exist even now: the De Lanessan in Hanoi and the Grall in Saigon. To a population of 23 million, 90 Europeans and 54 natives served as physicians and 92 Europeans and 1,462 natives as nurses. Two Pasteur Institutes, the Calmette in Saigon and the Yersin in Nhatrang, reached international fame for their research on tuberculosis and bubonic plague.

But the economic imperatives were such that to build the Indochinese government budget, the French allowed opium to become a critical resource. Bearing the RO (Regie opium) signs, countless opium dens were opened around the clock, offering the population a refined opium manufactured by special government laboratories.

Security

Lack of security was another problem eradicated by the French. Indeed, for half a century under the Nguyen, Vietnam suffered revolts and piracy. In 1851, the Chinese "Tam Duong," led by the three brothers Duong Quang Nghia, Duong Luc Thang, and Duong Duc Thang, spread destruction in Thai Nguyen. In 1854, the Giac Chau Chau (Grasshoppers Revolt) movement, led by former high mandarin and renowned poet Cao Ba Quat, controlled the province of Son Tay. In 1868, Ngo Con, a remnant of the Chinese T'ai Ping (Thai Binh Thien Quoc), plundered Cao Bang. His associates of the White, Yellow, and Black Pavillions (Tau O) terrorized the mountainous regions of Tonkin. In 1872, after Ngo Con and his associates were eliminated, the Black Pavillions under Luu Vinh Phuoc rallied to the Hue government. They fought the French, inflicting cruel losses by killing Francis Garnier and Henri Riviere. Thus, as Devillers pointed out, the French also brought back peace: "The nha que (peasant) could work in peace in his rice field without fear of pirates."[17]

But we shall later learn that in West Cochinchina, insecurity was originally identified as the consequence of the March to the South policy (Nam Tien). Indeed, the Don Dien settlements were the refuge for all kinds of misfits.

Education

If the Chinese had Si Nhiep to introduce Chinese culture, the French had also Doumer and Sarraut to teach the Vietnamese Western civilization. Of course the French did not cling to Chinese traditions even if they had any knowledge of them. They began to limit vernacular schools in which they introduced French programs. Their assimilation efforts had a curious aspect: In history class, the natives had to repeat "nos peres les Gaulois" (Our ancestors, the Gauls). Actually, education was simply designed to provide the colonial administration with the specialized man-power to rule the territory.

Justice

Justice under the French took a dual system. While French citizens were subjected to French law, the natives still depended on the Gia Long Code, renovated with the name of Annamite Code, which no longer included live dissection, but still maintained caning or pillory, hard labor or exile, strangulation, or decapitation. Yet the redemptive goal of these punishments was clearly visible: Those who were still alive went back to the society to live as if nothing had happened before.

COCHINCHINA

Cochinchina is the name coined by the Portuguese for what was Nam Ha or Dang Trong.[18] The country was also well known to the French missionaries and merchants.

The Colonial Society

Claude Farrere, writing about life in Saigon, made a vivid portrait of the colonial French: "Here (in Indochina) we give refuge to the miscreant and the worthless, the spongers and thieves. Those who settle in Indochina do not know how to work in France. Those who trade in Indochina were bankrupt. Those who lord it over the scholar mandarin flunk out of college. And those who sit in judgement and condemn have perhaps themselves been judged and condemned."[19]

As a modern colony, Cochinchina "enjoyed" a special status: It had a "depute" (representative) to the French National Assembly. To build up a French constituency, Henri Chavigny de la Chevrotiere imported shiploads of Indians from Pondichery (another French colony). By manipulating the electoral process, he acquired an unprecedented power. He was, in fact, the maker of Cochinchinese congressmen and above all the spokesman for the colons party who led a permanent opposition to indigenous emancipation reforms: On the one hand, in Cochinchina, they enrolled the local bureaucracy, the missionaries, and the Banks; on the other, in France, they aggressively lobbied with right-wing politicians and parliamentary groups. They courted the media, infiltrated other parties, and concluded alliances with the Catholic church. Thus, until the end in 1954, there was a "pattern of bureaucratic insubordination" (to borrow a term from Miles Kahler[20]) among the admiral governors, and especially Admiral Thierry d'Argenlieu, who fought all efforts for peace by creating the bogus Republic of Cochinchina.

Henri came from the island of La Reunion in the Indian Ocean, to make a private fortune in Cochinchina by recruiting coolies (laborers) for French rubber plantations in Indochina and in New Hebrides. He also owned the influential daily *La Depeche* through which he managed to secure a seat on the powerful Colonial Council. As the "de" particle of his surname was attributed to a noble origin, it drew a swift protest from author Ho Tai Hue Tam who knew better.[21] In fact Henry's only repute came from his superior swordsmanship, for at that time the art of fencing was the mark of a patrician background. And, indeed, Henry used his sword more than once to silence political opponents. He finally found his nemesis in Admiral Governor Decoux who for no clear reason put him behind bars. For that matter, Henry had no comment in his daily *La Depeche*. He had not asked the governor for an honorable reparation on the field.

In Cochinchina of the 1930s, the democratic process was supposedly carried out by the Colonial Council, an elected body of ten French and ten Vietnamese. But four additional members dispatched by the governor to represent French administration were always at hand to make sure that the votes remained in favor of the government. When, by this scheme, Governor Ernest Outrey passed a land law against the peasants, Le Van Trung and his colleagues resigned en masse. They were unanimously reelected by their Vietnamese constituency.

The French "societe coloniale" was a closed society, divided into three major groups: the colons, the civil servants, and the military. The first two had little consideration for the lower class soldiers. Indeed, for a long time, the Rue Catinat, pompously called Saigon's Champs Elysees, was off-limits to the troops. To these three classes, Devillers added a class of "women"[22] who, by their ethnocentrism, shaped the colonial mentality.

Sociological substrata developed with Marseillais, Parisians, Free Masons, Monarchists, Republicans, and even Dreyfusards and Antidreyfusards.[23] But above all, there were the ubiquitous Corsicans with some Sicilian traditions, under the well-known Franchini, owner of the Hotel Continental, which was the rally point of the colony.

Among the Asian colonial charms, there was the "midi-pastis,"[24] an absolute daily ritual, which then led French to consider hepatitis a "colonial disease." Opium was the other spell of Asia. And for a multitude of other reasons, many of those who had left their families in France, made up their mind not to return. As they had to divorce, all they needed was an adultery affidavit (constat d'adultere) duly established by a huissier (process server). Thus, a clever French lady, not necessarily young, made a lucrative career by offering her quarters exclusively for these legal proceedings. She was a significant part of Saigon folklore.

Vietnamese Peasants and French Land Policy

Before the French conquest, land ownership was the emperor's eminent right. Land possession was an appendage of the gentry status, as a result of imperial favors or as a kind of remuneration for services to the crown. The emperor also dispensed land to villages, which in turn allocated portions to the inhabitants under the conditions that they cultivated it and paid tax. Failure to comply resulted in a peasant's eviction. In this case, the estate went back to the communal lot for further redistribution. The don dien (military settlements) built up over Champa territory during the long March to the South,[25] were gradually integrated into the national plan, which consisted of Cong Dien (communal ricefields) and Cong Tho (communal lands). However, after an unspecified period—presumably over many years—the allocated land might become individual property of the farmers who had developed it.

By transferring his land ownership to the French in 1862 and submitting his rule to French control in 1874, the emperor provided background legitimacy to French spoliation. On June 22, 1863, by decision of Admiral Bonard, all estates left behind by their runaway owners were put on sale: From March 1865 to August 1866, 4,119 hectares were sold to Europeans. When there was a lack of Europeans buyers, Chinese came in to fill the gap. Soon, rich Vietnamese also joined the owner's club; hence, the fable that there was no systematic spoliation because natives could also become landowners . . . provided they had the means: Actually, the peasant could afford neither the high cost of the investment nor the exorbitant interest such an operation would yield.

As a result, the dispossessed peasantry split into two classes: the tenant farmers, who had to rent land to pursue their traditional livelihood, and a rural proletariat, who went to work on French industrialization projects. Indeed, there was a frenzy over building routes, canals, and railroads. From 1886 through 1936, the government of Cochinchina spent 59 million piastres to dig 4,000 kilometers of canals.[26]

Now in West Cochinchina, immense areas remain unexploited. In the vast swamp of Ca Mau, for example, except for mosquitos, crocodiles, snakes, and tigers, no life is possible. In 1964, a sampan trip through the region gave the author a firsthand confirmation of a 1879 report from province chief Briere: "The explorer's pirogue could slide indefinitely amidst the solitude over which lay the silence of death."[27] Indeed, at low tide, this silence is only disturbed, from time to time, by the faint noise of fish falling into the river. They were caught in the dense canopy at high tide.

The only vegetation consists of Tram shrubs rising from the dark green water. On half immersed mounds, under makeshift tents, groups of two or three bony humans vegetated, half naked. They were the woodcutters who provided Vietnamese households with the Cui Tram or Cui Don.[28] Yet, no one in the cities had ever suspected the existence of such living conditions.

Yet, to be fair, ownership inequality was not the result of French policy. It had existed long before under the monarchic regime, but the problem took an acute aspect with the introduction of modern agricultural technique, which allowed a minority of people to concentrate into their hands the majority of land. During the 1925–1930 period, the regime of great estates was already established: 6,300 large landowners, who lived in Vietnam cities or even in France, controlled 1,000,300 out of 2,300,000 hectares of cultivated surface. A rural proletariat developed among small landowners forced out by usury and government spoliations. They lived on wages earned mainly in time of harvest or in industrial developments. This led professor Pham Cao Duong to state that "In sum, the regime of great estates in Cochinchina presented a feudal pattern of operation."[29]

Indeed, the typical contract between landlords and tenants made the former only liable to provide the land and to pay the property taxes, while the latter had to bring in his own labor, housing, livestock, seeds, and farming tools. Because the rent was paid for with rice, the tenant might expect serious trouble if the land were of poor quality. Again, according to Pham Cao Duong, for an annual production of 3,000 kilograms of paddy, the tenant had to pay 1,500 kilograms of rice for the rent. With the balance, he had to make up for the care of his buffalo, the maintenance of his implements, the provision of seeds, and the livelihood of his family. Under the best conditions he would end up with 1,100 kilograms of rice for an average household of six, probably including his parents, his wife, and two children. This meant a daily intake of 500 grams per person. Besides, any expense for ancestors's cult, funerals, traditional festivities, such as the Tet or the Trung Thu (mid-autumn festivals), had to be "advanced" by the landlord at usurious rates. Even in case of natural disasters such as droughts, floods, or grasshoppers, the tenant was still liable for the rent.

When it came to the rich native landowners, their way of life reached legendary dimensions. It was public record that the so-called Cong Tu Bac Lieu (Son of the Duke of Bac Lieu) was known for his eccentricities: One night he used 100 piastre notes[30] as torchs to search out a five piastre bill inadvertendly dropped on the floor by a beautiful lady. Another day, he hired three rickshaws: one for himself, the second for his walking cane, and the third for his umbrella.

The Western "proprietaires" contributed to the folklore. Mr. Gressier, a French colon in West Cochinchina, set fire to a luxurious car, just imported from France, because his children were fighting for the driver's seat.

In the political realm, the independence of villages ended when the French created an administrative corps of Phu, Huyen, and Cai Tong[31] to control the country from provinces down to hamlets. This deprived the peasants of their traditional leadership; as some of the new notables were appointed by the Cai Tong or the Huyen, traditionally elected notables refused to sit among them. Finally, due to their absenteeism, power was shifted to those strangers who had no ties whatsoever with the village and therefore worked only for their own profits.

Yet if economic conditions have contributed to the rise of discontent, they were by no means the determinant factor of revolts. Traditionally, people's happiness is perceived as a result of harmonious relationship between Heaven and Earth, such harmony being empowered by a Mandate of Heaven. Since the French, as usurpers, did not have such a mandate, they could only bring misfortune and therefore had to be expelled.

Indeed, the French themselves had objected to the economic situation as the origin of peasant unrest. A governor of Cochinchina declared that the promoters of revolts "are men who have remained imbued with the ancient order of things predating French conquest and who have adamantly remained within the tradition and ideas of the past."[32]

NOTES

1. Joseph Buttinger, *Vietnam: A Dragon Embattled*, p. 79.

2. Ibid., p. 90.

3. Under previous administrations, there was one governor of Cochinchina and one resident general for Annam-Tonkin. With the newly created Indochinese Union, each of the four protectorates—Laos, Cambodia, Annam, Tonkin—were under a Resident Superieur. The Cochinchinese governor remained unchanged. All five reported to the Governeur general.

4. Later, the Vietnamese won representation on these councils.

5. Vietnamese subprefects.

6. Vietnamese prefects.

7. Ho Tai Hue Tam, *Radicalism and the Origins of the Vietnam Revolution*, p. 37.

8. Unskilled laborers.

9. Indians from the French colony of Pondicherry (India).

10. Prefect and subprefect.

11. Vietnamese having studied in France.

12. Philippe Devillers, *Histoire du Vietnam*, p. 47.

13. Ibid., p. 49.

14. Paul Bernard, *Le probleme economique indochinois*, p. 114.

15. D. G. E. Hall, *A History of Southeast Asia*, p. 742.

16. Phan Boi Chau, *Vietnam Vong Quoc Su*, p. 52.

17. Devillers, *Histoire du Vietnam*, p. 52.

18. See Oscar Chapuis, *A History of Vietnam*.

19. Buttinger, *Vietnam*, p. 442, citing Claude Farrere, *Les civilises*.

20. Miles Kahler, *Decolonization in Britain and France*.

21. Ho Tai Hue Tam, *Radicalism and the Origins of the Vietnam Revolution*, p. 118.

22. Devillers, *Histoire du Vietnam*, pp. 41, 42.

23. Ibid., p. 43.

24. Noon pastis is an alcoholic beverage made with anis.

25. See Chapuis, *A History of Vietnam*.

26. Ho Tai Hue Tam, *Radicalism and the Origins of the Vietnam Revolution*, p. 70.

27. Pham Cao Duong, *Vietnamese Peasants under French Domination*, p. 39.

28. Kitchen firewood.

29. Pham Cao Duong, *Vietnamese Peasants*, p. 70.

30. In the 1930s, the average rate of the piastre varied between 10 and 12 francs.

31. The Phu is a chief or prefect of a province, the Huyen is chief or subprefect of a district, and the Cai Tong is the head of several villages.

32. Ho Tai Hue Tam, *Radicalism and the Origins of the Vietnam Revolution*, p. 71.

5

REFORMS, REVOLTS, REVOLUTIONS

According to Truong Buu Lam: "The Vietnamese had developed over the centuries a conditioned reflex to surface threats."[1] Applied to old Asia, the above definition might relate to a pattern of xenophobia opposed to external ethnocentrism. Anyway, it became obvious to many scholars that their Confucian culture could not resist Western technology. Hence, the first logical step was to adopt modernization as a tool for organized resistance. This was the role of the first reformists.

THE REFORMISTS

The most famous reformist was Nguyen Truong To, who from 1863 to 1875 presented 43 projects covering commerce, industry, agriculture, and administration. A native of Bui Chu (Nghe An), To learned the French language from Catholic missionaries, while in turn teaching them Chinese characters. He sojourned three years in Paris where he acquired some insights on mining, water works, and architecture.

Ambassador to England, Pham Thu Thu also had a project for naval schools. Back from a mission in Hong Kong, Tran Dinh Tuc and Nguyen Huy Te proposed opening sea ports to foreign trade. At the same time, social issues appeared on reforms agendas: In 1868, besides recommending increases in mines explorations, and ship and locomotive building, Dinh Van Dien insisted on the reduction of corvées and on free medical care to the handicapped. In 1881, Phan Liem called for constitution of capitals to carry out international trade.

It was to no avail. Actually, it is not that Tu Duc was not interested in modernization: On the contrary, he had made sure that those with knowledge of the French language in explosives manufacturing and in locomotives exploitation were rewarded with various administrative positions, which unfortunately had no relation whatsoever with their experience. Furthermore, the country being

95 percent agricultural was not yet ready for immediate industrial transformations. Above all, the decision-making process was in the hands of the French who kept the right to make transformations suitable to their own interests. This led modern historian Pham Van Son to scornfully cite a popular saying: "The son of the king remains king while the son of a monk continues to sweep the pagoda courtyard" (Con vua thi van lam vua, con ong sai chua lai quet la da).[2] Be that as it may, the Hue Court first had to tackle revolts in Tonkin and Annam.

POPULAR MOVEMENTS IN TONKIN AND ANNAM

Throughout its history, Vietnam had to endure acts of banditry perpetrated by ethnic minorities and general devastation by sea pirates from Indonesia. Annam had to drive back multiple inroads from the Cham.

With regard to Tonkin, as a result of sharing the border with China, the country presented a kaleidoscope of various activities from pure banditry to tribes' revolts. This led to the tendency of confusing piracy and nationalist movements.

The remnants of the Tai Ping under Ngo Con, established in Cao Bang in 1868, spread havoc in the region. Upon complaints from the Hue Court, China assigned General Ta Ke Qui to help Vietnamese General Nguyen Viet Thanh. In 1870, Ngo Con died during his attack of Bac Ninh. Then his remnants divided into the Yellow Flags under Hoang Sung Anh and the White Flags under Luong Van Loi. But the most notorious group, the Black Flags under Luu Vinh Phuoc's (Liu Yu Fung) command, controlled the important centers of Tuyen Quang and Thai Nguyen.

After the commander of Lang Son, Doan Tho, was killed by the bandit To Tu, the Hue Court assigned Prince Hoang Ke Viem to command Ninh Binh, Lang Son, and Thai Nguyen, with Ton That Thuyet as interprovincial judge. Le Tuan was the imperial delegate. Later, in 1872, the famous Marshall Nguyen Tri Phuong came to represent the Hue government with the title of viceroy of Tonkin.

Besides the pirates, the minority tribes also were a continuous threat to regional peace. On April 12, 1884, ex-military officers Doc Ngu, De Kieu, and Nguyen Quang Bich rose at Hoa Binh, Yen Bai, Phu Tho, Bac Giang, and Son Tay. In August 1884, 300 Muong took arms at Hoa Binh under Doc Tam, Le Hoa, and Quach Chanh. Gradually, they were subdued; the last leader, Kiem, was sent to Poulo Condore for 25 years, and another, Bang, was banished to Lang Son for 20 years.

From 1887 to 1890, 800 Man, Meo, Tho, and ethnic Chinese revolted under Son A. In 1904, a woman named Man Pa Jeng led a coalition Man-Meo attack on Cao Bang. In 1911, again 2,000 Meo from Lao Kay and Ha Giang revolted at Muong Hua under Giang Quang Bao, a self-appointed king of the Meo tribe. He was captured in 1914. Colonel Joseph Gallieni, with three regiments, took That Khe and Na Sam.

In Annam, revolts took more of the form of "organized social protests" fomented by primitive rebels known as "Giang Ho," the equivalent of Hobsbawm "social bandits."[3] Heroes of Vietnamese folk culture, these Giang Ho came from the peasantry and thus were under village protection. Such protection was quite effective, for in Vietnam, "village customs prevail over King's decrees."[4] Their Robin Hood–style was not necessarily an altruistic concept: It was quite right that in exchange for peasants' help, the Giang Ho shared with them the products of their marginal activities. However, any violation of village mores automatically exposed the Giang Ho to villagers' reprisal. History shows that denunciation was the main weapon used by the peasants against their recalcitrant proteges. This shed a light on the pattern surrounding the capture of many fugitive leaders and the failure of their movements.

Under Minh Mang (1821–1840) there were 200 uprisings including the famous Le Van Khoi's episode; under Thieu Tri (1841–1847) only 50; under Tu Duc (1841–1883) 200 including the Hong Bao and Giac Chia Voi.

THE RESISTANTS

Because social bandits later moved into the political field as in the case of the Tay Son and De Tham, a blurred picture ensued enabling some authors to include them in the general category of nationalist resistants, although xenophobia had always predominated among the grassroots class.

De Tham

Among the northern rebels, De Tham was considered the epitome of a nationalist at the service of his king and his country. This may not be absolutely true, for he perfectly fit Hobsbawm's description of the social bandit. He did not begin his career with a political agenda but acted as an outlaw out of material paucity. His involvement in nationalist struggles, or more precisely anti-French rebellion, came only later after he met with Phan Boi Chau.

De Tham, or Hoang Hoa Tham, was born in 1846 at Son Tay to a miserable peasant family, like Luu Vinh Phuoc. At the age of 20, he joined a rebel chief named Ba Phuc whom he would later succeed. At 25, he allied with Cai Kinh. On July 6, 1888, Cai Kinh died leaving the command to De Tham who set his control over the regions of Que Vuong, Vo Giang, Hiep Hoa, and Viet Yen. In 1889, his forces amounted to 500 well-trained combatants. He then associated with two prominent chiefs: Chinese Luong Tam Ky from the Black Flags and the Thai warlord Deo Van Tri from Northern Tonkin. In addition to his headquarters at Yen The, he organized, not unlike the Buu Son Ky Huong in Cochinchina, farm camps in Phu Lang Thuong, Thai Nguyen, Vinh Phuc Yen, and Bac Giang.

In 1892, the French attacked Yen The without much success. De Tham's strength resided in his mobility, which enabled him to escape French pincer strategy. Thus, in spite of many expeditions, the French were unable to defeat De Tham.

On September 17, 1894, Chesnay, editor of the paper *Avenir du Tonkin*, was captured. Under pressure of the colons and given the impossibility of defeating Tham at that time, the French army had to negotiate to obtain his release. In fact, De Tham's conditions were not too harsh: The French had to pay 15,000 francs for ransom. They also had to withdraw from Yen The and leave the administration of the four cantons Nha Nam, Muc Son, Yen Le, and Huu Thuong to De Tham with the right to levy taxes for three years. The French accepted, and a lull took place during which their relations took quite an amiable turn, although during a common hunting party, De Tham was "almost accidentally" killed by a French officer. During this period, De Tham settled at Phon Xuong, where he cultivated rice on a large scale. A newcomer, Ky Dong, clandestinely provided him with new recruits from a French plantation he was managing.

At the end of 1895, Tham was involved in the attack of Bac Ninh and refused to return to the French the weapons he had seized as bounty. Thus, in November 1895, Colonel Gallieni sent a gunboat with troops to force Tham's surrender. After a vain attempt to negotiate, Tham retreated into the jungles.

In 1908, De Tham was involved in a revolt of the Garde Indochinoise (Linh Kho Xanh) at Bac Ninh, Nam Dinh, and Nha Nam where an French officer was killed. The same year he took part in a vain plot to poison the entire French garrison at Hanoi, with the help of the Garde Indochinoise.

The poisoning at Hanoi Citadel. This episode had generated a general commotion in Paris. On the evening of June 27, 1908, the Garde Indochinoise attacked the French garrison in Hanoi after careful planning: On the one hand, the nearby post of Don Thuy would be neutralized by heavy artillery, on the other hand, the important posts of Son Tay and Bac Ninh would be barred from coming to the rescue. As for De Tham, he would wait outside the citadel for the signal to attack Gia Lam and destroy railroad and telephone lines.

Inside the garrison, Corporal Nguyen Dang Duyen carefully mixed his poison with food. The French were having a party: Dinner was served exactly at 7 P.M. according to an established schedule. But the poison appeared to be only a strong purgative and the French were alerted. Outside, since he saw no signal, De Tham realized that the coup had failed and withdrew his forces. On July 8, 1908, 24 death sentences and 70 life sentences were pronounced against the rebels.

Thus, the long lull with De Tham was over: the French demanded his surrender and made sure this would be the last time they heard about him. Indeed, his star was dimming. On January 28, 1909, the Tonkin resident began a massive operation. From January 29 through November 11, 1909, De Tham lost 11 major battles and finally took refuge in Yen The, surrounded by the French. His wife was captured and deported to Guyana. Many of his party deserted, compelling him to call for help from his long-time friend Luong Tam Ky, who provided him with a personal escort. During the Tet[5] he sent everyone back home to enjoy the holiday, keeping only two Luong Tam Ky volunteers as bodyguards. It was February 10, 1913: That night, the two ruffians entered his bedroom and smashed his head with a farmer's hoe.

The Thai Nguyen revolt. The Thai Nguyen revolt was the work of Vietnam Quang Phuc Hoi, which had succeeded in infiltrating the military circles. This town, located between Hanoi and Cao Bang, was, like Poulo Condore in Cochinchina, the concentration camp for political prisoners from the Duy Tan Hoi to the Can Vuong and the Quang Phuc Hoi, among the latter, the prestigious Luong Ngoc Quyen who was a graduate from Japanese and Chinese military academies. He had been arrested by the French in Kwang Si and sent to Thai Nguyen where he became, with Sergeant Trinh Van Can, the instigator of the rebellion.

During the night of August 31, 1917, which was precisely a payday, Can began to take the city jail after killing French warden Loeu. All prisoners were freed and, like Luong Ngoc Quyen, joined the rebels. But if Trinh Van Can's loyalty was unquestionable, his military competence was rather limited: Instead of flying the Quang Phuc flag for six days, he should have retired in time to avoid a direct confrontation with French rescue forces. In the ensuing fight, Quyen was seriously wounded and since his transportation slowed down the retreat move, he decided to die on the spot. After a heated deliberation, the leaders had to acknowledge the inevitable, thus Can had a squad present military honors to Quyen before firing at him.

When he left Thai Nguyen, Can had had 131 Garde Indochinoise, 200 volunteers, 167 rifles and 15 swords. Under French pursuit, Can moved to the Vinh Yen jungle after losing 11 battles. Unable to resist French pressure, he went back to take refuge in Thai Nguyen, where he witnessed mass desertion from his side. On October 8, 1918, he found himself with only ten soldiers. When eight of them left, Can committed suicide. The entire revolt lasted only 38 days.

The Can Vuong

Vietnamese historians divide the Can Vuong into two periods: the actual Can Vuong (Royalist period), which was a direct response to Ham Nghi's call for struggle against the French before his capture, and the subsequent Van Than (Intellectual period), as an offshoot of the Can Vuong after the deportation of Ham Nghi.

From all corners of the country, the population responded with enthusiasm to the imperial appeal but not for the same reason: deserters of the Kwang Si army and remnants of the Black Flags[6] volunteered with the hope of further looting; bourgeois, scholars, mandarins were motivated by Confucian ethics; only the peasants from Nghe An-Thanh Hoa, ancestral abode of the Nguyen Dynasty, fought for love of their king. Soon, Vietnam began to show a picture quite familiar in 1945, when French ruled cities in the daytime while Viet Minh controlled the villages after dark. Likewise, the Can Vuong movement controlled the countryside by night.

In 1889, Doc Tieu and Doc Nghi, ex-military officers, were officially commissioned by Ham Nghi to head a 1,000 man force composed of officers and soldiers from the former imperial army. Notwithstanding their experience, they were routed by the French on August 31, 1889, at the village of Thuy Lam. In 1890, at Yen The, another officer, De Nam, engaged against the 1,300-man troop of Colonel Frey. After killing two officers, he retreated with his 400 men. All these remnant troops would later join De Tham.

The spontaneous support accorded to the Can Vuong was both its strength and its weakness. Proliferation of groups prevented a unified command, although Ham Nghi and Ton That Thuyet had appointed former Son Tay An Sat (provincial Judge) Nguyen Quang Bich to coordinate the movement. In fact, Bich was rather more preoccupied with begging aid from the Ch'ing than doing his job. Yet it was a vital function, for instead of waging war against the French, many Can Vuong leaders focused on the suppression of the Catholic population. At the end of the conflict, the civilian casualties would reach a staggering figure: 40,000 Catholic converts, 18 French missionaries, and 40 Viet priests were murdered, while 9,000 churches were destroyed.[7]

Enthronement of Dong Khanh, an elder brother of Ham Nghi, had resulted in a division of national consciousness and paved the way to an erosion of the will to fight for the Can Vuong. Yet when the French urged the new king to tour the country for appeasement, daily assaults on his life prevented Dong Khanh from going further than Dong Hoi. For his personal safety he had to interrupt the trip and go home by sea. To win Ham Nghi's cooperation, Dong Khanh offered him the three provinces of Thanh Hoa, Nghe An, and Ha Tinh, but Ton That Thuyet intercepted the message. Dong Khanh was luckier with Prince Hoang Ke Viem to whom he gave the control of Quang Tri and Quang Binh. In return, as he was well informed of Ham Nghi's detailed life, Hoang Ke Viem advised the French to contact the chief of Ham Nghi's bodyguards, a man named Truong Quang Ngoc. Ngoc came from a Muong tribe. His father, once a minor mandarin, was dismissed by the Court of Hue for some peccadilloes. Thus, some authors believe Ngoc in fact harbored a deep resentment against the emperor. Actually, the end was in view. Everyone knew they were fighting a losing war and were trying to find their way out. They had to face a double front: on the one hand, two entire French divisions and on the other, the Garde Indochinoise (Linh Kho Xanh)[8] under the awful mandarin Nguyen Than. In June 1885, the Can Vuong lost Dong Hoi to the French and Quang Nam to Nguyen Than. In July, the French took Quang Tri and in August they occupied Binh Dinh. General Prudhomme defeated the Can Vuong in Quang Binh and Ha Tinh. The cooperation of pro-French mandarin Tran Ba Loc led to a particularly bloody repression. In October, Cam Lo, Tan So, and Mai Linh were evacuated by the Can Vuong. In February 1886, with the participation of General Nguyen Than, the Can Vuong was beaten lock, stock, and barrel at Trai Na. By then, calm was reestablished, enough to allow the French to install telegraphic lines between Quang Nam and Hue.

Then came the end for Ham Nghi as already reported. His deportation opened another chapter of Vietnam resistance.

The Van Than

Ham Nghi's deportation was a fatal blow to the Can Vuong movement: By losing its king, the movement lost its raison d'etre. And yet, the Confucian scholars took over. Tien Si (PhD) Nguyen Xuan On in Ha Tinh, Nghe An, and Thanh Hoa; former Hanoi governor Le Truc in Quang Binh; nongraduate Dinh Cong Trang and his associate Cu Nhan (Master) Pham Banh with their famous Ba Dinh base; Tien Si Tong Duy Tan in Thanh Hoa; ex-mandarin Nguyen Thien Thuat with Admiral Ta Hien built the famous maquis of Bay Sai at the conjunction of Hung Yen, Hai Duong, and Bac Ninh.

After its defeat, the Van Than disbanded. Nguyen Thien Thuat went to seek refuge with Liu Yung Fu in Kwang Si. Tong Duy Tan was captured and publicly executed in September 1892. Their remnants joined Phan Dinh Phung and continued the struggle after he had succeeded in chasing the French out of Ha Tinh. In fact, Phan Dinh Phung had no illusions for a final victory and said: "It is our destiny. We accept it." To avenge Ham Nghi, in 1893, he publicly executed traitor Truong Quang Ngoc[9] at Tuyen Hoa.

Phan Dinh Phung. Once jailed and banned by Thuyet for having criticized the murder of King Duc Duc, Phan Dinh Phung forsook the past and joined Thuyet to support Ham Nghi. According to French accounts, although he was a distinctive scholar, Phan's military craft was also quite remarkable. His troops were well trained, wore a uniform, observed a military discipline, and were well equipped with locally made rifles. For ten years, from 1886 through 1895, they held Ha Tinh against French expeditions.

In 1887, Phan established contact with De Tham and settled in the Vu Quang mountains (Annam) where his assistant, Cao Thang, built an arms factory, which produced 350 French model rifles. His forces then amounted to 1,000 regulars.

But on December 28, 1893, Phan contracted dysentery and anticipating his death ordered his troops to disband. Taking advantage of the news, the French dispatched General Nguyen Than against Phan with 3,000 militia. When Nguyen Than arrived, Phan was already buried. He had Phan's corpse exhumed and burned; the ashes were mixed with heavy gun powder to fire at La Giang, the last Van Than outpost.

Granting that technological warfare was a cause of French victory does not explain Vietnamese defeat, for in more than one occasion they had shown their capability to defeat the French. The truth lies first in the lack of a Vietnamese unified command: It is a historic fact that Vietnamese lacked a sense of cooperation. Although there was some loose relationship between the 50 resistance groups, no consensus could be obtained over appointing a commander in chief and no individual leader had enough power to impose himself as such. Second, the role of collaborators, their intimate knowledge of the country, and their determination to serve the French in carrying out ferocious repression was the determinant factor of French victory.

THE COLLABORATORS

The role of collaborators was not advertised; perhaps for the sake of national pride, it had to be forgotten. Yet, through multiple instances, one has to recognize that no military conquest can succeed without some kind of cooperation from the opposite side, be that covertly under the form of espionage or openly under the form of political cooperation. In the intelligence field, the French had systematically used information extracted by the missionaries from their converts through the process of religious confession. Open collaboration came from three dissimilar groups: the North Tonkin tribes that had been excluded from the Vietnamese society as worthless minorities, the Le partisans anxious to restore their own dynasty, and the Vietnamese elite, either scholars attracted by Western culture or mandarins in disgrace or simply dissatisfied with the court. Among these, Nguyen Than, Hoang Cao Khai, Tran Ba Loc, and Do Huu Phuong were noted for their loyalty to the French and their bloody repressions against their countrymates.

Among the Le partisans, Le Duy Luong under Minh Mang and Le Duy Cu under Tu Duc were not associated with the French, while Pedro Le Duy Phung benefitted from support from the Catholic missionaries and Garnier against the Nguyen. He had been raised as a Catholic adept at a French Penang seminary. With the help of Father Legrand de la Liraye, he obtained a post of translator in the French forces. He later left to build an army of 20,000 controlling Quang Yen, Hai Duong, and Nam Dinh. Only in 1864, did Tu Duc succeed in getting rid of him.

Some scholars, Petrus Ky and Paulus Huynh Tinh Cua, for example, were accused by Vietnamese historians of being "traitors": Both had authored many Franco-Vietnamese dictionaries, hence working toward eliminating cultural obstacles to French assimilation policy. They both belonged to a French-speaking intelligentsia mainly composed of Christian adepts. This, incidentally, explains the predominance of Catholics within the colonial society and administration. This also explains the latent hostility between Buddhists and Catholics, which lasted until modern times and caused the demise of Catholic President Ngo Dinh Diem.

INTELLECTUAL MOVEMENTS

Only later, at the end of the 19th century, did the scholars begin to distance themselves from a crumbling ruling class and join the popular movements. Many had by then realized that they must protect an indigenous way of life without which they would not be able to preserve their interests as a dominant class.

If the Can Vuong was by no means the genesis of a true Vietnamese nationalism, it was nevertheless the expression of a multifaceted anticolonialism. Although they fought against the same enemy, it was not always for the same reason. Thus, it was to the credit of scholars like Phan Chu Trinh and Phan Boi Chau to identify the modern causes of Vietnam decadence. Through literary propaganda, the two Phans succeeded in convincing the peasants that their living conditions were not due to "heaven's anger," as Eastern philosophy had said for so long, but a result of economic exploitation. Yet, they put the blame on the French administration while they were well aware that it had been generated long ago from their monarchic regimes.

Phan Chu Trinh

Trinh was born in 1872 in Quang Nam where his father taught the martial arts. Like Phan Boi Chau, he was then too young to be involved in the Can Vuong movement, and his political career only began at the end of the Van Than period. Anyway, given his democratic conviction, it is doubtful that he would take any part in helping to restore the imperial regime.

In 1901, after having obtained a second-place doctorate at the national examination, he went on to occupy a post in the Ministry of Rites (Bo Le). Disgruntled by government corruption, he left to associate with Phan Boi Chau and other reformists. Political violence was not on their agenda yet. In 1902, Trinh met with De Tham during the latter's lull with the French, but disagreed with him on armed struggle. In 1904, he travelled to China to meet with Phan Boi Chau, and both visited Japan where after ten months of observation, he disagreed with Chau on calling for Japanese help. In 1906, he alone went back to Vietnam to carry on his own program. He wrote to the French Governor General Beau who was receptive to democratic reform. Indeed, democracy is a language well understood in the West, and Trinh was the only one to use this vehicle to reach the French government. Furthermore, his knowledge of the works of Rousseau and Montesquieu was of course in the French taste. Considering that education was vital to Vietnamese progress, Trinh founded the Duy Tan Hoi (Association for Modernization of Vietnam) under the presidency of Prince Cuong De while he kept the post of General Secretary for himself. To support the Duy Tan Hoi, the Dong Du movement (Eastward travel) was created under Prince Cuong De himself.

In March 1907 Luong Van Tuong and Nguyen Quyen opened the Dong Kinh Nghia Thuc (Free School of Tonkin) at Hang Dao Street (Peach Street) in Hanoi. The program called for reforms in education and examination, opening the country to new ideas of progress and democracy, based on the works of French authors Jean-Jacques Rousseau and Montesquieu. There Phan Chu Trinh lectured assiduously on comparative study of "Monarchy vs. Democracy" and on "Morality and Religion in Western and Eastern cultures." According to Trinh, monarchy provided no moral standard except the compulsory respect for the right of the might; since freedom and equality were the foundation of morality, only democracy was moral. Later many of Ho Chi Minh's followers would emerge from this institution.

In 1908, in Annam, following a 30 percent increase in taxes to commemorate Emperor Khai Dinh's birthday, Quang Nam erupted in violent demonstrations: Phan Chu Trinh was arrested with Tran Cao Van, Ngo Duc Ke, Huynh Thuc Khang, and Tran Quy Cap who were beheaded at Nha Trang. The Free School was closed under the pretext that it was a forum for anti-French propaganda. But from March to May 1908, revolts spread to Quang Ngai, Binh Dinh, and Thanh Hoa, causing destruction of government offices and death of government employees. Phan Chu Trinh, accused of being behind the riots, was sentenced to death by the Co Mat Vien (Privy Council) for incitation to violence. Thanks to the intervention of the French human rights association, his sentence was commuted to deportation to Poulo Condore. Ernest Babut of the human rights association continued to fight for his release, and in 1911, Trinh was freed but assigned with his son to residence in France. There he resumed his political activities, demanding a change in French politics in Vietnam. While praised by the leftists, he experienced harassment from the right: He lost his monthly government allowance and had to work in a photographic shop for a meager living.

At the beginning of World War I, Trinh was put into custody at La Sante prison to keep him out of the reach of German agents who were quite active in Vietnam. He was released in 1915 after the intervention of the Socialist Party.

In 1922, the presence of Dong Khanh at the Paris International Fair led Trinh to send him an open letter "blaming his indifference toward the plight of his country. He challenged his imperial prerogatives and called the emperor by his personal name Buu Dan," which is the most offensive insult in Sino-Vietnamese customs.

In 1925, he benefitted from an amnesty and went back to Saigon. That same year Phan Boi Chau was also freed from prison, and Phan Chu Trinh decided to go and meet him at Hue. At that time, his personal prestige enabled him to have an unofficial voice in Vietnam affairs. When Khai Dinh died, he cabled Resident Superieur Pasquier his decision to "reorganize the government and found a party" notwithstanding his lack of credentials. But instead he succumbed to illness and died on March 24, 1926, at the age of 55. For his funeral, all schools went on strike. As for the amount of mourners attending the funeral it varied from 25,000 to 140,000.[10]

Phan Chu Trinh, by his opposition to the use of force and his politics of noncooperation, appeared as the harbinger of India's Mahatma Gandhi.

Phan Boi Chau

Chau was born in 1867 to a family of scholars in Nghe An Province, the cradle of Vietnamese revolutionaries. At the age of 18, he clandestinely joined the Can Vuong movement and organized death volunteer groups. Yet at age 33, he became a laureate at the Nghe An examination but later failed the doctorate. Yet, he would become, by his own right, a prominent scholar.

After the death of Phan Dinh Phung, Phan Boi Chau picked up the torch of resistance. First he authored many writings, including the *Vietnam Vong Quoc Su* (History of the Decadence of Vietnam) in which with a style that was not always academic, he blamed Tu Duc's government for being "an impotent sleep-walker which treated the people as grass and garbage. If the French were in our house, it was our fault for we had invited them." As for the treaty of 1862, Chau said: "Phan Thanh Gian and his assistant Lam Duy Nghiem began to tremble at the view of the French. They would give away all their ranks and positions and their entire families if so the French wished, let alone the six provinces of Cochinchina."

In Phan Boi Chau's political scenario, Ton That Thuyet was the hero and Nguyen Van Tuong, the villain. He accused Tuong of being a French informant who, against remuneration, led the French troops against Thuyet. As for Queen Mother Tu Du, "she was a stupid and voracious woman . . . a crook that sent good mandarins to death or in retirement, and thus got upside down the affairs of the nation." If such a trivial language was not to scholars' taste, it obviously delighted a xenophobic populace.

The kaiser's appeal in 1905 for the independence of Morocco gave Phan Boi Chau an insight into France's political isolation in Europe. Moreover, Japan's victory over Russia moved the target of Vietnamese activists' expectations from China to Japan.

Considering that education was fundamental to reach independence, Phan Boi Chau founded the Duy Tan Hoi (Association for the Modernization of Vietnam) under the presidency of Prince Cuong De, while he kept the post of general secretary for himself. Later, in 1906, to support the Duy Tan, both founded the Dong Du movement (Eastward travel). Chau traveled widely in Tonkin, Cochin-china, China, and Japan. In August, at Phon Xuong (Tonkin) he met with De Tham who was having a lull with the French. Like the Buu Son Ky Huong, Tham was actively building self-sufficient farm camps.

In Cochinchina, Phan Boi Chau and Cuong De[11] went up to the That Son (Seven Mountains), the cradle of millenarian rebels, to meet with enigmatic monk Tran Nhut Thi. As it happened, Thi's other name was Monk Phung, who, under the saffron robe, was fomenting anti-French crusades in Cochinchina.

In China, with Phan Chu Trinh, Phan Boi Chau and Cuong De paid a visit in 1906 to Luu Vinh Phuoc (Liu Ying-Fu) who was living in retirement in Kwang Si. Here, in spite of their close friendship, the two Phans were for the first time confronted with their ideological difference: Trinh was for a demo-cratic regime, while Chau remained monarchist. Yet, they would stay together to pursue the common goal of the liberation of Vietnam. Thus, that year, all three went to Japan.

The Dong Du Movement

At Yokohama, Chau assured the Japanese that the Duy Tan Hoi was essentially monarchist. He easily won the protection of Inukai Tsyoshi, an influential member of the monarchist Dobun Shoin party. Tsyoshi would sponsor Cuong De's stay in Japan, where he would direct the Dong Du organization.

When Chau came to Tokyo with Cuong De and Trinh, things were not as easy as they appeared at the first meeting in Yokohama. They were told by the government that Japan had just come out of a war with Russia and therefore was experiencing financial difficulties, which prevented Japan from granting them any subsidies. Furthermore, any open activity against France could bring Japan back to war with the Western bloc. Nevertheless, as they had championed a Pan Asian cause, the government would not oppose Vietnamese undertaking if carried out with prudence and discretion.

The Dong Du project immediately attracted a large support: in Tonkin, Nguyen Thuong Hien and Nguyen Quyen; in Cochinchina, Nguyen Than Hien and Gilbert Tranh Chanh Chieu; and in Annam, Phan Chu Trinh, Ngo Duc Ke, and Huynh Thuc Khang. In spite of Cuong De's presence, Phan Chu Trinh heartily supported the movement.

In Japan, under the protection of the Do Buu Kwai organization (Eastern Cultural Institute—Dong Van Thu Vien) they were steered to study academics at the Do Buu Shoin University or military science at the Shimbu Gakko (Military Academy—Chan Vo Hoc Hieu). During the period 1906–1908, more than 100 volunteers, mainly Cochinchinese, arrived in Japan.[12]

To provide necessary funds for Dong Du, commercial organizations mushroomed: In Hanoi there was the Dong Loi Te organization, in Quang Nam, the Thuong Mai Hop Xa. In Cochinchina, Gilbert Tran Chanh Chieu built up a lucrative network of restaurants, hotels, and export-import companies: the Nam Dong Hung and the Nam Trung Hotels in Saigon; the Hoi Te Nam and the Minh Tam inns at Mytho.

But Gilbert's arrest put a halt to these activities. Furthermore, to undermine the Dong Du movement, the French granted Japan some commercial advantages but in return, demanded the eviction of Vietnamese from Japan, including Cuong De and Phan Boi Chau. Thus, all anti-French action in Japan stopped and Vietnamese revolutionaries had to move back to Canton where they found themselves in the middle of revolutionary turmoil. The suspicion of the warring parties forced them to take refuge in Siam. But their isolation in Siam on the one hand and the arrest of Gilbert Chieu and 40 of his followers in Cochinchina on the other hand put an end to the Duy Tan and the Dong Du movements. In 1907, Phan Boi Chau and Cuong De moved to the Kwang Si under Luu Vinh Phuoc's protection. There was only one way left: armed struggle.

In 1925, following a mysterious denunciation, Chau was arrested by the French security in Shanghai and was transferred back to Tonkin. Incarcerated at the Hoa Lo jail in Hanoi, he was sentenced to death. In France and in Vietnam, mass protestations in his favor led Governor Varenne not only to release him but also to offer him the post of minister of education, which he refused. He preferred to retire from politics to his home at Hue.

The conclusion of Chau's and Trinh's political careers seemed to confirm that they had both reached a logical conclusion on the inevitability of the French departure from Vietnam. They perceived the gradual participation of the natives in the administrative process as the harbinger of Western renunciation of direct rule, thus, paving the way to self-government in the future. When delegates of the newly created Viet Nam Quoc Dan Dang came to visit him, they found in Phan Boi Chau a cautious old man who could only advise them prudence and moderation.

The Catholics and the Dong Du Movement. The involvement of Catholics and Buddhists was minimized in order to show that French had the support of the two leading religions in Vietnam. Yet, if these two faiths, being more or less courted by the occupant, officially refrained from taking any antigovernment action, their adepts did not always follow suit. And if from a political point of view, the participation of Buddhists in the revolutionary cause is understandable, given Asian ethnical symbiosis, the involvement of Catholics was beyond common expectation.

In France, the antagonism between Church and government stemmed from the opposition of anticlerical groups, represented in Indochina by Paul Bert and other officials. This conflict escalated with the rapid expansion of the Foreign Mission as a politico-economic power. In Indochina, a large amount of estates and industries were in the possession of the Mission. In Hong Kong, the Mission owned the famous Bethanie House, which served as a rest and recreation center for Catholic missionaries from all over Asia. There was also the prestigious Nazareth Editions House that published Christian propaganda in more than 40 Asian languages.

The hostility took a sharp turn with Bishop Pineau, the vicar apostolic of southern Tonkin, when the colonial police first arrested and accused French protégé Father Magat of seditious activities. In fact, Magat was trying to protect his converts from the Can Vuong by raising some armed groups. Magat's case was not unique; other French missionaries had done likewise, but the real target was Bishop Pineau himself.

For obvious reasons the colonial bureaucracy was not ready to see any Catholic church rise to power, let alone Pineau's efforts to promote De Rhodes principles for the creation of an indigenous clergy. In this respect, the administration found some allies among the young priests dispatched by Paris. The newcomers claimed a defective "material and temporal gestion" of their aging superiors. They opposed the promotion of "ignorant natives." Internal strife surged when Pineau surrounded himself with three prominent Vietnamese: Father Nguyen Van Dong, pastor of his Xa Doai Cathedral; Father Nguyen Van Tuong, procureur of his mission; and Father Do Linh, his own confessor and chaplain.

Upon denunciation of the French priests, the French resident personally came to search the Bishop's premises, looking for proof against Father Linh. The inquest ended on June 12, 1909, with the three native priests accused of having close connections with Phan Boi Chau and collecting money for the Dong Du movement. They were sentenced to nine years deportation to Poulo Condore. Tuong, the eldest one, soon died on the remote island. Later, the two others were freed during a general amnesty at the end of World War I. As for Bishop Pineau, after a decent interval to spare Church prestige, he resigned, ending 44 years of apostolate.

THE VIETNAM QUANG PHUC HOI

In 1912, Cuong De and Phan Boi Chau invited some 100 émigrés to Luu Vinh Phuoc's residence in Kwang Si where they founded the Vietnam Quang Phuc Hoi (League for the Restoration of Vietnam). The new organization took the form of a government in exile under Tong Dai Bieu (General delegate), Cuong De, and General Secretary Phan Boi Chau. The government council was divided equally between the three Kys: Tonkin was represented by Nguyen Thuong Hien, a school teacher; Annam by Phan Boi Chau himself; and Cochinchina by Nguyen Than Hien. Ten commissioners shared the departments of army, economy, education, finance and others. The government flag consisted of five red stars on a yellow background.

The army (Quang Phuc Quan) was under the command of graduates from Chinese and Japanese military academies, among which was the famous Luong Van Quyen. Weapons were purchased abroad and a plant was erected to manufacture bombs.

In the name of a Vietnam military government, promissory notes were issued in the amount of 5, 10, 20, and 100 piastres with a warranty to reimburse at 100 percent interest once the democratic government was installed. Counterfeiting was subject to harsh penalty. In Cochinchina, Cuong De circulated common stocks well accepted by the peasants and merchants.

Three delegates, Lam Quang Trung (Annam), Dang Binh Than (Cochinchina), and Dang Xung Hong (Tonkin), were in charge of propaganda in Vietnam. Tran Cao Van was assigned to approach the 16-year-old Emperor Duy Tan himself, who readily accepted to join the revolutionists. The young monarch was so enthusiastic that he even decided himself that the uprising would take place on May 3, 1916. But through an indiscretion from a "blue militiaman" (Linh Kho Xanh), the French got wind of the plot. As a result, after a few days in the mountains, Duy Tan had to surrender. Fourteen rebel leaders were executed by firing squads and more than 200 deported to Poulo Condore. As for Tran Cao Van, he was beheaded.

On April 4, 1913, a bomb killed the Thai Binh prefect Nguyen Duy Han. Twelve days later, a grenade hurled into the Hanoi Hotel killed two retired French officers, Montgrand and Chapuis. This triggered off a huge reprisal: 254 arrests, 7 executions, 52 deportations. Phan Boi Chau and Nguyen Hai Than were sentenced to death in absentia.

Then World War I broke out in 1914, giving Chau the opportunity to come back to Vietnam. On February 4, 1915, he sent three columns of Vietnam Quang Phuc Hoi to the Sino-Viet borders: the first one from Lung Chow to Yen Bai, the second from Lung Chow to Lang Son, and the third from northern Thailand to Lai Chau. All three units were beaten lock, stock, and barrel. Leaders Tran Hieu Luc, Hoang Trong Mau, and Le Duc Mau were captured one after the other. They were publicly executed in Hanoi shortly afterward.

It goes without saying that the party had to step back. Under French demand, the Canton governor general placed Chau under arrest, but he was freed in September by the military government of Sun Yat-sen.

In 1915, German agents in Thailand gave 10,000 piastres to the Phuc Quang Hoi to conduct an attack on Mong Cai and Ha Khau; both failed. The following year, a brutal French offensive forced the local leaders to flee to Canton and Hong Kong. But under their influence, the tribes at the border regions carried on for four more years with eight attacks against Luc Nam, Mong Cai, Nho Quan, Lao Kay, and Ha Giang. As already reported, the uprising of Thai Nguyen was also a work of a Quang Phuc officer.

In China, the Quang Phuc Hoi had no luck either: In 1917, they staged an attack at the Yunnan-Tonkin border and again failed. The movement receded until 1940 when, taking advantage of the arrival of Japanese in Tonkin, they started an uprising under Tran Trung Lap, who expected Japanese support. It was to be their last mistake: The Japanese were twiddling their thumbs, leaving the French with free hands to crush the revolt. As the French tightened their control over the Lang Son-Cao Bang area, the Quang Phuc fled back to China and disintegrated.

EVOLUTION OF POLITICAL PARTIES

Past failures brought up new ideas orienting the Vietnamese revolutionists toward multiple and confusing changes, which nevertheless showed a trend toward socialism as a tool for reaching independence.

From Tam Tam Xa to Thanh Nien and the Indochinese Communist Party

During the early 1920s, Canton was Phan Boi Chau's headquarters. In 1923, together with two communists, Ho Tung Mau and Le Hong Phong, he organized the Tam Tam Xa (Heart to Heart Association). They sent a young member,

Pham Hong Thai, on a suicide mission to kill French Governor General Merlin during his visit in Canton. Thai failed and threw himself into the Pearl River.

In 1924, Chau also held a meeting in Canton with political refugees, among who was Ly Thuy, a Komintern interpreter who had just arrived from Moscow. Ly Thuy suggested the creation of a party similar to the Third International but was ruled out because Vietnam, as an agricultural country, lacked the typical divisions of class of an industrial society.

In May 1925, to replace the extinct Vietnam Quang Phuc Hoi, the Vietnam Thanh Nien Cach Mang Dong Chi Hoi (Vietnam Revolutionary Youth Association), or Thanh Nien for short, was founded in Hong Kong with Phan Boi Chau as president, Nguyen Hai Than as advisor, and Ly Thuy as general secretary. The immediate purpose was to train specialists in agitprop (i.e., communist propaganda) for Vietnam.

Two months later, an incident of extreme importance put the Thanh Nien on the marxist track. In July 1925, Phan Boi Chau was lured into a Shanghai French concession where he was arrested by the French police. Chau's demise allowed Ly Thuy to take over the Thanh Nien and thus the rumors that he had masterminded Chau's capture in order to cash in the 100,000 piastres of French reward[13] and also to seize control of the Thanh Nien party.

Before the Tam Tam Xa, the Phuc Viet (Restoration of Vietnam) was founded in August 1917 in Poulo Condore by political detainees Le Van Huan, Tran Hoanh, Nguyen Dinh Kien, and Pham Cao Dai. Later in 1925, the Phuc Viet took the name of Hung Nam Hoi (Vietnam Renaissance Association) and changed again into Vietnam Cach Mang Dang (VNCMD, VN Revolutionary party) after absorption of the 60-man Tan Viet Dang (New Vietnam party) from Quang Nam-Quang Ngai. In 1927, hunted down by the French, leaders of the Vietnam Cach Mang Dang moved to Hong Kong to merge with the Thanh Nien.

In 1928, at a general meeting in Hong Kong, the VNCMD delegation from Vietnam demanded the adoption of the common name of Dong Duong Cong San Dang (DDCSD, Indochinese Communist party). Upon opposition from the Thanh Nien of Hong Kong, the two Vietnamese delegates, Ngo Gia Tu and Tran Canh The, abruptly left. Back home in Tonkin, they discarded all vestiges of the Thanh Nien, founded the DDCSD, and sought Komintern's recognition.

In Hong Kong, for fear of losing influence, the Thanh Nien command also changed its name to Vietnam Cong San Dang. Its Tonkin-Annam section became the Annam Cong San Dang (Annam Communist party) and Cochinchina had Dong Duong Cong San Lien Doan (Indochinese Communist League). They also asked for Komintern sanction.

Annoyed by these unprecedented proliferations, the Komintern assigned Ho Chi Minh to solve the problem. At that time, Ho was in Bangkok busy organizing the Thai Communist party. Thus, he went back to Hong Kong, where he succeeded in unifying all parties under the name of Vietnam Cong San Dang. But for two reasons the Komintern preferred the name of Indochinese Communist party (ICP). First, the word Vietnam was a display of nationalism, which was not in line with party policy. Second, a serious incident occurred in 1928 to jeopardize the prestige of the Vietnam Communist party. Nguyen Van Phat, chief of the newly created Vietnam Cong San Dang, was accused of sexual abuses by his private secretary Miss Nguyen Trung Nhut. Thus, the central committee under Ton Duc Thang sentenced Phat to death. One night in September 1928, three men strangled Phat in his house at 10 Barbier Street in Tan Dinh (Saigon).[14] To thwart French investigation, they burned his face. This event made the front page of local newspapers. As for Miss Nguyen Trung Nhut, she immediately moved in with Do Dinh Tho, another member of the party. Although their affair was by mutual consent, her behavior left some doubt about her loyalty. Fearing punishment, the couple went to the French police and gave them all of the party's secret documents in exchange for protective custody in France. The episode ended with French execution of five members of the Thanh Nien, including leader Ho Ngoc Lam. Three others were sentenced to hard labor in Poulo Condore, among them Ton Duc Thang who would later succeed Ho Chi Minh as president of the Democratic Republic of Vietnam. In a definitive act, the ICP replaced the Thanh Nien in March 1930.

Yet, the Thanh Nien had so far recorded unprecedented success: It had successfully carried ten walkouts in Vietnam, which included the Saigon water plant, the Haiphong Franco-Asiatic Petroleum Company, and the Loc Ninh (Cochinchina) rubber plantation. Needless to say, the diversity and magnitude of these strikes showed evidence of the ICP's strength. As it openly opposed recruitment of coolies for the New Hebrides and Caledonia, the French reacted by executing two of their female cadres. In March 1929, the tribes killed the French manager of the Delignon plantation together with his assistant. In the process, 2,000 rubber trees were destroyed. On May 9, 1929, the Thanh Nien called for France to give back all powers to "the workers and the peasants," thus revealing its marxist orientation.

In 1930, the ICP Central Committee moved to establish its headquarters in Hai Phong. In that year, taking advantage of a bad harvest and a plunge in prices in Annam, the ICP fomented a riot in Nghe An, Ha Tinh, and Quang Ngai. On September 12, 1930, 6,000 peasants took the city of Vinh where they replaced the local administration with "soviets." The French quelled the movement. Many ICP leaders were arrested including Truong Chinh and Pham Van Dong, while Hong Son was sentenced to death.

The Viet Minh

On May 19, 1941, the day which Ho Chi Minh's panegyrists emphasized as his birthday, the eighth session of the ICP Central Committee was convened to create the Vietnam Doc Lap Dong Minh Hoi, or Viet Minh (Vietnam Independence League). The red flag with a golden star was then adopted.

The Viet Minh's program was to fight both French and Japanese, to restore independence, to establish a Democratic Republic of Vietnam, and to seek alliance with other democracies against fascism. Thus, at the outset, the Viet Minh clearly appeared to be a nationalist movement. There is no clear explanation about the origin of the Cochinchinese opposition to the Viet Minh except that it was a "Tonkinese" organization. As a matter of public record, the Cochinchinese population nurtured strong xenophobic sentiment against the natives of Tonkin, which stemmed from the economic and cultural dichotomy between the two.

The Lien Viet

In 1947, Lu Han went back to Yunnan leaving behind his protégés, the Viet Nam Quoc Dan Dang and the Dong Minh Hoi. Ho Chi Minh organized the Lien Viet (League for National Union) to include the VNQDD, Dong Minh Hoi, Democratic and Socialist parties, and independents. As for the ICP, it was split into three parties: Cambodian, Laotian and Vietnamese, the latter one still keeping an eye on the two others. Sensing a communist trap, the two Nationalist factions refused to join and the Lien Viet became an ailing party.

The Dang Lao Dong (Workers' Party)

In November 1945, to realize union of all parties for a common action against the French, the ICP disappeared—in name only—to be officially replaced by the incongruous Marxist Study Association.

In 1950, to step up the war, the Viet Minh government demanded that all women became part of the militia, which so far included only men from ages of 18 to 55. At the end of the year, a realignment with China was outlined by declaring that the policy of the Chinese government was the policy of the Vietnam government.

In 1951, the ICP reemerged to make two major decisions: First, the Workers' party (Dang Lao Dong) was created as the official facade of the ICP. Second, to give a boost to the Lien Viet, the Viet Minh was integrated into the Lien Viet. Obviously, it was a camouflage destined to put these parties under communist control.

HO CHI MINH

Ly Thuy was one of numerous aliases so efficiently used by Ho Chi Minh to cover his true identity in such a way that later on, even the Office of Strategic Services (OSS) did not know that he had 20 other assumed names.

Ho was born in 1890 in Nghe An. His birthname was Nguyen Sinh Con. His father, Nguyen Sinh Huy, a Pho Bang,[15] had been forced to retire from school teaching because of his anti-French ideas. Soon Ho, following his father's example, began to criticize the French and had to leave the Quoc Hoc (National

School) in 1908 without a degree. He sailed off to France on September 15. Under the name of Ba, he found a kitchen job on a French steamship, *Admiral Latouche Treville*. Upon his arrival in Paris, according to some Vietnamese historians, he tried in vain to register at the distinguished Ecole Coloniale. This event was unlikely to happen, for even given his extraordinary intelligence, Ho certainly realized that without proper credentials, there was no chance for him to pursue superior study. In fact, he vegetated in various trivial occupations while attending political courses held by the French Socialist party (SFIO). Obviously, he did quite well in these studies, for in 1919, under the name of Nguyen Ai Quoc (Nguyen the patriot) he addressed a petition to the Society of Nations asking independence and civil rights for the Vietnamese people.

Inside the French Communist party, Ho obviously enjoyed much consideration. Under such prominent leaders as Marcel Cachin and Paul Vaillant-Couturier, Ho specialized in colonial studies. For that matter, he was dispatched to Moscow as representative of the French Communist party at the 1922 meeting. There, for the first time, he met with Lenin and Chou En-lai.

By the end of 1923, he was one of the ten members of the Peasant International Krestintern. He went back to France for a short time and returned to Moscow at the news of Lenin's death. Thereafter he studied at the famous Eastern Workers University in Moscow.

In 1924, Ho was part of the Borodine delegation to China, but it seems that his title of interpreter was a cover for more important activities. Indeed, upon his arrival in Canton, he took over the Tam Tam Xa (Heart to Heart Association), which was vegetating after the failure of Merlin's assassination. He also created the A Te A (League of Oppressed People of Asia) to control all communist activities for the account of the Komintern. Then, with Phan Boi Chau, he founded the Vietnam Cach Mang Thanh Nien Dong Chi Hoi, or Thanh Nien.

The year 1930 was not propitious for Ho. A French Komintern agent, Joseph Ducroux, had fallen into British hands and came clean. A huge operation was launched against communist networks, and Ho Chi Minh was arrested on June 5, 1931 and sentenced to a six-month-imprisonment by the Hong Kong British court. His case was successfully argued at the Privy Court by Sir Stafford Cripps. Considering that Ho was a political refugee, the council had him released and refused to return him to France. To thwart further French action, his British lawyer, Frank Loseby, managed to hide him in Hong Kong until he was able to return to Moscow in 1933. But Bernard Fall did not rule out the idea that, to obtain his freedom, Ho had made a deal with the British intelligence.[16]

Back in Russia, Ho entered, in 1934, the famous Lenin Institute, a breeding ground for communist leaders. In China, it was the time of anticommunist repression by both French and Chinese governments, and many dissidents went underground or moved to Thailand for safety.

There is no accurate report on Ho's private life. According to some rumors, during the period 1933–1941, he was involved in a romantic relationship with

Vo Nguyen Giap's sister-in-law, Nguyen Thi Vinh (Minh Khai). She was a graduate from Stalin University and as such was assigned to the Komintern under Ho Chi Minh's supervision. Later she was executed by the French.

In 1938, Ho was back in China where he worked in the entourage of Chou En-lai under the name of "Comrade Hu." In February 1940, as Comrade Vuong, Ho took over the Kun Ming underground ICP. In June, Pham Van Dong (Lam Ba Kiet) and Vo Nguyen Giap (Duong Hoai Nam) joined Ho in Kun Ming. Both were sent to be trained at the Whampoa military academy.

The French defeat in World War II and the beginning of Chang Kai-shek's anticommunist drive led the trio, Ho–Giap–Dong, to move back to Tonkin in February 1941. They secretly settled in Pac Bo near the Chinese border. Ho began to organize the Cuu Quoc Hoi (National Salvation Association), which included youth, women, workers, and intellectuals.

In mid-August 1942, Ho made the fateful decision to go back to China to seek help from both China and the United States. Leaving the Viet Minh in the care of Pham Van Dong and Vo Nguyen Giap, he crossed the border to be arrested by the Kwang Si authorities, under the fallacious pretext that he was both a "French and Japanese spy."

From October 1942 to September 1943, life was no bed of roses for Ho when incessant transfers from jail to jail compelled him to drag his heavily shackled legs over some 400 miles. To General Chang Fa-kuei, commander in chief of the fourth war zone (Kwang Si-Kwang Tung), he said: "I am a communist, but my present concern is for Vietnam's freedom and independence, not for communism. I give you a special guarantee. Communism will not operate in Vietnam for fifty years."[17] He was subsequently released.

General Chang Fa-kuei revealed himself a man of wisdom. At that time, like Ho, he was not so much concerned with communism as with the Chinese domination of Indochina. Thus, he needed Ho's cooperation. Given his immense popularity, Ho would serve as a catalyst to round up all disparate parties and allow Chang Fa-kuei to create, on August 10, 1943, the Vietnam Dong Minh Hoi (Vietnam Revolutionary League). Thus the DMH included the VNQDD, the Viet Minh, and other smaller units, but the Indochinese Communist Party was conspicuously absent from this Kuo Ming Tang organization. By the same token, Ho was prudently kept away from any effective authority, and the command of the Dong Minh Hoi was given to a Chinese-born Vietnamese, Nguyen Hai Than, who like Cochinchinese General Xuan, did not even speak his native tongue.

As a result of the quid pro quo with Chang Fa-kuei, Ho obtained an introduction to the OSS and to U.S. General Claire Chennault at Kun Ming. To Chennault, he pledged to help American pilots shot down over Indochinese territories. To the OSS, he offered Viet Minh services for collecting intelligence. Shortly thereafter, the OSS began to drop advisors, arms, and ammunition to the Viet Minh in Pac Bo. This aid would gradually intensify with the U.S. involvement.

VO NGUYEN GIAP

Giap was born in 1912 in Quang Binh. In 1924, he joined the short-lived Tan Viet Cach Mang Dang (New Vietnam Revolutionary party). On November 25, 1930, he was sentenced to two years imprisonment by the tribunal of Thua Thien.

The years 1932 to 1937 seem to be the formative period of Giap's revolutionary career: Although graduated in law, he chose to teach history at the Hanoi Thang Long school, where he gained fame for his course on Napoleonic military campaigns. He then adhered to the Indochinese Communist party, cooperated with the newspaper *Le Travail,* and married Nguyen Thi Quang Thai (Minh Thai) whose sister was Nguyen Thi Vinh (Minh Khai). In 1940, while he was in Kun Ming with Ho Chi Minh, both his wife, Minh Thai, and her sister, Minh Khai, were captured by the French. After a summary judgment, Minh Khai was executed, while Minh Thai was sentenced to 15 years, but she died under torture in prison.

PHAM VAN DONG

Born in 1908 to a Quang Ngai mandarin family, Dong studied at the famous Truong Buoi (College du Protectorat Hanoi). In 1925, he secretly sneaked out to China to acquire political training at the Vietnam Cach Mang Thanh Nien Dong Chi Hoi (Thanh Nien). Back in Hanoi, he was dismissed from the college for engineering student's strikes during Phan Chau Trinh's funerals. Afterward, he headed off toward Saigon to find a job. In 1929, he was arrested during a police investigation of the Barbier Street execution involving the Thanh Nien and was sentenced to ten years at Poulo Condore.

THE VIET NAM QUOC DAN DANG (VNQDD)

In 1927, under the influence of K'ang Yu Wei (Khang Huu Vi) and Liu Shao Ch'i (Luong Khai Sieu), Nguyen Thai Hoc, an exteacher, and Hoang Pham Tran, founder of the publishing house Vietnam Dong Thu Xa, created on December 25, 1927, the Vietnam Quoc Dan Dang (Vietnam Nationalist party) patterned after the Chinese Kuo Ming Tang. The first adherents came from the Nam Dang Thu Xa formed by liberal professionals such as journalists, writers, students, and by defectors from the Thanh Nien party. Of course the publishing house served as a cover for their activities.

The VNQDD appeared at the outset as a secret society. Admission was by cooptation, candidates being sponsored by regular members. Some practices followed Triad tradition of blood oath. At that time it seems that the party drew some suspicion; thus, Chinese Kuo Ming Tang's help was only lip service, and even Phan Boi Chau, then in house arrest in Annam, advised prudence. However, he agreed that his portrait be sold to the public to provide funds for the new organization.

An event changed the fate of the VNQDD: In Bac Ninh and Bac Giang, Nguyen Khac Nhu founded the Vietnam Dan Quoc (VNDQ) with an important following. They began to fabricate bombs but soon human error caused the destruction of the plant and the death of many members. The accident revealed their existence to the French, who hunted them down. Some were executed, others sentenced to life imprisonment. Thus, when solicited by the VNQDD, Nhu readily accepted to fuse his VNDQ with the VNQDD.

The rally of the Nhu group allowed the VNQDD to secure a strong foothold in the two northern provinces of Tonkin. They began to vainly compete with the Thanh Nien in Thanh Hoa, but were luckier in Cochinchina where they controlled the vast agglomeration of Saigon, Cholon, and Gia Dinh.

In 1928, more than 40 members met in Hanoi to elect Nguyen Thai Hoc as president. The Central committee included two branches: the legislative under Nguyen Khac Nhu and the administrative under Nguyen The Nghiep. Hoang Pham Tran was in charge of propaganda and Hoang Van Tung became head of the assassination committee; he would spend more time retaliating against the party traitors than attacking the French. It was the Central Committee's opinion that retaliations be given large publicity to serve as a deterrent to potential traitors: All victims must carry written death sentences signed by the party. Nothing could better help the French police investigations.

During the mid-1920s, rubber plantations became the major resource of Indochina. They covered the area of Terre Rouges (Red Land) northwest of Saigon from Bien Hoa to Tay Ninh extending to adjacent Cambodia. Collection of latex began in early morning. A special knife was used to remove a thin spiral portion of the bark to allow the latex to drip down into a bowl attached underneath. It is obvious that the industry required a huge number of coolies who had to be imported from Annam and Tonkin. The Cochinchinese themselves refused to venture into regions beset with malaria and poisonous water.

In Tonkin and Annam, a Frenchman named Herve Bazin specialized in recruiting cheap labor not only for Cochinchina but also for the French colonies of New Hebrides and New Caledonia. The peasants who signed for a three year contract rarely came back home for many reasons: They had to work 10 to 12 hours everyday and lived in shabby constructions without sufficient food. Soon they became victims of beriberi, malaria, and contaminated water. The sick received no medical care and were forced to work until exhaustion. Then they were left to die alone in the forests. Rare were those who survived the three-year contract; they were not permitted to go home and were forced to continue.

All political parties were well aware of this situation but only the VNQDD took the matter into its own hands. On February 2, 1927, at 7 P.M., two men were waiting for Bazin in front of his house. One of them handed him a piece of paper bearing his sentence to death duly signed by the VNQDD, while the other gunned him down. The two men belonged to the VNQDD assassination squad of Nguyen Van Vien. Arrested a few days later, Vien hung himself in his prison cell. Many members of his organization were sentenced to life imprisonment. As for the two great leaders, Nguyen Thai Hoc and Nguyen Khac Nhu, they received a death sentence in absentia.

To mislead the French, Nguyen Thai Hoc sent them a man with false information on his whereabouts. But instead, the emissary came clean and this led the VNQDD tribunal to condemn him for treason. Ky Con, chief of the assassination team, put a bullet in his head and a message in his pocket. It read, Did not observe the oath.

As they had blown their cover with these public executions, Nguyen Thai Hoc and Nguyen Khac Nhu decided to stake everything in a general uprising: Nguyen Thai Hoc would attack Ha Nam, Thai Binh, Ninh Binh, Nam Dinh, Pha Lai, Hai Duong, Ninh Giang, Bac Ninh, and Lang Son while Nguyen Khac Nhu would take control of Yen Bai, Lao Kay, Vinh Yen, Phuc Yen, Hung Hoa, and Son Tay. This episode is known in Vietnam history as the Yen Bay mutiny.

The Yen Bai Mutiny

At Yen Bai, all the French posts were manned by the Tirailleurs Annamites (Red militia) who were part of the French military forces. As for the Gardes Indochinoise (Blue militia), they were under a Franco-Vietnamese command operated by residents and mandarins. A significant amount of those Indochinese guards had rallied VNQDD thanks to a propaganda network led by two women, Co Giang (Nguyen Thi Giang) and Co Bac (Nguyen Thi Bac), who were wives of their officers. The insurrection planned by Nguyen Thai Hoc himself but under Nhu's command was scheduled for the Tet holidays.[18]

On the night of February 9, 1930, they attacked right after the bugler sounded taps. They forced the tirailleurs to take refuge on the hills. A fight ensued between the Vietnamese themselves. When the French rescue arrived, the rebels retreated: 4 corporals, 22 privates, 15 civilians were captured and executed on the spot.

At Hung Hoa, the insurgents did not fare better: Nguyen Dac Nhu was wounded and captured. On his way to jail, he bit off his tongue and died.

In Hanoi, the Indochinese guards were confused by incoherent orders and did not take action. As for Nguyen Thai Hoc, he made an attempt to escape but was captured on February 20, 1930.

An unprecedented repression ensued: The French used five aircraft to throw 57 10-kilograms bombs over the village of Co Am. Ten other villages were likewise leveled. The Foreign Legion and the infantry had received orders to kill all prisoners "to scare the population."

On June 17, 1930, 439 were executed including Nguyen Thai Hoc and 13 other VNQDD leaders; 7,439 were sent to concentration camps of Poulo Condore, Son-la, Lai Chau, and Lao Bao. In the following year, 80 more were executed, 383 deported, 106 sentenced to life, and 50 to hard labor. In 1933, the Saigon tribunal sentenced 8 to death, 19 to life imprisonment, and 970 to hard labor.[19]

The news of Yen Bay reached France on February 11, 1930. In Paris, a few weeks later, the inauguration of the House of Indochinese students in the presence of President Doumergue and Emperor Bao Dai was interrupted by student demonstrations against French reprisals.

After the death of Nguyen Thai Hoc and Nguyen Dac Nhu, many leaders fled to China, including Vu Hong Khanh who founded a second VNQDD in exile.[20]

SECTARIANS AND SECRET SOCIETIES

In Cochinchina, popular unrest took root during the frenzied March to the South (Nam Tien). Indeed, the colonization of Cham and Cambodian territories was not without bloody resistance from the natives. In these first colonies, besides the unruled peasant-soldiers, there were deserters, social misfits, exconvicts, and political malcontents. For some reason, they were apprehensive of government control, and many went to join with the 8,000 rebels trained in the That Son Mountains under Lam Son, their Cambodian leader. This half Chinese, half Cambodian Buddhist monk claimed to be the heir to the Khmer throne; he also proclaimed that his magic protected people against bullets and swords. In 1840, his arrogance led the Hue Court to move against him. Two years later he was defeated but some of his followers remained in the mountains to teach occult sciences.

The That Son Mountains rise to the west of Cochinchina, as a chain of seven hills—none of which is higher than 700 meters, but the dark misty crests emerging from a dense vegetation cast an enigmatic shade of menace and danger. Indeed, to the animistic souls, mountains are first the abode of spirits and gods. For the Vietnamese, the Nui Cam (Forbidden Hill) is the residence of Maitreya Buddha, who is awaiting his turn to reincarnate on earth. Thus, the That Son is the birthplace of Vietnamese messianism.

The That Son Mountains (Seven Mountains) are known for their folklore in which Khmer magic blends with esoteric Buddhism and popular Taoism of the Chinese White Lotus. There was a popular belief that some of its hermits, through long periods of meditation, had developed the same supernatural power that had allowed, 2,500 years ago, Sakyamuni Buddha to see viruses in the water. In such a closed society, isolated from the world by natural obstacles, where, as John J. Collins suggests, "social relations are created and sustained by supernatural beliefs and practices . . . people have beliefs and so they express them in practices; they have practices that they justify by beliefs."[21] This is exactly what the Vietnamese saying means, "Co linh moi co tinh, co tinh moi co linh."

The That Son also played a vital role in Vietnam history: Once it was the refuge of Emperor Gia Long, when, as Prince Nguyen Anh, he was running for his life under the frenzied pursuit of an invincible Nguyen Hue. Later, Phan Boi

Chau and Cuong De went to the Nui Cam (Forbidden Hill) to consult with with a mysterious monk who was presiding over the destiny of Cochinchinese resistance.

Two major groups originated from the mystical Nui Cam: the Buddhist sectarians dominated by the Buu Son Ky Huong (Strange Fragrance of the Precious Mountain) and the secret societies represented by the Thien Dia Hoi (Heaven and Earth Society). In spite of an apparent dichotomy, these groups were historically connected by the traditional link existing between the White Lotus and the Triad in China when they were fighting for the Ming against the Ch'ing.

The Sectarians

Cochinchinese sectarians are easily identified as an offshoot of of the Chinese White Lotus through the reading of the mythical Phong Than (Investiture of the Gods), the semihistorical Tam Quoc Chi (Romance of the Three Kingdoms), the worship of Dieu Tri Kim Mau Mother (Wu Sheng Lao Mu), Ngoc Hoang Thuong De (Jade Emperor) and the messiah Di Lac (Maitreya Buddha). Therefore Maitreya Buddha was not only a celestial entity but also a political symbol of final independence from the French as in Vietnam or from the Ch'ing as in China.

Dieu Tri Kim Mau (Wu Sheng Lao Mu) as the Unborn Mother is the major deity who created human beings. She had sent many Buddhas, from Dipankara to Maitreya, to save her 96 myriad children still trapped in the red dust (sins) of the earth. The Phong Than (Investiture of the Gods; Chinese, Feng Shen yen-i) is like the Greek *Illiad*, "stories about the Gods and their activities." It depicts the cosmic conflict between the corrupt Shang Dynasty supported by heretical genies Xien, and the Sons of Heaven Chou protected by the Jade Emperor and his army of gods and saints. The other text, Tam Quoc Ch'i (Romance of the Three Kingdoms; Chinese, San Kuo), had by and large more impact on the grassroots Vietnamese than any of the five Confucian classics. It has become the canon of the Buu Son Ky Huong and its offshoots.

The Buu Son Ky Huong

Actually, economic claims, while justified, were not the real motives of the anti-French movement. A French governor of Cochinchina himself admitted that "individually, the leaders of the movement have no personal motive to invoke in order to justify their xenophobic sentiments. Some of them are men who have remained imbued with the ancient order of things predating the French conquest and who have adamantly remained within the tradition and ideas of the past."[22] In a nutshell, it had more to do with Confucian traditions and culture than with socioeconomic theory.

The Buu Son Ky Huong (Strange Fragrance of the Precious Mountain) was founded by Buddha Master of the Western Peace (Phat Thay Tay An). The words "strange fragrance" have a clear connotation with the "incense smelling" sect, an offshoot of the Chinese White Lotus religion.

In spite of Vietnamese denials about the Buu Son Ky Huong role in political uprisings, Georges Coulet had produced judiciary reports, according to which the Buu Son Ky Huong amulets were widely used as passports among members of the resistance, regardless of their affiliation.

Moreover, the principle of the Four Debts (Tu An) was a standard oath of initiation practiced among Chinese secret societies. To the question: "Where do you go?" the postulant answered: "I go to volunteer, to avenge my Emperor, to pay my debt to my parents, to avenge my brothers.[23]

Buddha Master. The origin of the Buddha Master is a matter of controversy: Some have him born in Annam (Trung Ky) with the name of Tran Nguyen. He was a self-appointed monk whose deviant behavior induced Emperor Minh Mang (1820–1841) to banish him to the That Son Mountains. But the most popular version goes back to 1679, when the Ming refugees under Duong Ngan Dich were authorized by the Nguyen Lord to settle in Gia Dinh where a Vietnamese colony already existed since 1658. It is in that Khmer-Sino-Viet melting pot that Doan Minh Huyen was born in 1807, the day of the full moon, at the time of the Horse (Gio Ngo).[24] This might also explain his high proficiency in Chinese characters and esoteric Buddhism. But the Tong Son annals show that he was born in the village of Tong Son (Sadec) under the name of Le Huong Thien.[25]

The region was far from being peaceful. In 1841, Cambodian monk Luc Sam and his Buddho-Taoist group[26] rose up in Tra Vinh. The Hue Court dispatched Nguyen Cong Tru and Nguyen Tien Lam to quell the revolt. In 1847, as the movement continued to expand, Emperor Thieu Tri assigned Nguyen Tri Phuong to keep peace in An Giang. This was not Thieu Tri's only problem: At that time, Colonel Lapierre was sinking the Vietnamese fleet in the Bay of Danang.

As for Doan Minh Huyen, until the age of 43, he led an ordinary peasant life, but beginning in 1850, he began to show a pattern of abnormal behavior with "nervous and psychic aberrancies," to borrow a term from John J. Collins.[27] These physical signs, which are still seen in many cultures as a shamanic disposition, set him apart from the population. Alone, he began to roam the local rivers in a small junk. Then a cholera epidemic broke out, giving him the opportunity to demonstrate his healing power. Soon his reputation as a miracle healer led the people of western Cochinchina to revere him as the Phat Thay Tay An (Buddha Master of the Western Peace). According to Ho Tai Hue Tam, the title Phat Thay betrays the syncretism of Buddhism (Phat-Buddha) and popular Taoism (Thay-Master).[28] Indeed, he practiced Buddhist meditation Thien (Zen) blended with shamanistic Taoism.

His prestige was such that "around his retreat, the sick jammed rivers and canals with their sampans; on the ground, appeared thousands of makeshift huts."[29]

Soon it became necessary to build what Buddha Master called trai ruong (farm camp) to house his patients. Actually, this decision was an attempt to put the peasants out of the reach of land speculators and to build independent communities economically self-sufficient. Yet, those lands did not allow rice cultivation, and the dwellers had to subsist on sweet potatoes and maize. But at least they were happy to live in a society no longer ruled by the four tiers system but only by peasants and artisans.[30] Because it was against French land policy, Buddha Master was placed behind bars. To gain his release, he accepted to be ordained into the Lam Te, a Buddhist order under government control. He later took refuge in an isolated Lam Te pagoda on the Nui Sam. His followers also settled in that area.

At the outset, the Buu Son Ky Huong was guided by primitive Buddhism with the slogan "Cuu Dan Do The" (Rescue the people, save the world). Later it evolved into the specific Four Debts (Tu An) dogma,[31] which encompassed Confucianism, Taoism, and Buddhism.

Buddha Master died in 1859 at the age of 50, leaving a millenarian message to his disciples: "When the cinnamon tree blossoms and the Bo De[32] bears fruits, I shall be back" (Chung nao cay que tro bong, Bo de co trai thi ong tro ve).

Historians Dat Si and Nguyen Van Hau report a list of four Buddha Master incarnations. They are confined to traditional healing and preaching; keeping away from politics except the famous Su Vai Ban Khoai (Potato-selling monk), who used to disguise himself as a nun; roaming the Vinh Te canal during the years 1901 and 1902, and distributing Buu Son Ky Huong amulets as passports for insurgents. Perhaps his economic views were seen as dangerous enough to cause him to disappear suddenly in 1902. But he left 11 volumes of verse in Cochinchinese vernacular. Ho Tai Hue Tam affirms that these 11 volumes "present an interesting interpretation of the cause of suffering." Indeed, for the first time in Cochinchina, some Buddhist adepts saw suffering in direct relation with socioeconomic conditions.

The Buu Son Ky Huong tradition faded away as a result of the leaders' aging. Used to travel to recruit followers, they reached a point where they were no longer able to physically carry out their missionary work. Thus, many of them went into peaceful retirement, having made enough profit to deserve some material comfort for themselves and their families. Perhaps they also realized that it was time for new ideas, which require a different type of charisma compatible with modern mass action. The last one, Huynh Phu So, did his best to bring his sect, the Hoa Hao, into modern times.

Tran Van Thanh. Buddha Master died in transmitting the sacred mold of his amulets to his first disciple, Tran Van Thanh. Indeed, the transmission of the mold, together with the robe and the brown flag, could be seen as a succession ceremony, but Thanh was more oriented toward secular accomplishments. He went on to build a farm-camp at Lang Linh, which later played the major role in the Buu Son Ky Huong insurrection.

As an exofficer of Indochinese guard, Thanh was recalled to duty to quell the popular Self-Defense movement. Instead, he joined with them and attacked Cai Be and My Tra in May 1865. In 1864, Truong Cong Dinh died in battle, and two years later, in 1866, Vo Duy Duong died of disease. Tran Van Thanh took over the command.

In 1867, under la Grandiere, the French seized Vinh Long, the movement of Self-Defense began to disintegrate and Thanh returned to his Lang Linh stronghold but did not give up the fight.

In late 1867, Thanh entered an unsuccessful alliance with Pu Kombo, a pretender to the Khmer throne, and the following year, Thanh allied with Nguyen Trung Truc. After Truc's demise in 1868, Thanh again returned to Lang Linh and took over the command of the Dao Lanh.

The Dao Lanh

The Dao Lanh derived from the original "Tu Tien" sect with the attractive slogan "Lam lanh lanh du" (Do good, avoid evil). Dogmatically, it was separate from the Buu Son Ky Huong. Yet, to simplify the picture, one may see the Dao Lanh as the revolutionary arm of the Buu Son Ky Huong because of Tran Van Thanh's leadership orientation.

After the execution of "laureat" (Thu Khoa) Nguyen Huu Huan, his followers joined the forces of the Thien Dia Hoi and the Dao Lanh. Under Thanh, the sect became the major anti-French group, although it was not without serious problems: They tried to manufacture guns, but lacked know-how. They attempted to purchase arms from Siam, but Siam had just signed a peace agreement with France.

In 1868, with the greatest secrecy, Thanh organized the Bay Thua village with 1,200 people. His wife directed the digging of a canal to join Bay Thua to Lang Linh. With such an important population, it was difficult for the Bay Thua village to remain clandestine: In 1873, the French burned it to the ground, killing Thanh in the process. The Dao Lanh was banned. On August 22, 1873, Admiral Dupre, French governor of Cochinchina, declared that apostles or adepts of the Dao Lanh would be prosecuted in accordance with section No. 6 of the Gia Long Code, which concerned secret societies.

The sect regrouped in the village of An Dinh in the That Son (Elephant Mountains). With 150 families claiming to be farmers, the An Dinh village was legally recorded on the French census. But in 1882, the news of the Hanoi attack by Riviere caused a general unrest. A cholera epidemic and the apparition of a comet, which popular belief associated with war, gave the Dao Lanh the opportunity to resurface.

At the same time, the remnants of Thu Khoa Huan who on the one hand had joined the Dao Lanh and on the other took over the Thien Dia Hoi (Heaven and Earth)[33] created the triumvirate Thien Son Trung.

The Dao Lanh continued to work from its An Dinh base until 1887, when the French attacked. An Dinh was razed and the sect went underground. But it is with Nam Thiep that the Dao Lanh rose up as a major sect.

Nam Thiep. His name was Ngo Loi, from a peasant family of the Nui Doi, which was also Thanh's abode. Because he used to fall into trances, he was also called Nam Thiep (Sleeping monk). Like Buddha Master, he began to practice healing with water and yellow-paper mantras. He later moved to Cu Lao Ba Island.

After the death of Tran Van Thanh, Nam Thiep, calling himself Duc Bon Su (Holy Master), took over the wavering Dao Lanh. At Cu Lao Ba, where he lived, his healing success won him an immense following.

In 1876, after an association with Heaven and Earth in an inconclusive revolt and probably under the influence of his Chinese advisors, Nam Thiep went back to An Dinh village to build a new temple dedicated to Wu Sheng Lao Mu (Dieu Tri Kim Mau), whom he called Dia Mau (Earth Mother).

In February 1877, he took the title of Minh Vuong (Prince of Light), in accordance with the Potato-selling monk's prophecy: "When Cochinchina becomes prosperous, the Prince of Light (Minh Vuong) will ascend to heaven."[34] This prophecy betrays the Buddho-Taoist origin of sectarianism; while it unveiled the Manichaeism of darkness and light, ascension to heaven in broad daylight is a Taoist tradition since the time of the Huai Nan king.

In 1878, two adepts of the Dao Lanh, Ong and Kha, attempted a revolt in My Tho, Can Tho, Dinh Tuong, and Vinh Long. Armed with bamboo spears and Buu Son Ky Huong amulets, they converged on My Tho, carrying an altar loaded with talismans and a tablet for Thien Vuong To Su (Heaven King patriarch). The rioters were quickly routed and their leaders Ong and Kha were publicly beheaded.

On February 8, 1883, the Dao Lanh assasinated the chief of Hoc Mon district, Doc Phu Ca, together with his family. The same year, the Dao Lanh joined with the Cambodian monk (Luc) Hien, and after a rally in Soc Trang, 100 of them marched on the nearby village of Phu No. During the three days' attack, they killed three collaborators but did not carry out any hostile acts toward the population. The revolt was quickly put down. On January 22, 1885, they were involved in the arson of the Saigon central jail.

In 1884, Nam Thiep sided with Si Votha, another pretender to the Cambodian throne, and both were defeated. In 1887, after another vain revolt, the Dao Lanh ceased to exist and Nam Thiep disappeared in the That Son. In 1909, he died at the Elephant Mountain (Nui Voi). The French took advantage of a dispute between his disciples over the custody of his remains to raid the area, and, again, the Dao Lanh went underground.

The Dao Phat Duong. After the death of Nam Thiep, the Dao Lanh reemerged as a part of the Dao Phat Duong. Again, this event disclosed the intricacies of sectarian traditions: According to Cao Daist author Dong Tan, the Phat Duong (or Minh Duong) derived from the Minh Su sect, an offshoot of the White Lotus. When a Minh Su affiliate, Ngo Van Chieu, founded Cao Daism in 1923, he brought in with him the entire Minh network. At that time, the Dao Phat Duong had already acquired some celebrity among the anti-French movement.

In 1908, the Phat Duong leader Nguyen Giac Nguyen, abbot of the Long Tuyen Pagoda in Can Tho, lent his religious authority to a plot inspired by Gilbert Chieu.

During the great riots of 1916, 300 members of the Phat Duong attacked Tri Ton and Chau Doc, while in Saigon, the Thien Dia Hoi was carrying out the same scenario. It was not pure coincidence that under the name of Bay Do, Cao Van Long was found at the center of the action in Cholon.

The Orthodox Buddhists

Judiciary records do not show the role of the official Buddhist church in politics. Apparently, by and large, Mahayana and Theravada sects stayed away from politics. It is also quite possible that their absence from judiciary chronicles is due to French deliberate strategy, to conceal Buddhist hostility in order to claim they had the support of the two major religions, Buddhism and Christianity.

Yet, French police investigations revealed that many of those arrested for anti-French activities were self-appointed monks, who had never gone through the Truong Ky (monk's ordination) but somehow had knowledge of Buddhist rituals and some command of Chinese characters. In this respect, they were more or less sectarians. They served as couriers and distributors of Bua chu (amulets) together with anti-French tracts. Their pagodas were centers of seditious plots.

Monk Phung. The pagoda of Rach Tre in the province of Sadec controlled ten adjacent villages. In 1910, the abbot announced that a Truong Ky[35] would take place at Rach Tre, and he received some 4,000 piastres from the villages to organize this big event. The Truong Ky never occurred but by faking insanity, the monk was not made to justify taking the funds. He died a few years later to be replaced by a young handsome monk named Phung.

Among Phung's devotees, there was a gorgeous lady who shared her favors between two rich Cai Tong (Chief of Canton). She succeeded in grabbing some 20,000 piastres from both. In February 1916, they realized that their money had gone to monk Phung who was in fact her true lover. Because they also discovered that the money served to finance Phung's anti-French activities, they went to denounce him to the French. Phung was arrested at his Rach Tre pagoda, and the documents found on him attested that he was chief of a 50-man secret society named Dong Bao Ai Chuong (Men of the same race). Phung was sentenced to five years of hard labor.

Monk Bay Do. In 1904, a certain Cao Van Long, alias Bay Do, built on the top of the Nui Cam a huge pagoda, with 32 shrines and 300 separate meditation cells. On the first floor were his own quarters, complete with Western-style equipment. Although his entire family, including wives, children, and grandchildren, lived there with him, the dwelling was named "Nam Cuc Cuc pagoda," but initiates called it "Buu Son Ly Huong temple." Life was made easy there, for Bay Do spent his time traveling at will with no known agendas. While he never stayed more than a week at the Nui Sam, and during his journeys he never sojourned to any place for more than three days, he had different names at different places: Besides Bay Do and Long, he was known as Ma Vang and monk of Nui Sam.

In fact, the French obtained some information according to which Cao Van Long was the chief of the Cochinchinese resistance network. He was the mastermind behind most of the uprisings in Cochinchina. He had a secret meeting with Cuong De and Phan Boi Chau when they came to the Nui Cam. He had clandestinely organized a weapons factory at Nam Thua.

During World War I, in February 1916, all the monks of the Buu Son Ly Huong went back home, each one dwelling in a separate province. As for Cao Van Long, on February 14, 1916, at the height of the revolt in Saigon he found himself at the command post in Cholon. When the smoke cleared, many insurgents were connected to Bay Do: At My Tho, the rebel abbot of the Buu Son Tu pagoda was a Bay Do patient. At Chau Doc, the abbot of the Phi Lai pagoda was his close friend.

Finally, on March 17, 1917, Bay Do was arrested in a house located behind the Chau Doc court of justice. Lack of prosecution witnesses compelled the French to limit his sentence to only five years of detention.

Later, during World War II, under Long's instigation, entire villages fought against the French military draft and rejected tax increases.

SECRET SOCIETIES

By contrast with the sectarians, religion played a peripheral role in secret societies, for it was not so much an ideology of faith as a mechanism for unity and harmony between members. In colonial Cochinchina, before its decline under Western materialism, the Confucian culture was still clinging to a monarchic regime. According to Jean Chesneaux: "The anti-French secret societies displayed a very traditional patriotism and aimed only at restoring to Vietnam an independent monarchy founded solely upon the Mandate of Heaven.[36] This was not the case with the Thien Dia Hoi, but it was clearly the principle of the sectarian Buu Son Ky Huong with its four-debts dogma.

Yet, as absence of the king made the classic relationship of subject-king obsolete, the king was replaced by the nation in the Vietnamese Triad slogan "Phan Phap, Phuc Nam" (overthrow France, restore Vietnam), which reflected the Chinese Triad "Fan Ch'ing, Fu Ming" (overthrow the Ch'ing, restore the Ming).

In secret societies, more emphasis was put on the notion of brotherhood, which is the Confucian eldest brother–younger brother relationship. Thus, the traditional blood oath was designed to secure surrogate kinship between the members. By contrast, in sectarian organizations, such as the White Lotus, for example, there was no need for a blood oath since all members were children of the same mother Wu Shen Lao Mu (Dieu Tri Kim Mau). Another reason for the blood oath was to protect organization secrecy, the infraction of which was punished by death.

While sectarianism mainly derived from folk Buddhism traditions, the secret societies leaned on popular Taoism. This may explain the choice of the classic Thuy Hu,[37] which is a glorification of the Giang Ho. These social bandits fought against "the State (i.e., soldiers and policemen, prisons, tax collectors, and civil servants) class differentiation, which allowed peasants' exploitation by landlords, merchants, and the like."[38]

Rejected by the legal authority, the rebels formed a counterculture abhoring collaborators. "The sages stay in the ricefields but worthless men become civil servants."[39] Among their deeds, the Giang Ho promoted equality between sexes, which was quite an innovation given the Confucian tradition of the time.

As with their Chinese Triad parents, the Vietnamese Thien Dia Hoi society carried elaborate initiation rites, hands and fingers secret codes, and silent dialogues by manipulating tea cups in a particular manner.[40] Besides their Robin Hood fashion, their secret rites exerted on popular imagination the same attraction as sectarians' religious rituals did. This explains, among other things, the success of the Thien Dia Hoi in Cochinchina.

The Thien Dia Hoi (Heaven and Earth Society)

At the end of the 19th century, with the White Lotus, the Triad migrated to the South and adjacent countries like Taiwan, Singapore, and Cochinchina (South Vietnam).

But the pursuit of a materialistic mode of life had led the Triad to be involved in less than honorable activities. In Cholon and other cities, wherever there existed an important Chinese population, the Triad settled to do business that had to do with gambling, extortion, prostitution, and other illicit practices. In the provinces, they controlled transportation on land and rivers and even turned to outright sea piracy on the South China Sea and the Gulf of Siam. In villages, they raided landlords' farms, heartily supported by the peasants they had won over by their Robin Hood style.

One of the Triad successes consisted in initiating a loan system to provide low-interest funds to the population. Later it evolved into a small loan association of 10 or 15 persons called "hui," still in effect today even among Vietnamese colonies in America. They claimed, not without evidence, that their commercial network served dispossessed peasants, rural workers, jobless artisans, and disbanded soldiers.

At the end of the 19th century, after the admission of the Nguyen Huu Huan remnants, the leadership changed hands in favor of a Vietnamese ethnic majority and thus, the political agenda became Phan Phap, Phuc Nam (overthrow France, restore Vietnam). But its history can only be traced from secret archives of the French services.

If the connection between Thien Dia Hoi and Buu Son Ky Huong can be confirmed by their use of Buu Son Ky Huong amulets, its relationship with Cao Daists can also be traced to the time Nguyen Van Truoc, alias Tu Mat, converted to Cao Daism. He was the chief of a major gang of Cholon, and as the right hand of Phan Xich Long, he led the botched 1916 revolt in Saigon. He was jailed for five years, and upon his release was converted to Cao Daism by Pope Le Van Trung with whom he had maintained cordial relations since the time Trung was the representative of Cholon at the colonial council. Tu Mat even became an important adept having donated his own house to serve as a Cao Daist oratory with the name of Chua Tu Mat or Minh Ly Dan: There is no information on whether he had retired from the gang after his conversion, but the fact that he could afford such a liberality suggests that he still enjoyed a comfortable income.

After the 1916 riot, the Thien Dia Hoi began to phase out. However, at the Cho Lon Da Phuc temple in which the Living Buddha had dwelled for a while, Nguyen Van Huong ran a loose society. After Huong died, the Sino-Cambodian Chem Keo, who was already the Head of the Cambodia Heaven and Earth, took over the Cochinchinese branch. With him it was no longer piracy but big business. He opened estates in Phan Rang and launched other industries based on cheap labor. Some offshoots, like the Coconut and Bananas sect under Chinese leadership, kept closer ties to the Buu Son Ky Huong practices, reciting prayers from the *Tam Quoc Chi* novel (Romance of the Three Kingdoms).

Phan Xich Long

Although Phan Xich Long was the leader of Heaven and Earth in Vietnam, it is not clear whether he had any direct connection with the original Triad. Anyway, French police reports revealed that he was provided arms and munitions by some Chinese businessmen from Annam.

He was born Phan Phat Sanh in 1893 in Tan An. In spite of the fact that his father was a minor policeman, Sanh claimed his descendence from Emperor Ham Nghi. At 14 years of age, he already earned a living as a fortune teller.

In 1911, at Tan Chau (Chau Doc) under the name of Nguyen Van Lac, he began to plot against the French with two misfits, Nguyen Huu Tri and Nguyen Van Hiep. Both were in awe when he flashed a golden plaque, which carried the words "Heir to the throne." Then, Sanh moved to Cambodia and Siam where he learned sorcery and magic, supplemented with pyrotechnic training for making not just simple fireworks but also bombs.[41]

Left behind, Hiep and Tri managed to install in the village of Da Phuc an old, sick drifter they proclaimed the Living Buddha. Later, they moved to the populous Thuan Kieu Street in Cholon, where they expected to collect more religious contributions.

Because the Living Buddha died a few months later, the two men went to Battambang (Cambodia) to enthrone Sanh as emperor Phan Xich Long. By then they had a plan: first, to spread the news of the apocalypse in which only those wearing white cloth would be spared; second, under the protection of genies summoned by emperor Phan, a riot would take place in 1913 with the participation of a thousand people armed with swords and Buu Son Ky Huong amulets; and third, the bombs would be detonated not by Phan Xich Long himself but by the genies he would summon.

Indeed, in 1913, eight bombs exploded in the Saigon-Cholon area. While 600 men and women, clad in white and carrying swords and Buu Son Ky Huong amulets, were marching on Saigon, Sanh was arrested by the police 100 miles away in the coastal town of Phan Thiet.[42] The rioters were defeated: 111 were arrested, 63 were sentenced to imprisonment.

Then World War I erupted in time to prevent the French from deporting Phan Xich Long, who remained confined in the Saigon Central Prison.

In 1916, at the news of the Verdun disaster, 13 provinces of Cochinchina rose up: In January, Gia Dinh Province openly refused to pay taxes. In Saigon, on February 16 at 3 A.M., 300 peasants clad in white and carrying Buu Son Ky Huong amulets, spears, and farming tools walked toward the Saigon Central Prison to free "Anh Ca" (Big Brother) Phan Xich Long. The leader was the chief of the Cholon gang named Nguyen Van Truoc, alias Tu Mat. That was not to be the unique event, for further investigations revealed many sites in town where people rallied for action. In Bien Hoa, the rioters succeeded in freeing all prisoners from the provincial prison. But the goal of the leaders was to first blow up key positions in Saigon and second to release Phan Xich Long who had provided them with a detailed plan for action from his jail.

The 1916 riots resulted in serious casualties; eight men were killed on the spot, 65 arrested, and 38 were executed. As this was only part of a general plan, the French intensified their search and succeeded in making 1,660 more arrests and 261 incarcerations. Tu Mat was sentenced to five years' imprisonment. This was a serious setback for the Thien Dia Hoi, compelling them to join the Cao Daist and the Nguyen An Ninh sects.

POLITICAL MOVEMENTS IN COCHINCHINA

In Cochinchina, spoliation of the natives took a sweeping aspect. The land was originally divided into individual properties as a result of the colonization of Cham and Cambodian territories during the March to the South. In other words, in contrast with tradition, by which land was bestowed as an imperial favor or an administrative remuneration, here the land truly belonged to those who had personally developed it. But the village might decide to reclaim the land in case of non-cultivation.

Popular Resistants

Although the French land reform had unfair consequences for the Vietnamese peasants, it is also true that there was a crucial need for modernization as many reformists had called for. Notwithstanding the ambivalence of popular revolts as products of religious sects and secret societies, those having a nationalist character were in direct reaction against the 1862 Saigon treaty by which Vietnam was forced to abandon the three eastern provinces of Cochinchina to France.

Thu Khoa Huan. Immediately after the Saigon treaty, Nguyen Huu Huan (known also as Thu Khoa Huan[43] called for an uprising. In 1863, he led attacks against the French posts of My Quy, Tan Binh, Thuoc Nhieu, and Cai Lay. Defeated, he withdrew to Chau Doc where he was captured and deported to Poulo Condore. When he was released, the French took the rest of the three provinces. Huan revolted again to be finally captured and publicly executed at the Phu Kiet market place in My Tho.

Nguyen Trung Truc. Even before the treaty, Nguyen Trung Truc, a fisherman-farmer, had been rebelling in Tan An since 1861. On December 11 of that year, he gained fame by burning the French vessel *L'Esperance* and was promoted by the Hue Court to chief of Ha Tien Province. When the last three provinces fell into French hands, he retired to the island of Hon Chong across Ha Tien.

Later, on June 15, 1866, in a surprise raid, he killed five French officers and seized 100 rifles, then retired to Ha Tien where he built up a maquis (peasant movement) at Cua San. After many attempts to capture his stronghold, the French seized his mother as hostage to force him to surrender. On October 27, 1868, he was executed at Rach Gia.

Truong Cong Dinh. Truong Cong Dinh was named Quan Co (top adjutant) by the Hue Court for having built a don dien (military colony) in the south.

After the fall of the Ky Hoa (Chi Hoa) citadel and the ensuing suicide of his commander, Vo Duy Ninh, Dinh reorganized the remnant force and consequently was promoted by the Hue government to the rank of Pho Lanh Binh (lieutenant colonel). Frequent inroads of his 600 resistants in Tan An and Go Cong kept the French on constant alert and the court granted them the honor banner of Nghia Quan (Righteous Soldiers).[44] After the 1862 treaty, Truong Cong Dinh allied with Vo Duy Duong to form the Movement of Popular Self-Defense (Phong Trao Nhan Dan Tu Ve) and with 6,000 volunteers chose the Dong Thap Muoi as his operational base. There is a controversy over the role of Tu Duc against pursuing resistance after the signing of the 1862 treaty. Since their actions tended to jeopardize Phan Thanh Gian's negotiations with the French for the return of the three eastern provinces, Emperor Tu Duc tried to remove Dinh from the field by naming him chief of the remote Phu Yen Province in Annam. He refused, and twice Tu Duc allegedly issued secret orders to capture both Dinh and Duong. Phan Thanh Gian also wrote to Truong Cong Dinh: "Since the Court has signed the treaty, you should cease hostilities and should not violate the King's order." To which Dinh replied: "The population of the three provinces would not accept the partition of its country. This was why it chose me as its military commander. As long as you speak of peace and surrender, we are determined not to obey the court's orders."[45] Although the court took no open action against Dinh, records shows that, in many cases, clashes did occur between government forces and other resistance groups. Yet the French kept on making the court responsible for the insecurity in the region in order to validate their claims over the rest of Cochinchina.

In 1863, under the pressure of Bonard's forces, Truong Cong Dinh left Go Cong for Bien Hoa where he committed suicide.

After his death, his widow went back to her native village where she received from Hue a monthly allowance of 20 francs and 60 liters of rice.[46]

INTELLECTUAL POLITICIANS

The anticolonialist protest came late with the Western-educated class—generally called "retour de France." It came late because as members of the bourgeoise, this class enjoyed social privileges, which it did not wish to lose by a violent confrontation with the French. But even the intelligentsia deprived of material advantages would first observe Western discursive tradition before opting for armed struggle ideology. As a result, they soon split into bourgeois politicians (Bui Qunag Chieu) and mass agitators (Tran Van An, Nguyen An Ninh and Ta Thu Thau, Duong Bach Mai, and Tran Van Thach).

Bui Quang Chieu

The epitome of the Cochinchinese bourgeois intellectuals, Bui Quang Chieu graduated in 1923 from the famous Ecole Coloniale in Paris, then went home the same year to found his Constitutionalist party. His slogan, Phap Viet De Hue (Harmony between France and Vietnam), showed his belief in the electoral process. He demanded freedom for his country and an equal representation between the French and Vietnamese in elected assemblies. He published the daily *Tribune Indigene* as the organ of his conservative party. He also cooperated with a French opportunist, Colonel See, to build various commercial enterprises.

His party was composed of various elements of the local bourgeoisie: Nguyen Phan Long, a journalist and politician; Truong Van Ben, owner of Xa Bong Vietnam cong ty (Vietnam soap company); and Tran Van Don and Nguyen Van Thinh, both medical doctors, to cite a few. From 1923 to 1927, they relentlessly asked for a constitution but Diep Van Cuong, one of Chieu's partners, was more specific in suggesting that voting rights be granted to landlords or to those who had a French education or to those who had business licences. This prompted

Ho Tai Hue Tam to complain that Chieu was fighting for his own class, not for the peasant and this constitution would pave the way to the rule of the bourgeoisie, after the departure of France at the end of her "mission civilisatrice."[47] She adds: "Inequality was a fact of life. It was the ordering principle among individuals as it was among nations and races." To the vast mass of peasants and workers, Chieu conceded only "the right to exist."[48] Cao Daist Nguyen Phan Long and his journal *Echo Annamite* joined a quavering anti-French clamor but, like Chieu, he failed to catch popular attention.

At the opposite camp appeared the independents Tran Van An, Gilbert Chieu, and marxist agitprop partisans Nguyen An Ninh, Ta Thu Thau, Duong Bac Mai, and Tran Van Thach. As for Tran Van An, he pursued whimsical alliances with various parties to end up as an agent of the Japanese Kempetai.

Tran Van An

Tran Van An was born in Long Xuyen in 1903. After a short stay in China, he went to Aix-en-Provence where he enrolled in the College of Arts. Returning to Saigon in 1928, he published the anti-French *l'Annam Scolaire* and cooperated with the Duoc Nha Nam (Torch of Annam). In 1935, he built a liaison with the La Lutte group led by Ta Thu Thau and Tran Van Thach, whom he had met in Aix-en-Provence.

In February 1941, he was arrested for his connection with the Marxist movement, Vietnam Nhan Dan Thong Nhut Cach Mang Dang (Vietnam Unified Revolutionary People Party), founded by the Trotskyites in October 1940. On April 18, 1941, he was acquitted by the Saigon justice court. Three days later, the French security sent him to the Ba Ra detention camp for two months.

1942 was the turning point in An's career: He began to work for the Kempetai and became a leader of the Vietnam Phuc Quoc Dong Minh Hoi (Vietnam Restoration Alliance) founded by pretender Prince Cuong De.

In 1943, as he was "third most wanted" on the French police black list, he moved to Singapore where he proclaimed himself commander in chief of the Phuc Quoc. After the March 9, 1945, coup under Japanese protection, An moved back to Saigon and declared that from then on, Phuc Quoc's slogan would be: "To live and to die with Japan."

On May 25, 1945, with Nguyen Van Sam, An founded the Vietnam Quoc Gia Doc Lap Dang (Vietnam Independence party). He then disappeared after presiding over the Conference of Cochinchina (Hoi Nghi Nam Bo). He remerged later as a member of the Vietnam Dan Chu Xa Hoi Dang (Social Democratic party) and was appointed propaganda minister on October 1, 1947, with the General Xuan government. He was part of the 24-man delegation to Bao Dai in Hong Kong. In 1948, he left the Xuan cabinet and in 1950 he became allied to the Binh Xuyen. In 1954, after the Geneva conference, he vainly fought to have Ngo Dinh Diem replaced by ex-professional pirate Bay Vien.

To repay Pham Cong Tac for all his help to the Phuc Quoc, Tran Van An secretly fed him information about Diem's plans to arrest him: Thus, the Cao Daist superior fled to Cambodia where he died.

Nguyen An Ninh

In December 1923, a new journal, *La Cloche Felee* (The Broken Bell), appeared under the name of Nguyen An Ninh. It was supposed to be an organ for the propagation of French ideas. This is true in the sense that he was disseminating the principles of the 1789 French revolution.

An avowed Trotskyite, Ninh began as an anarchist during the three years he spent in France, from 1920 through 1923. After having obtained his "licence en droit"[49] he went home to marry, then went back to France to achieve his doctorate. Limited resources led him to work for the Parisian newspaper, which had had among its staff Ho Chi Minh himself. When his finances worsened, Ninh made a living as a fortune teller. Finally, he went home completely bankrupt.

Nguyen An Ninh was born in Cholon but was raised in Hoc Mon, a village located 11 kilometers from Saigon and reputed for its bloody anti-French revolt in 1885. After working to raise popular consciousness, he began calling for anti-French rebellion.

Ninh created a secret organization called Hoi Kin Nguyen An Ninh (Nguyen An Ninh secret society), the activities of which were still unknown since they were secret. Indeed, as a lawyer, Ninh was shrewd enough to hide his organization behind the Heaven and Earth Society, which he used as a facade to recruit members for himself. But publicly he exerted the freedom of speech within the limit of the French law. Be that as it may, his sympathy for Phan Boi Chau was not to the French taste.

When Chau was brought to trial, Nguyen An Ninh declared: "What is needed is not clemency or generosity but justice and equality." On November 30, 1925, he continued: "Liberty is to be taken, it is not to be granted. To wrest it away from an organized power, we need to oppose to that power an organized force."[50]

In spite of his legal precautions, the French had enough evidence of his secret activities and on March 24, 1926, Ninh was finally arrested along with 115 village notables and rural workers of his organization. He was deported to Poulo Condore where he died in 1943. The Nguyen An Ninh secret society did not survive its founder.

Gilbert Tran Chanh Chieu

Gilbert Chieu was what the French called a "transfuge." By his French citizenship and his position as one of the first attorneys at law in Saigon he, instead of siding with Bui Quang Chieu, followed a different path. He was an early disciple of Phan Boi Chau, since the time he met him in Hong Kong. Thus, he supported the Dong Kinh Nghia Thuc (Free Tuition Tonkin University) and the Dong Du movement. He published the *Huong Cang Nhan Vat* (Hong Kong Personalities), a text in which he made a fascinating portrait of Phan Boi Chau. To preach modernization and revolution, he went to publish the famous *Luc Tinh Tan Van* (Journal of the Six Provinces). Besides these open activities made possible by his French citizenship rights, Gilbert Chieu was involved in clandestine action by creating a network of commercial enterprises to supply funds for the Dong Du: the Minh Tan Cong Nghe Xa (Modern handicraft) at Cholon and the hotels Minh Tan Khach Sang (Modern Hotel) at Saigon and Mytho. In 1913, he was behind an uprising, which was quelled: He escaped capital punishment thanks to his French nationality but was deported to Poulo Condore, and the Dong Du movement ended for lack of financial support.

Ta Thu Thau

Thau was one of the early promoters of marxist agitprop. He was a native of Long Xuyen in Cochinchina. Son of a village carpenter, he had a wretched childhood, losing his mother at age 11. When he reached age 17, his father became totally incapacitated, and besides his studies at the prestigious Chasseloup Laubat Lycee he had to do tutoring for family subsistence. He succeeded in winning the two highest secondary diplomas, and at age 22 he left for France to study general mathematics at the Sorbonne. With some friends he formed Le Jeune Annam (Young Annam) group, who distinguished themselves by wearing yellow armbands.

In 1927, he founded another journal, *Le Nha Que* (The Peasant), which was soon closed by the government. He succeeded Nguyen The Truyen as the leader of the Viet Nam Doc Iap Dang (Vietnam Independence Party). When the news of Yen Bai arrived in Paris, he organized student protests in Paris, demanding the release of the Yen Bai prisoners and boycotting the inauguaration of the House of Students.

In 1930, he was expelled from France. Back in Vietnam, he joined Ho Huu Tuong and his Trotskyite party. Both published the newspaper *La Lutte*, but their cooperation soon ended in bitter confrontation when Tuong left to publish his *October* newspaper. Besides, Thau took over *La Lutte* and clandestinely set up the Young Annam group to bolster his Trotskyite party.

Soon the Cochinchinese political checkerboard showed three groups: (1) the Trotskyite-La Lutte group with Ta Thu Thau and Duong Bach Mai; (2) the bourgeois bloc with Bui Quang Chieu, Nguyen Phan Long, and Tran Van Kha who had founded the Caucus of Cochinchinese representatives (Hoi Nghi Dan Bieu Nam Ky); and (3) the liberal party with lawyer Trinh Dinh Thao, physician Tan, and publisher Nam Dinh, editor of the famous *Duoc Nha Nam*. When all three factions formed the Indochinese Committee with 35 delegates, Cochinchinese Governor Pages was angry enough to summon everybody to his residence where they were properly lectured. Nguyen An Ninh and other leftists were sent to Poulo Condore while Ta Thu Thau fled to Bangkok where he was arrested and returned to Saigon in 1939 to receive the same hard labor sentence. Later, Nguyen An Ninh would die of disease in the concentration camp, while Thau would be executed in 1945 at Quang Ngai by Viet Minh Tran Van Giau.

Duong Bach Mai

Native of Baria (Cochinchina), Duong Bach Mai had stayed in Aix-en-Provence for two years before heading off to Moscow in 1929. There he took the Bolshevik name of Bourov. In 1931, he went back to Vietnam via Shanghai. In 1939, together with Nguyen An Ninh, he failed in the election to the municipal council of Cholon. But with the advent of the Viet Minh, Mai found himself a political inspector in the eastern provinces on September 25, 1945; director of national defense (Quoc Gia Tu Ve) in October; and Viet Minh delegate at Dalat and Fontainebleau conferences in 1946. As Viet Minh representative, he remained in France with Tran Ngoc Danh, who bore the Russian name of Blokov.

In spite of the protection of communist leader Marcel Cachin, he had to leave France, and on his way back to Vietnam he was arrested on March 25, 1947, by the French police at Djibouti. Banished to Kontum in May 1949, he was delivered by Viet Minh commandoes on October 5, 1949. He died in Hanoi in 1965.

POLITICO-RELIGIOUS SECTS

The term *politico-religious* caused much confusion, for it failed to differentiate between a religion carrying out political activities, such as the White Lotus in China or Cao Daism in Vietnam, or a political party using religion as a cover, such as the Triad in China or the Thien Dia Hoi in Vietnam.

The Hoa Hao

Around 1939, the Hoa Hao sect emerged as a Buu Son Ky Huong offspring under the leadership of Huynh Phu So. World War II had first created a division among Western nations. The Japanese occupation of Indochina had definitely destroyed the myth of white supremacy in Asia. There was a consensus among all colonized people that they must recover their independence from alien domination.

Huynh Phu So. Huynh Phu So was born in 1919 in the village of Hoa Hao (Chau Doc) where his father was the Huong Ca (mayor). At age 15, he developed serious mental and physical disorders, which, to quote Anthony Wallace, made him a "potential shaman."[51] Thus, he went up to the That Son Mountains where he learned about traditional medicine and herbs. From a man named Le Hong Nhat, he discovered a popular type of acupuncture using knives or broken pieces of ceramic bowls instead of the traditional needles. Later, he learned Khmer magic and sorcery from masters of the Ta Lon Mountain, the highest center of occult training across the Cambodian border. These trips to the mountains forged the qualifications he needed to be later the Hoa Hao leader, for he was a reincarnation of Buddha Master, and as such he had to prove his ability to display Confucian virtues, to heal, to make prophecies, and to practice magic.

In 1939, Huynh Phu So went through a complete transformation. One day after bowing to the Ban Thong Thien,[52] he revealed to his father that he was the reincarnation of Buddha Master. Afterward, he delivered a long speech on Buddhism, which upset family and neighbors alike. Although his words were a mere repetition of Buu Son Ky Huong's teachings, according to Ho Tam Hue Tai, "the mark of a true prophet, besides an ability to heal and to perform miracles, was the ability to revitalize the tradition by articulating a commonly held body of beliefs."[53] By 1919, So succeeded in securing more than 10,000 followers who came from the Buu Son Ky Huong background.

What Ho Tai calls a stroke of good luck[54] for So happened in 1940 when 30 members of the Thinkers sect began a riot by beheading a minor village notable and his wife. The leader, Nguyen Thanh Dao, was killed with two of his adepts; 11 others were wounded. The rest of the sect rallied behind Huynh Phu So.

The advent of World War II had made the French more sensitive to sects and the rallies of the Thinkers which prompted them to order So out of the area. So left Chau Doc and on his way to banishment, he converted two rich landowners, Le Cong Bo and Lam Tho Cuu. But the best of his acquisitions occurred in Cantho with Nguyen Giac Ngo from Cho Moi (Long Xuyen), Lam Thanh Nguyen from Nhon Nghia (Can Tho), and Tran Van Soai from Cai Von (Long Xuyen). All three would later appear on the Cochinchinese political scene as leaders of the Hoa Hao movement. Tran Van Soai, called also Nam Lua for his hot temper, would become the commander in chief of the Hoa Hao armed forces.

With magical cures by water and herbs, Huynh Phu So spread religious teaching with political overtones. He predicted the apocalypse in 1945 and the occupation of Indochina by the Japanese. But he also predicted that the invincible Japanese would not be able to swallow the chicken.[55] He was the only religious leader to raise economic issues. By contrast with Cao Daists, his "nationalism" was rather close to peasant thought about self-defense rather than political ambitions. When he published his *Ke Dan Cua Nguoi Khung* (Litanies of the Mad Man), he won the name of Dao Khung (Mad Monk). It was the moment the French were waiting for. They discarded him by placing him under medical care at the Cho Quan psychiatric hospital near Saigon. There, by displaying his occult power, he converted his entourage including his physician Dr. Nguyen Van Tam. The latter enjoyed his company so much that he kept him at his side for ten months.

Afterward, So was assigned residence in Bac Lieu. There he resumed his apocalyptic prophecies, making the province a center for a millenarian pilgrimage. There people could secure Buu Son Ky Huong amulets by enrolling en

masse into So's sect and by paying handsome contributions, which were chan-
neled to So himself. Thus, the So organization grew to become known as the
Hoa Hao sect.

In 1941, an event determined So's future. Probably without his knowledge,
a Hoa Hao adept captured an innocent beggar and opened him live in sacrifice
to the spirits. In retaliation, the French decided to deport So to Laos. This
induced his advisor. Luong Trong Tuong to approach the Kempetal[56] for help.
Because the political parties—Phuc Quoc and Dai Viet—had failed to attract
the masses, the Japanese were quite happy to try the religious card. Thus, the
French car transporting So on his way to deportation was intercepted by the
Kempetai. This official support from the invincible Japanese was instrumental
in maintaining So in religious leadership. From Saigon, where he was in Japanese protective custody, he organized, with Japanese advisors, an expansion
program, which consisted of swallowing one by one the other Buu Son Ky
Huong sects, left unruled by the retirement of their old leaders. Personally, he
took no rest from displaying his magical power; having learned that the wife of
wealthy landlord Chung Ba Khanh was undergoing an appendectomy, he succeeded in preventing the operation just by giving her a few oranges to eat. To
express their gratitude, the couple joined the Hoa Hao sect. The religion reached
such power that according to Ho Tai, the majority of landowners had to convert
under the pressure of their sectarian peasants.

While So was confined in Saigon, his adepts used any means to infiltrate the
rural administrations, a step that allowed them to carry out large scale recruit-
ments. In 1943, Huynh Phu So had the entire Buu Son Ky Huong under Hoa
Hao control. As they rebuilt the Lang Linh temple destroyed 30 years ago by
the French, the latter reacted by sending leaders Nguyen Giac Ngo and Lam
Thanh Nguyen to the Ba Ra concentration camp.

As for So himself, he had never concealed his preference for the Trotskyites,
because their leader Ta Thu Thau also came from Long Xuyen, So's native
province. But his Japanese protectors compelled him to remain in the field of
pure religion.

In 1943, his adepts built the Bao An (self-defense) forces, a prelude to the
Hoa Hao army. Tran Van Soai took command of the Hoa Hao forces after
having secured the cooperation of Le Quang Vinh, later famous under the name
of Ba Cut. Around that time, the Hoa Hao sect numbered some one million and
developed competition with the Communist party. Although So himself was
under the influence of Trotskyites Ta Thu Thau and Nguyen An Ninh, he was
above all concerned with his religious title of Minh Vuong Tri Vi (King of
Light), again, a White Lotus tradition.

The unexpected Japanese coup of March 9, 1945, created an entire political
vacuum. The social structure erected by the French collapsed, leaving off guard
foes and friends alike. Liberated from French concentration camps, Nguyen Giac
Ngo and Lam Thanh Nguyen scrambled back to the West to build up their own
army. Nguyen Giac Ngo, calling himself Dao Ngoan, began healing fraud: To

cure malaria, he secretly added to the supposed pure water quinine powder provided by the Japanese.

Free of French constraints, entire regions fell into anarchy. Hoa Hao sects mushroomed, causing major concern to the Japanese. Rice cultivation declined. Because the Japanese needed rice alcohol as fuel for their logistics,[57] So was given the role of touring the provinces and calling for resumption of rice cultivation.

He also launched the Vietnam Phat Giao Lien Hiep Hoi (Vietnam Buddhist Federation) but could not secure cooperation from the orthodox Buddhist organizations.

Later, So struck a deal with communists Ung Van Khiem and Thanh Son for a common action toward independence. The cooperation turned out to be a competition between the two parties, first about fundraising, later about military power.

In 1945, So agreed to have his forces trained by the Viet Minh. When, in August, the Japanese surrendered to the Allies, a United National Front (Mat Tran Quoc Gia Thong Nhut) was created to oppose French return. But the front collapsed a few days later when in Can Tho many Hoa Hao leaders were arrested by the Viet Minh. A clash occurred on August 29, 1945. To reestablish peace, a new Revolutionary People's committee (Uy Ban Nhan Dan) came up with a Hoa Hao delegate as commissar for social affairs while the Viet Minh and their associates, the Thanh Nien Tien Phong (Vanguard Youth), held major political and military posts.

On September 8, 1945, Hoa Hao and Viet Minh clashed again. Hoa Hao key leaders were captured and sentenced to death. Some managed to escape, including Lam Thanh Nguyen, Tran Van Soai, and Huynh Phu So. Their revenge was appalling: Rivers and canals carried communist bodies around the clock. Some makeshift stalls displayed parts of Viet Minh bodies for sale. These gruesome details were photographed by the Viet Minh and presented to French Minister Marius Moutet to evidence persecution perpetrated by Hoa Hao.[58]

On September 23, 1945, under a French offensive, Tran Van Giau had to retreat to the West but the Hoa Hao forces were blocking his way. The agreement of March 6, 1946, between France and the Viet Minh forced So to accept an alliance with the local Viet Minh represented by Nguyen Binh.

Nguyen Binh, who replaced Giau, organized the Allied National front (Mat Tran Quoc Gia Lien Hiep). This time, So was named chairman, but again all key positions were assigned to the Viet Minh members. Perhaps, So was lost in euphoria for he wrote a poem celebrating union and peace and took a communist turncoat, Nguyen Van Chuyen, as his political advisor. He also accepted the post of special commissioner in the Nam Bo executive committee. But when he undertook to reorganize his forces and gave the command of his fourth division to Tran Van Soai, tension surged again with the Viet Minh because they wanted the post for themselves.

In April, So was invited to a Nam Bo committee meeting where he was told to tour his area to call for peace; he was to use a Viet Minh escort, leaving behind his own bodyguards. Suspecting a plot, he flatly refused and left. On his way back home, he was intercepted by the Viet Minh. On May 18, 1947, when there was no hope to have So back, Tran Van Soai entered an agreement with the French to fight the Viet Minh. Two days later, on May 20, 1947, the Viet Minh announced Huynh Phu So's execution. According to rumors, his body was dismembered and separately buried in secret places.

As a former disciple of the Buu Son Ky Huong, So had agreed in his lifetime with the coming of Maitreya and the teaching of Sakyamuni. But following the "Potato-selling Monk" and probably influenced by the communist propaganda, So was the first to translate millenarian prophecy into the socioeconomic context: "The poor worry about paying their debts, about being ill, hungry and homeless."[59] In the aftermath of the Great Depression, his announcements gave a startling impetus to Vietnamese millenarianism; like the White Lotus in China, his apocalyptic visions had a decisive impact on the uprising of rural masses.

In spite of his close ties with Nguyen An Ninh and Ta Thu Thau, the two communist leaders, So limited his equalitarian world view with appeals to the rich to share their wealth with the poor. His Dan Xa (popular socialism) party, although with a Trotskyite accent, was based on the Buu Son Ky Huong rural community experience. It acknowledged the division of society into classes but at the same time emphasized two-way interrelationship. Thus, the Dan Xa favored social reforms rather than class struggles.

THE CAO DAISTS

Because of its opportunism, Cai Daism was not popular with many culture-bound critics. Bernard Fall was severe in his comments,[60] Graham Greene was rather humoristic,[61] and Gabriel Gobron was a rare panegyrist: In fact, he was Brother Gago, bishop of the Cao Daist Holy See, and his noncritical work,[62] "was based on inadequate and sometimes inaccurate source materials."[63] In fact, Gobron did not wash dirty linen in public and carefully reserved his criticisms for his religious partners: To them he bluntly suggested that "certain external aspects should be modified in order to be able to effectively keep the attention of persons susceptible to take it into consideration." Among these external aspects to be discarded, Gobron pointed to the "symbolic and shining eye,"[64] the image of Cao Dai himself.

This shining eye appeared in 1920 to the Doc Phu Ngo Van Chieu when he was chief of Phu Quoc Island, a kind of paradise lost in the Gulf of Siam. Expert in spiritism, Chieu would later, in 1925, train the first three converts, Pham Cong Tac, Cao Hoai Sang, and Cao Huynh Cu, also known as the Pho Loan group. With them, Chieu founded Cao Daism: The eye was adopted as the symbol of the Cao Dai God, and the Ngoc Co (beaked basket) was used to communicate with God and his saints during medium seances.

This religion claims to be a syncretism of the three Eastern religions: Confucianism, Taoism, and Buddhism. But the worship of Ngoc Hoang Thuong De (Jade Emperor) and Dieu Tri Kim Mau (Wu Sheng Lao Mu) betrays an original link to the Chinese sectarian White Lotus.

Based on Cao Daist Holy texts, the sect activities, like those of the White Lotus, were not exclusively religious but also covered the social and political realm; above all, this syncretic faith would not be confined to Vietnam but must spread all over the world.[65] Indeed, according to the Thanh Ngon Hiep Tuyen (selected Holy texts), Cao Dai had proclaimed that his religion was the national religion of Vietnam.[66] "Once there was a country in bondage and thanks to Me it will be the Master of the world."[67] Cao Daist leaders clearly understood that this universal hegemony could not be without first putting up a good fight against foreign invaders.

Yet, at the outset, the Thanh Ngon Hiep Tuyen Holy texts revealed a determined Cao Dai God preaching in 1926 a Franco-Vietnamese unity.[68] But in 1927, Cao Dai began to preach a need for justice "because justice defeats oppression."[69] Thus, there is ample evidence that a consensus existed between Cao Dai God and his disciples over the liberation of Vietnam. Obviously, this consensus was the key to Cao Daism's success: They were not only Vietnamese nationalists, they were also crusaders of God. Hence, in the aftermath of the French demise in March 1945, Cao Daism emerged as the major political party in Cochinchina.

Cao Daists are still not comfortable dwelling on their past politics and especially their collaboration with the Japanese. But as truth unfolded, with the advent of Vietnam independence, fear for French reprisals vanished to leave room for more and more accounts of Cao Daist participation in the fight for freedom, perhaps with some myth and legends. For one thing, high dignitary Cao Hoai Sang, one of the three Pho Loan veterans, thus, a key witness, publicly confessed that he, Cu, and Tac were "harboring hatred for foreign domination and had chosen spiritism as a way to gain some knowledge of the fate of their country."[70] As for the original founder, Ngo Van Chieu, 40 years after he died, his spirit proclaimed that he had left the Tay Ninh church to "seek some magical power for the liberation of his country."[71]

Superior Pham Cong Tac

Among the Pho Loan trio mentioned above, Pham Cong Tac was at the outset an unexpected partner, for he was a Roman Catholic. For a while he managed to keep a low profile, playing a background game, which would take him to the top of the organization. Indeed, he would be the most powerful leader of the Cao Daist church.

According to his official biography,[72] Pham Cong Tac was born in 1890 in the village of Binh Loc, district of Tan An. In 1905, the victory of Japan over Russia led the Vietnamese to hope for some Japanese aid. Tac belonged to Bui Quang Chieu's Constitutionalist party and was also involved with the Dong Du movement in 1906. The following year, as the French police moved against the Dong Du, Tac scrambled for cover to his ancestral abode at Tay Ninh. Later he married and found an entry-level job as an office boy in the Saigon custom services,[73] but his Holy See biographers insist that his inextinguishable compassion for the underdogs led him to borrow some money in order to bail out a group of young prostitutes who were working in cathouses to clear their parents' debts. Beside these rather mundane performances, Tac also made a journey to heaven where he talked to God.[74]

Although as Ho Phap (law protector) he was second in command after Pope Le Van Trung, he held an edge over Trung because of the preference given by Cao Dai to his Hiep Thien Dai, the legislative body of the Holy See. But it is more realistic to believe that his power derived from his control over the College of Mediums, who were the only connection between Cao Dai and this world.

In 1935, after the death of Pope Trung, a general assembly voted for Tac's "dictatorial policy" (Chanh sach doc tai).[75] This propelled him to a position of dictatorship, since he gathered in his hands legislative, executive, and judiciary powers. Later, Philippe Devillers would assert: "Within four years, Tac made Cao Daism a formidable political power."[76]

From then on, Pham Cong Tac concentrated on steering Cao Daism toward national politics.

Trinh Minh The

Trinh Minh The appeared to be an exceptional figure rather unknown to the public. Formerly chief warrant officer in the Nippon army, The had been trained for three years by the Kempetai as a marksman and a jiujitsu expert. Upon the return of the French, he retired with his troops in the Tay Ninh jungles. When Pham Cong Tac came back from exile, under his protection, The was promoted to the rank of colonel chief of operations and commander of Tay Ninh and the eastern provinces of Cochinchina.

At that time, Tran Quang Vinh refused to transfer the Cao Daist administration to Tac; thus, in 1948, The secretly organized the Black Shirts to support Tac in his contest with Vinh. In 1949, with Tac's blessing, he settled separately and proclaimed independence for his zone. He was probably the secret contact between the Viet Minh and Pham Cong Tac. At the end of 1949, he became the leader of the Phuc Quoc Hoi. In 1950, The lent to the Viet Minh sufficient weapons to attack a French convoy. In 1951, his prestige allowed him to call for a meeting where various influential leaders, such as VNQDD Vu Hong Khanh and Uy Ban Kien Quoc Nguyen Xuan Chu, came and founded with him the Front of National Resistance (Mat Tran Quoc Gia Khang Chien Vietnam) in which his party took the name of Cao Daist Alliance (Lien Minh Cao Dai).

According to Pierre Darcourt—a French journalist born in Vietnam—The was the mastermind behind the execution of priests Tricoire, Jeanson, and Boulard. On another day, his patrols intercepted a French Jeep: The two military occupants were dragged out, their ears were severed, their eyes gouged, their fingers chopped off and stuffed in their pants pockets.

Another time, he told his personal friend: "You are my best friend. I want to reserve the highest honors for you." Then he had him drugged, loaded him with explosives, and sent him to Saigon as a human bomb to kill General Chanson, the French commander in Cochinchina. But his notoriety originated with the assassination of Colonel Peter Dewcy, chief of the OSS in Cochinchina.[77] For all these deeds, The became the quiet Vietnamese in the celebrated Graham Greene novel *The Quiet American*.

Yet, it was Trinh Minh The that OSS Colonel Lansdale set out to deal with. Lansdale had just come out of the Philippines where he had made Magsaysay president. In Saigon, against Ambassador Collins's advice, he single-handedly supported Diem. However, according to Pierre Darcourt, anticipating Diem's possible demise, Lansdale prudently looked for a potential replacement and believed he found him in Trinh Minh The, "a man of the people"[78] like Magsaysay. After he had been shown The's arms factory where Western weapons and even American M1s were handsomely reproduced out of the ten kilometers of steel rails wrenched away from the Saigon-Loc Ninh railroad line, Lansdale promised to supply The with one radio station, three air bases, and a seaport at Ha Tien in the Gulf of Siam. The idea was to provide The with military strength to take over in case Diem failed.[79]

But for the time being, The preferred to pocket Diem's $2 million reward for his submission. When his 2,000 guerrillas entered Saigon in an official parade, the French shouted from the tribune: "Here are the tramps bought off by the CIA," and Lansdale replied: "We bought them because you could not beat them."[80]

During the showdown between Diem and the Binh Xuyen, The, who had just been promoted to brigadier general of Diem's army, was defending the Tan Thuan bridge between Saigon and Nha Be. He was shot behind the ear and died in his Jeep. Although Ngo Dinh Diem had ordered a state funeral for The and publicly wept at The's coffin, rumors persisted that he and his brother Nhu were behind the kill. This speculation does not seem ludicrous at all, given Lansdale's supposed scheme to replace Diem by The.

As for the French, the Second Bureau[81] had enough ugly details on The to also be interested in his execution.

NOTES

1. Truong Buu Lam, *Patterns of Vietnamese Response to Foreign Intervention 1858–1900*, p. 2.
2. Pham Van Son, *Viet Su Tan Bien*, Vol. V, p. 40.
3. Eric Hobsbaum, *Primitive Rebels*, p. 13.
4. *Luat vua phai thua le lang.*
5. The Vietnamese New Year, which occurs in January or February.

6. Their chief, Liu Yu-Fung, was retiring to China after the Li-Fournier Treaty.

7. Pham Van Son, *Viet Su Tan Bien*, Vol. VI, p. 76n.

8. The armed forces were divided into three branches: the Red Militia (Linh Kho Do) was part of French expeditionary forces; the Blue Militia (Linh Kho Xanh), with French and Vietnamese officers, was under the French civilian authority (Residents); and the Regional Militia (Linh Kho Luc) was under Vietnamese command in districts and provinces.

9. Truong Quang Ngoc was Ham Nghi's bodyguard. He handed his emperor to the French.

10. For Chesneaux 25,000 mourners; for Pham Van Son 140,000.

11. Born Nguyen Phuc Dan, Cuong De was a direct descendant of heir apparent Prince Canh, who died of smallpox during the battle of Qui Nhon. For some reason, his family fell into disgrace under Minh Mang but was rehabilitated by Tu Duc in 1848 with the rank of Hau (Marquis).

12. 75 from Cochinchina, 30 from Tonkin, and 10 from Annam.

13. Chen King C., *Vietnam and China, 1938–1954*, p. 18, citing Hoang Van Chi, *From Colonialism to Communism*, p. 18.

14. Some 300 meters from author's house.

15. Second degree doctorate under Tien Si (doctorate).

16. Bernard Fall, *The Two Vietnams*, p. 118.

17. Chen King C., *Vietnam and China*, p. 118.

18. Tet is the Vietnamese New Year, which coincides with the Chinese New Year. Both belong to the lunar calendar.

19. Pham Van Son, *Viet Su Tan Bien*, Vol. VII, p. 180.

20. Another splinter group, the Vietnam Quoc Dan Cach Mang Dang VNQDCMD (Nationalist Revolutionary party), was founded by a Cuong De sympathizer, Hoang Nam Hung, but in January 1930, Nguyen Ai Quoc included it in the Indochinese Communist party.

21. John J. Collins, *Primitive Religion*, p. 33.

22. Ho Tai Hue Tam, *Millenarianism and Peasant Politics in Vietnam*, p. 71.

23. Georges Coulet, *Les Societes secretes en terre d'Annam*, p. 112.

24. Between 12 P.M. and 2 P.M.

25. Trinh Van Thanh, *Thanh Ngu Dien Tich danh Tu-Dien*, Vol. II, p. 1060.

26. The White Lotus was a Buddho-Taoist organization.

27. John J. Collins, *Primitive Religion*, p. 170.

28. Ho Tai Hue Tam, *Millenarianism and Peasant Politics in Vietnam*, p. 35.

29. Trinh Van Thanh, *Thanh Ngu Dien Tich Danh Tu Dien*, Vol. II, p. 1062.

30. Ho Tai Hue Tam, *Millenarianism and Peasant Politics in Vietnam*, p. 16.

31. 1. Debt to the ruler 2. Debt to the parents 3. Debt to the Three Jewels 4. Debt to mankind.

32. The Bodhi tree under which Buddha was meditating. It is 10 to 12 meters high, with round leaves. Its stony fruits are used to make Buddhist beads.

33. The Vietnamese members took over because of their numeric superiority over the Chinese.

34. Ho Tai Hue Tam, *Millenarianism and Peasant Politics in Vietnam*, p. 64.

35. Ordination ceremony for Buddhist monks.

36. Jean Chesneaux, *Secret Societies in China*, p. 127.

37. Vietnamese translation of Chinese Shui-hu Shuan (Water Margin).

38. Eric Hobsbaum, *Primitive Rebels*, p. 3.

39. Jean Chesneaux, *Secret Societies*, p. 129.

40. Serge Hutin, *Les Societies secretes en Chine*, p. 96.

41. Georges Coulet, *Les Societes secretes*, p. 39.

42. Ibid., p. 41.

43. Laureate of competitive examinations.

44. *Nghia Quan* also means loyal forces or resistants.

45. Truong Buu Lam, *Patterns of Vietnamese Response*, p. 74.

46. This was a very generous assistance: A ninth rank mandarin's wage was only 18 francs and 48 liters of rice. Obviously, the court did not see her deceased husband as a rebel.

47. Ho Tai Hue Tam, *Radicalism and the Origins of the Vietnam Revolution*, p. 40.

48. Ibid., p. 43.

49. A master in law.

50. Ho Tai Hue Tam, *Radicalism and the Origins of the Vietnam Revolution*, p. 143.

51. Anthony F. C. Wallace, *Religion: An Anthropological View*, p. 145.

52. A typical Heaven altar erected in front of each house.

53. Ho Tai Hue Tam, *Millenarianism and Peasant Politics in Vietnam*, p. 119.

54. Ibid., p. 120.

55. According to the Chinese Zodiac, the year 1945 was the year of the rooster; thus, he meant that the Japanese control would not last until the year's end.

56. Japanese secret police.

57. Rice alcohol was used to replace gasoline.

58. The author saw these pictures a few hours before they were presented to Moutet. But it was simply impossible to say whether they belonged to Viet Minh or Hoa Hao victims.

59. Ho Tai Hue Tam, *Millenarianism and Peasant Politics in Vietnam*, p. 151.

60. Bernard Fall, *Political and Religious Sects in Vietnam*, p. 241.

61. Graham Greene, *The Quiet American*, p. 85.

62. Gabriel Gobron, *History and Philosophy of Caodaism*.

63. Victor L. Olivier, *Caodai spiritism*, p. 4.

64. Gabriel Gobron, *History and Philosophy of Caodaism*, p. 146.

65. *Thanh Ngon Hiep Tuyen*, p. 46.

66. Ibid., p. 39.

67. Huong Hieu, *Dao Su Xay Ban*, Vol. II, p. 242.

68. *Thanh Ngon Hiep Tuyen*, p. 109.

69. Ibid., p. 84.

70. Huong Hieu, *Dao Su Xay Ban*, Vol. I. p. 1.

71. Do Van Ly, *Tim Hieu Dao Cao Dai*, p. 120.

72. Dai Dao Tam Ky Pho Do, *Tieu Su Duc Ho Phap*.

73. Chinh Dao, *Vietnam Nien Bieu Nhan Vat Chi*, p. 417.

74. Toa Thanh Tay Ninh, *Tieu Su Pham Cong Tac*, pp. 6–18.

75. Tran Van Rang, *Dai Dao Su Cuong*, Vol. II, p. 42.

76. Philippe Devillers, *Histoire du Vietnam de 1940 á 1952*, p. 69.

77. Pierre Darcourt, *Bay Vien the Master of Cho Lon*, pp. 387–388.
78. Ibid., p. 387.
79. Ibid.
80. Ibid., p. 396.
81. French Army intelligence.

6

THE FRANCO-
INDOCHINESE WAR

In 1940, France collapsed, leaving her overseas possessions virtually without leadership. In Indochina, as vital merchandise was brought into China by the French Yunnan railroad, it was the moment the Japanese chose to demand control of the Tonkin border from French Governor General Catroux. Catroux's calls to the United States were in vain as President Roosevelt had made up his mind that France, having "milked Vietnam for one hundred years, should never be allowed to come back."[1] Thus, a defenseless Catroux had to abide the Japanese ultimatum. For this he was dismissed and replaced by Admiral Decoux.

AN UNEASY ALLIANCE

On August 30, 1940, France had to sign an accord with Tokyo recognizing the preeminent position of Japan in the Far East. Because the details would be negotiated later between the two local military commanders, Decoux was secretly instructed to delay the negotiations. The conference between Generals Martin and Nishihara began on September 5, 1940, and dragged on for two weeks. On September 18, an impatient Nishihara sent his Kwantung army to attack Lang Son and Dong Dang. Haiphong was also bombarded. After two days of fierce fighting, when French casualties reached 800 lives, Vichy ordered Decoux to immediately accept Japanese conditions. The ensuing Martin-Nishihara agreement enabled 6,000 Japanese troops to stay in north Tonkin and 25,000 to transit toward Yunnan. But it would not take long for the Japanese to come back with more demands.

The following year, 1941, Japan requested the rights to station in Cochinchina for "common defense" against possible Allied attacks from Singapore. Vichy unsuccessfully sought help from the Germans. On July 28, 1941, French Prime Minister Admiral Darlan had to accept the Japanese presence in south Indochina.

This 1941 "common defense treaty" enabled the Japanese army to control

French military installations and economic resources in Indochina. Assigned by the Japanese to the defense of the Tonkin borders, the French also had to provide them with logistic support, which gradually depleted Indochinese resources and perverted the local economy. Indeed, there would be a drastic 60 percent reduction compared with the 1938 exports, which included more than 1 million tons of rice, 58,000 tons of rubber, 548,000 tons of maize and more than 1.5 million tons of coal.

By 1944, import reduction directly affected the food supply. Europeans had to use ration tickets. Soy beans became substitutes for milk, and the shortage of wheat flour led many families to replace bread with burned rice (Com Chay). The shortage of medicines was critical for the Europeans who were not used to traditional medicine. Native pharmacist Ho Dac An managed to manufacture a few items he put on sale at his Tan Dinh store. Allied pilots also contributed by dropping critical products against dysentery and bacterial infection. Scarcity of gasoline resulted in the use of charcoal and rice alcohol as fuel for motor vehicles. Thus, rice cultivation was under the firm control of the Kempetai. In Saigon, the two major distillery plants (Mazet and Binh Tay) had to process huge amounts of grain. In 1942, alcohol production in Indochina reached some 16,000 tons, depleting the population's basic sustenance. Applied to Tonkin, it brought dramatic consequences: A famine followed with the death of thousands of peasants. Even in the south, by 1944, the Japanese occupation took its toll: Now a peasant household had only one "short," which members wore in turn when they had to go to the city. For them, it was the return to the pre-Han period more than 1,000 years ago, when they only wore loincloth.

THE JAPANESE COUP (MARCH 9, 1945)

Resistance against Japanese occupation was in the pocket of Allied strategists since the beginning. In the Far East, Allied intelligence gathered a host of services including the American OSS and naval Group Miles, the Chinese Tai Li secret services, the French Military Mission (M5) in Kun Ming, and DGSS (Direction Generale des Services Speciaux) in Kandy (Ceylon) to cite a few.

In early 1944, de Gaulle appointed General Roger Blaizot commander of the CEFEO (Corps Expeditionnaire Français en Extreme Orient) with the mission to recover Indochina. To prevent American opposition, the CEFEO was made a part of the Southeast Asia Command (SEAC). The DGSS was to organize resistance in Indochina, and Lieutenant de Langlade, chief of DGSS-Far East, parachuted into Tonkin to confirm Mordant's appointment as chief of Indochinese resistance. But because each local organization was sponsored by a specific Allied service, it was impossible to have a unified command. General Mordant was linked to the Free French DGSS, while the director of Caltex Oil Company, Gordon Laurence, created the GBT[2] group to work with the OSS and the Chinese. In Cochinchina, French planters and their British counterparts in Malaya also formed clandestine organizations. Like the GBT, they worked independently from Mordant.

At the outset, Franco-Japanese cohabitation was apparently a decent relationship, mainly within bureaucracy and business concerns. But antagonism soon developed with the European community. They had to leave their luxurious habitations for Japanese functionaries and businessmen. By interfering in French police activities, the Kempetai aroused fear and humiliation.

In 1943, a retired General Iwane Matsui publicly invited the Vietnamese to join his Great Asian sphere of coprosperity, declaring that Japan would free all Asian countries whether or not the United States, Great Britain, or France liked it.

To compound French misery, the Japanese allowed Thailand to invade Cambodia on January 9, 1941. Caught by surprise, the French had to retreat on land, but a naval engagement took place on January 17, near the island of Koh Chang. In half an hour, from 18:14 to 18:45, the French warship *Lamotte Picquet* sent the entire Thai fleet to the bottom. To save their associates from more humiliations, the Japanese imposed their mediation and forced France to return Siem Reap and Battambang provinces, which were ceded to Cambodia by the treaty of March 23, 1907.

By accepting Mordant's resignation, Decoux was well aware of the existence of anti-Japanese resistance. He was also happy to have General Tsushihashi and Ambassador Matsumoto for dinner, while Allied air forces were dropping arms and munitions to the resistants.

But in 1944, the Allies' landing in Normandy, the U.S. bombing of Haiphong and Saigon (where the Japanese lost 24 ships), the naval defeat in the Gulf of Leyte, and the loss of the Philippines were serious causes of concern for the Tokyo high command. Moreover, Decoux's systematic delay in supplying logistic support and his obstinate refusal to turn over Allied pilots shot down over Indochina aroused Japanese suspicion. Because Decoux and Mordant failed to give assurance of French cooperation in case of the Allied invasion of Indochina, the Tokyo high command began to plan for a takeover. General Tsushihashi was then assigned to reorganize the 38th Army in Indochina.

Actually the Indochinese army was not geared for conventional war for its purpose was to maintain peace among the tribes and patrols along the Tonkin border. Thus, a direct confrontation with modern Japanese forces might have been ruled out.

On March 9, 1945, in a well-orchestrated plot, the commander in chief, General Tsushihashi ostensibly gave a reception at his residence. In the middle of the party, he surreptitiously left for his headquarters. At the same time, Japanese ambassador Matsumoto was signing an accord with Decoux on supplying rice to Japan. After the ceremony, at 7 P.M., Matsumoto handed Decoux an ultimatum to surrender within the next two hours.

Before the French could react, the Japanese attacked. The entire French high command, including Governor General Decoux, Generals Mordant and Ayme, was imprisoned. Generals Alessandri and Sabattier managed to escape to China with their troops. General Lemonnier was captured and beheaded during the Cao Bang-Langson massacres.

On March 24, 1945, de Gaulle's provisory government promised that, after the liberation, all former territories would be associated with France in a new economic order. Made after the Japanese coup, this declaration did not impart the assurance that the French were sincere. Indeed, their later efforts to reoccupy Indochina would come to justify such reserve.

The March 9 coup was also the moment of truth for the Vietnamese. Once in command, the Japanese forsook all the promises of the Great Asian sphere of coprosperity. Instead of transferring the administration to the Vietnamese, as their propaganda had led the natives to expect, the Japanese went on to place the French at every level of administration. In response, the Viet Minh began to attack Japanese isolated posts.

On August 6, 1945, the American atomic bomb exploded over Hiroshima. The following day, Ho Chi Minh converted his guerrillas into an army of liberation. In Saigon, on August 14, 1945, the Viet Minh called for a united front with participation of Cao Daists, Hoa Hao, and Thanh Nien Tien Phong.

On August 16, 1945, the Japanese surrendered. They began to transfer weapons and combat materiel to the sects. But they were outpaced by Ho Chi Minh. On August 19, 1945, in a show of strength, the Viet Minh Liberation Army seized the city of Thai Nguyen in Tonkin. By August 20, the Viet Minh were firmly installed in Hanoi. Two days later in Saigon, the United Front became the Viet Minh Front.

On August 25, 1945 news of British arrival spread. To place the Allies in face of a fait accompli, Tran Van Giau, a member of the ICP, created the Viet Minh Executive Committee of Cochinchina (Uy Ban Hanh Chanh Nam Bo) as a Cochinchinese administrative body.

THE BRITISH

At the Potsdam Conference in July 1945, to accept Japanese surrender, the Allies had decided to send the Chinese to Tonkin and the British to Cochinchina.

On September 6, 1945, British General Gracey and his Gurkhas troops arrived in Saigon. He immediately made the Japanese commander Terauchi personally responsible for the restoration of order. The Viet Minh in Cochinchina were to immediately yield their weapons. In response, on September 11, a congress of the Communist Party took over the direction of the Viet Minh front. On September 24, Tran Van Giau called for the population to evacuate Saigon.

THE CHINESE

At the Potsdam Conference, the Chinese were given occupation of Tonkin in compensation for the Russian occupation of Manchuria decided previously at the Yalta Conference. It was also a convenient arrangement since Vietnam belonged to the Chinese zone of influence.

But General Lu Han, chief of the Chinese expeditionary troops, came to Tonkin with definite ideas. First, he ignored an order from the Chung King Central Government to let French General Alessandri and his troops accompany the Chinese back to Vietnam. Later at the signing of Japanese surrender ceremony, while the Viet Minh were conspicuously present, the French were practically ignored and their flag was not even displayed among Allied colors.

Indeed, at that time, by contrast with Cochinchina, the French political position in the North was in shambles: The Viet Minh government stubbornly refused to negotiate on anything except independence, the Japanese were understandably indifferent, the Americans as always ambivalent, and the Chinese decided to ignore their French ally. Indeed, Lu Han's view of the war was the narrow perspective of a provincial warlord, not preoccupied with international opinion. Perhaps, by contrast with Chiang Kai-shek, he wished to add Vietnam to his native Yunnan. Anyway, given the financial profits he made in Hanoi, he was definitely in favor of a long occupation. Yet, he was well aware of the native anti-Chinese sentiment: On September 5, when his troops arrived in Cao Bang, they were met with hostile demonstrations.

Soon Lu Han realized that the French, although weak from a political standpoint, remained financially strong, with their two major banks (the Bank of Indochina and its affiliate the Franco-Chinese Bank) being the only financial resources on which Indochina depended. To begin with, Lu Han had 1200 million Chinese gold units (Kuan Chin)[3] to be exchanged on a 1 to 1 rate with the Indochinese piastre. Without consulting with the French, he raised the exchange rate to 1.5 piastre for one gold unit. Thus, each army unit followed suit and put pressure on the Bank of Indochina branches to obtain piastres at the new rate. Furthermore, every single day, Chinese aircraft from Kun Ming brought into Hanoi huge quantities of Kuan Chin banknotes to be exchanged against 500-piastre bills, which had been printed before by the Japanese on the BIC emission equipment they had seized during their March 9 coup. In November 1945, to put an end to Lu Han's traffic of piastres, Sainteny withdrew the 500-piastre banknotes from circulation. Jean Laurent, the new Director of the BIC (Banque de l'Indochine), in Hanoi and his assistant were jailed by the Chinese for refusing to advance an allowance of 15 million piastres for Chinese troops. Intervention of U.S. General Gallagher had France comply with the Chinese request and the BIC officials were released. Nevertheless, these incidents led Lu Han to realize that Chinese occupation without French financial support would not be so easy, given the fact that the Viet Minh were unable to provide the 96 million piastres needed for Chinese monthly expenditures. The only cash they had on hand was 1,250,000 piastres seized previously from the colonial treasury.

THE FRENCH RETURN

In mid-1945, the French intensified their drop of arms and personnel to the local resistance. On the night of August 22, 1945, the French commissioner in Cochinchina, Jean Cedile, landed near Tay Ninh and was immediately surrounded by Cao Daist peasants who handed him over to the Japanese, refusing rewards.

In Hanoi, on September 2, 1945, to present the French with a fait accompli, Ho Chi Minh declared the independence of Vietnam at the Ba Dinh place. Down to the south, Saigon erupted in a huge demonstration: Anticommunist suspects were massacred. Two French priests, Fathers Jeanson and Boulard, were murdered. The popular Father Tricoire, pastor of the Saigon Basilic, was executed in front of his parish office by a hysterical crowd. The monuments to French war heroes were desecrated by order of dissident Cao Daist Trinh Minh The. As head of the executive committee, Tran Van Giau had to publicly condemn these incidents.

Fighting for supremacy broke out among various factions in the provinces: Hoa Hao and Viet Minh clashed violently. During August and September, the Cao Daists joined the fight against the Viet Minh.

SAINTENY

Major Sainteny was one of the most prestigious names in the French resistance. A prominent member of the Reseau Alliance, he won more fame with a unique escape from the notorious Gestapo headquarters in Rue des Saussaies. His three-year stay in Indochina before the war led the DGER (Direction Generale des Etudes et Recherches) in Calcutta to appoint him, in April 1945, as head of the French Military Mission (M5) at Kunming. As a French equivalent of the OSS, the DGER in China enjoyed a close cooperation with the U.S. organization.

The first thing Sainteny worked on was to build up an intelligence line along the Tonkin border with the remnants of Alessandri forces, which had succeeded in crossing the border after the March 9 Japanese coup. An intact Indochinese navy, under Captain Commentry, was relocated to Pakhoi. Reinforced with heavily armed junks, they contributed to the harassment of Japanese in the Bay of Ha Long.

In July 1945, when the Viet Minh put in a request to the OSS for arms and munitions, Sainteny saw it as an opportunity to start a dialogue with Ho Chi Minh. A French liaison officer was dispatched to Ho's command post. The first encounter between Ho and Sainteny was postponed due to weather conditions, which prevented the French aircraft from landing on a makeshift runway. The arrival of Lu Han troops seemed to be a determinant factor for Ho to resume the dialogue. Problems with the Chinese occupation army coupled with the lessons of history largely contributed to his decision. The Vietnamese wanted unity and independence, and the French government accepted the principle of "self-government within an Indochinese Federation and a French Union."

The arrival of Leclerc troops and the overwhelming pressure of the Chinese mission were also other reasons for Ho to sign the March 6 accord.

The March 6 Accord

When Sainteny came to Hanoi by air in September 1945 with Major Archimede Patti as head of the OSS mission, he had enough trump cards to expect some success in dealing with Ho: First, from Kun Ming, he had developed significant dialogues with the Viet Minh; second, as a "New French," he was not responsible for past politics in Indochina; third, he was a wartime resistant as much as Ho could be; and last but not least, he was the son-in-law of socialist Albert Sarraut, well respected among the Viet Minh.

It is not clear whether Sainteny had received any specific instructions from the French government about recovering the Hanoi governor general's mansion. It seems that he took it upon himself to settle in a place that, after all, had been the symbol of French sovereignty in Indochina. Besides this show of authority, perhaps it was a design to test Viet Minh resolve. Since they did not oppose, Sainteny believed he had scored a psychological victory. But harsh reality would soon force him to pack up and make room for Chinese General Lu Han who arrived on September 9, 1945, with a force of 152,000 men.

The French fleet arrived at Haiphong in the early hours of March 6, 1946. As the local Chinese troops opposed their landing, a two-hour artillery dual resulted in the sinking of two French ships with 500 casualties on one side and the burning a Chinese arms depot, on the other. Fearing responsibility for the incident, the chief of the Chinese mission, Shao Pai-ch'ang, pressured Ho for an immediate conclusion to his negotiations with the French. Thus, the same day (March 6, 1946), Ho Chi Minh signed an accord with Sainteny, authorizing the presence of 15,000 French troops in North Vietnam. As for France, she recognized Vietnam as a free state within the Indochinese Federation and the French Union. Vietnam had a government, a parliament, and finances. Reunion of Cochinchina with the North would be subject to further referendum.

Obviously, this agreement was not satisfactory to any Vietnamese including Ho Chi Minh himself. He told Sainteny: "I am not happy about it; after all, it is you who have won; you are well aware that I wanted more than that. In fact, the problem of Cochinchina appeared as the major obstacle to Franco-Vietnamese peace." Hence, in June 1946, Ho Chi Minh told General Salan: "Do not make Cochinchina a new Alsace-Lorraine, otherwise we will have the 'guerre de cent ans.' "[4]

In Hanoi, the people were not happy. It took all of Giap's eloquence to explain about a Free Vietnam. "Freedom is not autonomy, it is more than autonomy. Of course it is not yet independence, but with it we shall reach independence." As a result, he received an overwhelming ovation. The March 6 accord was accepted by the people. Later, the Viet Minh would rationalize that "the decision to sign the March 6 accord was correct, expedient and genial. This act of peace was imperative at that time as the act of war would be imperative on December 19.[5] As for Ho, he bluntly told his critics: "It is better to smell French wastes for a short while than to eat Chinese feces for life."

In Saigon, the March 6 accord also had its detractors, but they did not belong to the party: Dr. Tran Tan Phat, a member of Cochinchina Council, voiced his opposition to what he called an infringement to the autonomy of Cochinchina: He was immediately murdered by Tran Van Giau's squads. Later, Bui Quang Chieu and Ho Van Nga found the same fate.

Of course, the accord would not easily resolve the situation, for after the December attack, according to General Salan "in 1947–1948, the goal of France was to chase the Viet Minh away from the Tonkin delta, to destroy the Viet Minh organization and its prestige, to protect Tho's and Nung's ethnic minorities, and to secure the border."[6] Thus, in spite of Leclerc's peaceful efforts, d'Argenlieu stubbornly favored the solution by force. He sarcastically repeated: "I am amazed—yes, that is the word, amazed—that France's fine expeditionary corps in Indochina is commanded by officers who would rather negotiate than fight."[7] Thus, he was not in any hurry to implement the March accord, and when a suspicious Giap met with Salan over French logistic arrangements, he gave him an insight on Viet Minh guerilla strategy: "This type of war is quite compatible with our nature, customs and environment. We are at home here. Nature and people belong to us."[8] Salan knew Giap was right. And that is why he sided with Leclerc for a peaceful solution.

ADMIRAL THIERRY d'ARGENLIEU

Priest-Admiral Thierry d'Argenlieu, formerly Free France naval officer and de Gaulle's representative in the Pacific, was recalled to duty from his Carme monastery where he was known as Father Louis de la Trinite. He arrived in Saigon on October 30, 1945, to take the command as French high commissioner for Indochina. Like de Gaulle his mentor, d'Argenlieu nurtured a certain idea of "la grandeur de la France." Perhaps his nomination also reflected de Gaulle's aspiration to restore the traditional admiral governor's rule in Indochina.

According to Philippe Devillers, d'Argenlieu arrived in Saigon "full of generous intentions. He wanted very sincerely the liberation of an associated Indochina. He had prepared speeches which could have real psychological impact. For unknown reasons, they were not pronounced."[9] That same day, he created the Indochinese Federation with himself at the top and Leclerc as deputy high commissioner. Colonel Cedile was commissioner of the Republic in Cochinchina, while Sainteny assumed the same function in Annam and Tonkin.

After de Gaulle left the government, d'Argenlieu systematically ignored Leon Blum's leftist cabinet. In fact, as a priest, he could not resolve to deal with the communists. But socialist minister of colonies Marius Moutet supported the

Sainteny plan to negotiate with Ho Chi Minh. Until the end, d'Argenlieu would undermine all Sainteny's efforts. He would, with the support of the colon party, favor an independent Cochinchina, separated from Tonkin and Annam.

His first search pointed toward restoration of the monarchy. Since Bao Dai had been involved with Ho's government, d'Argenlieu decided to enthrone crown prince Bao Long but he met with the stubborn opposition of his mother. Indeed, Empress Nam Phuong maintained that Bao Dai was alive and therefore remained the legitimate ruler. D'Argenlieu then founded a republic with Nguyen Van Thinh as president.

THE REPUBLIC OF COCHINCHINA

Nguyen Van Thinh was a prominent personality in the south. He was not only a well-known medical doctor, but also a great landowner. President of the Cochinchinese Democratic party, he belonged to a host of prestigious organizations. He was vice president of the Chambre d'Agriculture, director of the Office du Riz, and member of the Grand Conseil des Interets Economic and Financiers de l'Indochine.

The first Republic of Cochinchina was to be adjoined by a "consultative council" organized by Thinh himself. As it was public record that French controlled the entire process, Thinh was not able to recruit volunteers even in his own party. Thus, the Consultative Council had to be created by Federal ordinance on February 4, 1946. It consisted of 12 members out of which four were French natives and seven were French citizens. On March 26, under the presidency of attorney Beziat, the assembly elected Thinh as chief of the Provisory Government of the Republic of Cochinchina.

On May 30, upon Beziat's insistence, d'Argenlieu took it upon himself to recognize the Republic of Cochinchina as a free state, having its own government, parliament, army, and finances. These were exactly the terms of the March 6 accord between Ho and Sainteny. On June 1st, the Republic of Cochinchina was proclaimed by Dr. Nguyen Van Thinh. On July 26, the Consultative Council took the name of Cochinchina Council with a total of 42 members. Soon differences arose, with the Vietnamese members asking for more political reforms and the French unwilling to change. They went on to build a defense organism called the Union pour la Defense de l'Oeuvre Français en Indochine (UDOFI) of which Beziat and William Baze became the spokesmen within the council. A systematic opposition developed to put in check Thinh's efforts to organize a democratic government. Finally, under William Baze's direction, the council gave an ultimatum to Thinh to reshuffle his cabinet before November 15, well aware that Thinh was unable to comply. Indeed, since the beginning, Cochinchinese intellectuals had refused their collaboration, considering his government a tool of the French. Placed against the wall on November 9, Thinh asked for an audience with d'Argenlieu. The high commissioner was not available for a man he had placed in such a terrible predicament. That very night, Thinh hanged himself in his Saigon residence. He was replaced by Dr. Le Van Hoach.

Hoach was an M.D. graduate from the Hanoi University. His choice came from the fact that he belonged to the Cao Daist sect, the only party capable of keeping the Viet Minh in check. He also retained from his Cao Daist formation a unique sense of opportunism. After the March 9 coup, as police chief of Can Tho, he took the French community under his protection. In June 1946, he was paid back with the function of delegate of Can Tho province at the Consultative Council. Thereafter, he was named vice president. On November 29, 1946, he succeeded Nguyen Van Thinh as president of the Provisory Republic of Cochinchina.

The following year, Cedile was also replaced by Torel, a man favorable to Bao Dai's return. On January 14, 1947, under Torel's advice, d'Argenlieu proposed to Paris to restore monarchy. He sent envoys to Hong Kong, but Bao Dai remained aloof. Thus on February 1, 1947, without consulting Paris, by federal ordinance, d'Argenlieu recognized the government of Cochinchina as a free state within the French Union. Consequently, the admiral was "recalled for consultation."

There was no problem for Cao Daists to now support Bao Dai as they had once supported Cuong De in 1945. On March 25, 1947, Le Van Hoach declared that, legally, Bao Dai remained emperor since his abdication was not a voluntary act. As this was not to the liking of the UDOFI group, the Cochinchina Council worked to replace Hoach. To pave the way for General Xuan, Baze forced Hoach to take the officer into his government. Thus, on September 15, 1947, Xuan arrived from France to take up his post as vice president. Then a smear campaign spread, linking Hoach to past collaborations with the Japanese. Furthermore, given the havoc created by terrorist Nguyen Binh, the council preferred a military man at the top. Taking the hint, Hoach resigned on September 29, and left for Hong Kong to join Bao Dai. On December 25, 1947, Hoach founded the National Union of Vietnam (Vietnam Quoc Gia Lien Hiep) to prepare for Bao Dai to come back.

On October 1, 1947, General Xuan was elected president. Nguyen Van Xuan was a graduate of the prestigious Ecole Polytechnique. Raised in France and married to a France woman, he had trouble speaking his native tongue. He soon realized that a Republic of Cochinchina under French control had no chance of surviving and that the only way out was either to go to Ho Chi Minh or to Bao Dai. As he had once escaped death from the Viet Minh in Hanoi, he was not ready to renew the experience. Yet, he first attempted to create a national convention as a Third Force to mediate between Bao Dai and Ho Chi Minh. Well aware that UDOFI would be in minority within a national assembly, Baze publicly accused Xuan of treason. But it was too late; anyway, the Bao Dai solution had gathered enough momentum to change the situation.

As for d'Argenlieu, his Catholic instinct and the advice of the colons' party led him to denounce the Ho Chi Minh government as a communist plot, thus placing his colonial war at the level of an anticommunist crusade. But Leclerc retorted: "Anticommunism will be a useless tool in our hands as long as the problem of nationalism remained unsolved."[10] In other words, as long as France refused independence and union of the three Kys, anticommunism remained only a fallacious pretext for her imperialistic war.

The failure of Thinh's experience coupled with the recognition of the Xuan Republic led the French government to lose patience. Following a series of slaps on his wrist, d'Argenlieu resigned in March 1947. This led Leon Blum to state that had he submitted his retirement earlier, the government would have happily accepted.

GENERAL LECLERC

On October 5, 1945, General Leclerc, commander of the celebrated second DB (Second Armor Division) arrived in Saigon in the midst of a typhoon, under the hysterical acclamations of a French community soaked to the skin. Invested with the mission of pacifying Indochina, Leclerc would not let grass grow under his feet. Twenty days later, he began a swift reoccupation campaign. The fact that he had assigned My Tho and Tay Ninh as priority targets showed the French concern about both communist and Cao Daist predominance in Cochinchina. The Viet Minh were winning ground. On December 8, 1945, religious delegates, including Cao Daists, Hoa Haos, Buddhists, and Christians flocked to Hanoi to pledge support for the Viet Minh.

On February 5, 1946. Leclerc declared: "The pacification of Cochinchina is accomplished" and turned toward the North. However, as long as the Chinese remained in Tonkin, they were a dangerous obstacle to French landing. Furthermore, the landing was limited by the Red River tide table, which indicated the date of March 6 as the last favorable time for the year 1946, so went the tale. Hence, Leclerc urged for the departure of the Chinese troops.

On March 1, 1946, a Franco-Chinese agreement was signed by which the Chinese would leave Vietnam without delay but with substantial gains: France had to return to China the Shanghai concession, the Kwang Chou Wan territory, and the Chinese portion of the Yunnan railroad. Interests of Chinese residents in Indochina were protected with regard to taxation, real estate, residence, and education. Above all, a free transit zone in Haiphong was reserved for Chinese merchandise under Chinese customs control. (Later, the French would violate this specific disposition and trigger the Franco-Viet Minh war.) As a last condition of the agreement, the French must have the approval of the Ho Chi Minh government to land in Tonkin.

On March 16, 1946, Leclerc arrived in Hanoi with a first contingent of 1076 men. Probably infuriated by the Haiphong incident, he bluntly declared to the Viet Minh reception committee. "We had left. With or without your approval we would come." Hence, the welcome meeting lasted no more than five minutes. But later, at his first encounter with Ho, he succeeded in displaying the charm for which he was so much loved. All smiles, he hastily walked toward the Vietnamese leader with hands stretched out and cordially said: "Hello, Mr. President, we all agree now." Ho would later confide to his entourage that he liked Leclerc for his simplicity.

To exacerbate the situation, in April 1946, d'Argenlieu asked chief of staff General Juin to remove Leclerc and Salan, who opposed his policy of force. Before leaving Vietnam, Leclerc declared: "Negotiations and agreements are necessary. At this stage there is no question of imposing oneself by force on masses who desire evolution and change. Otherwise military operations would continue for a long time.[11] Upon his return, Leclerc had a stormy session with de Gaulle. Based on d'Argenlieu's willful reports, de Gaulle accused Leclerc of having surrendered Indochina to the Viet Minh. Outraged, Leclerc banged the table and in turn accused de Gaulle of having abandoned Syria.

Upon d'Argenlieu's departure, Leclerc was offered the succession. Although convinced that no military solution could resolve the Indochina problem, Leclerc insisted on having 500,000 troops, not to obtain a victory, but to secure a stalemate, which could bring Ho Chi Minh back to the negotiation table. But as Paris could not bear to accept his terms and conditions, a civil servant, Emile Bollaert, was appointed instead. He arrived after the Fontainebleau conference and its disastrous consequences.

THE MODUS VIVENDI (SEPTEMBER 14, 1946)

As for Ho Chi Minh, the March 6, 1946, accord began to prey on his mind, and on March 24, he met with d'Argenlieu on board the warship *Emile Bertin* in the Ha Long Bay. They discussed the choice of a place for further talks. While Ho favored some location in France, d'Argenlieu insisted on Dalat for a preliminary conference.

On April 18, 1946, Vo Nguyen Giap and his delegation met with the French at Dalat. The first disagreement occurred with the definition of the French Union: According to the Vietnamese, it must be a free association of independent states that would grant France commercial and economic privileges in exchange for technical and financial assistance. Also, independence for Giap must be the return of Cochinchina to Vietnam. The discussion became hopeless when the French not only insisted on the separation of Cochinchina but also asked for the autonomy of the Muong and Thai minorities in Tonkin. Three weeks later, on May 11, the two parties "agreed that they disagreed on key issues" and decided to meet again at Fontainebleau in France.

In May 1946, Ho Chi Minh and his men left Hanoi for Fontainebleau. At Saigon, in a public meeting with his fellow countrymates, Eurasian William Baze promised to shoot at Ho Chi Minh if on his way to Fontainebleau he ever stopped there (in Saigon).[12] Baze won notoriety in the local resistance and was now the founder of the Gardes Volontaires de la Liberation, or GVL (Liberation

Volunteers), apparently to help colonial troops disarm the Japanese but in fact to fight the Viet Minh.

While Ho Chi Minh was on the high seas, d'Argenlieu officially recognized the autonomous Republic of Cochinchina. It was a blatant rejection of the March 6 accord, but Ho Chi Minh chose to consider it a "misunderstanding" to be later clarified at Fontainebleau.

The Fontainebleau conference opened on July 29, 1946, with the news of occupation of Kontum and Pleiku by French troops. While the Vietnamese delegation, led by Pham Van Dong, insisted on the discussion of the Cochinchinese problem, the French eluded it. In fact, at that time, the Paris government was in profound disarray: The events in Vietnam had set in motion huge riots in Algeria, Tunisia, and Madagascar. Again, to make matters worse, in Saigon, d'Argenlieu was actively fanning the flames: On August 1, 1946, he called for a second Dalat conference from which the Ho Chi Minh government was conspicuously excluded.

At Fontainebleau, after a few days of incoherent exchanges, judging the parley inconsequential, Pham Van Dong and all his delegates went back to Hanoi, leaving Ho Chi Minh behind to salvage the conference. On September 14, in the middle of the night, Ho finally agreed to sign a "modus vivendi" with Marius Moutet by which the parties agreed to end acts of hostility, leaving the issue of Cochinchina pending for further negotiations. This was barely cause for celebration.

Back in Hanoi, Ho and his men were now convinced that the problem of unification could be resolved only by force. As a result, on September 13, 1946, the Nam Bo committee of resistance was created under the command of Nguyen Binh.

Nguyen Binh's real name was Nguyen Phuong Thao, a native of Haiphong. In 1929, as a member of the VNQDD, he was deported by the French to Poulo Condore for five years. In 1940, as a member of the ICP, he led many uprisings in Tonkin. In September 1945, as commander of the Viet Minh fourth zone (Mong Cai, Cam Pha, and Hon Gay), he fought against the Lu Han troops. To placate the Chinese, Ho dispatched Binh to replace Tran Van Giau in Cochinchina. For the Viet Minh, this was a good choice, for Binh was an exceptional military commander. He created such havoc among the French expeditionary corps that General Salan himself gave him a rating above Vo Nguyen Giap.

On October 13, 1946, Nguyen Binh organized the Mat Tran Quoc Gia Lien Hiep (United National Front) into which he lured other sects with offers of insignificant posts, while keeping for the Viet Minh finances, army, and police. Although Nguyen Binh had secured Hoa Hao collaboration, a love-hate relationship developed to climax with the execution of Hoa Hao leader Huynh Phu So. This was the last straw, throwing the sect into the arms of the French. In January 1948, both Hoa Haos and Cao Daists joined to support Bao Dai.

For his failure to make peace with the sects, in April 1951, Binh was removed.

Thereafter, he went on to survey in Cambodia to establish the southern operational base (Trung Uong Cuc Mien Nam) On September 29, 1951, he was killed in an accidental encounter with a Cambodian squad. Yet documents seized by the French after his death pointed to another version: Binh was executed by secret order of the Ho government. His insubordination was against party rules.

POLICE OR WAR?

The failure of the Fontainebleau conference and Nguyen Binh's activities in Cochinchina were for both French and Viet Minh subjects of bitter complaints. According to Vietnamese historians, on October 30, 1946, the French command devised plans for a showdown. To begin with, in the following November, they strongly opposed arrests of pro-French elements. They again protested when the Viet Minh seized an illegal stock of salt belonging to a French smuggler. In anticipation of an attack, on November 8, the Haiphong Tu Ve (militia) and highway defense posts were reinforced.

On November 20, 1946, in violation of the March 1, 1946, Franco-Chinese treaty, a French patrol boat seized a Chinese junk smuggling gasoline into Haiphong Harbor. The Tu Ve militia reacted by capturing the boat with its French occupants. This time General Valluy ordered Hanoi commander Colonel Debes "to give a good lesson to the Viet Minh." Here history repeated itself: Like Riviere, 60 years before, Colonel Debes delivered an ultimatum on November 23, giving the local Viet Minh two hours to evacuate Haiphong. The Tu Ve installed defensive barricades. They also killed some French soldiers who were buying food supplies at the Haiphong market. Then French paratroopers swept the Chinese quarter where the Tu Ve were entrenched. The warship *Suffren* bombed the city with high-caliber shells. Fighting spread to the nearby Cat Bi airport, Lang Son, and Nam Dinh.

When the battle ended, a large area of Haiphong had burned to ashes and Vietnamese casualties amounted to 10,000, including 6,000 dead.[13] From Paris, where he was on a visit, d'Argenlieu cabled back, praising "the determination of French troops and their sacrifices."

In Hanoi, the French occupied government buildings. Ho Chi Minh had to move out of the city with his regular troops, leaving the defense of the capital to the Tu Ve militia. On December 19, in response to a former demand for disarming the Tu Ve, Vo Nguyen Giap decided to launch a surprise attack: at 8 P.M. the Hanoi power station was blown up, giving the signal for a general offensive. Forty French were massacred, 200 were taken away as hostages. At the same time, the Viet Minh attacked Nam Dinh, Bac Ninh, and Hue. When Sainteny tried to reach Ho Chi Minh for a cease fire, his personal carrier ran over a Viet Minh mine. As for Ho, while Vo Nguyen Giap called for war, he made frantic calls to the French for peace. On December 21, having received no reply, Ho Chi Minh declared a "total war for independence."

What is called the first Indochinese war had begun. In Cochinchina, Viet Minh representative Nguyen Binh intensified attacks of French outposts and isolated villages.

On January 2, 1947, minister of colonies Marius Moutet and General Leclerc arrived in Hanoi on a factfinding mission. For some reason, Moutet failed to establish contact with Ho. He declared, however, that after assessing Viet Minh destructions in the northern capital, he doubted their resolve to negotiate. In fact, he had made up his mind when he gave his blessing to the bombing of Haiphong.

Later, analyzing the circumstances, General Salan questioned: "Since 1945, the principal actors knew that there was no strictly military solution to the Indochinese problem. Our troops made police or war to reestablish peace. But what peace?"[14]

VIET MINH MILITARY DOCTRINE

The French Army was fighting under the dictates of politicians. According to Salan, "the decision to undertake or not undertake such and such military campaign was essentially a political act."[15] The problem was that these political lines were uncertain for quite a long time.

The Vietnamese revolutionaries' unwavering policy stemmed from their obsession for independence. Thus, for Vo Nguyen Giap, the army came from the people, and they had to fight for a war prosecuted by the people: "People war, people army." It consisted of mobilizing all forces available in the nation, without distinction of age or sex, as long as one could launch a grenade, plant a mine, or use a rifle.

To begin with, villagers aged 18 to 55 were formed as local militia and made, in turn, responsible for the military training of peasants to conduct limited guerrilla warfare. They also served as tactical reserves for the regional and regular troops, or they provided manpower for supply columns on the battlefield. They were, in a sense, the replica of peasant soldiers during the 18th century march to the South. The entire population was mobilized: Some elderly and children served as couriers or watchguards, while others were dispatched for mining operations. Women excelled in intelligence gathering or took full part in combat units.

Above this level, there were the regional troops, which posessed a structure similar to the regular army but remained specialized in regional guerilla operations. They helped the regulars in preliminary exploration of the terrain, as well as replacing casualties during battles.

At the top of the organization, the regular army received orders directly from the Central Government. At the outset, they were trained in mobile maneuvers, but from 1949, as an increase in Chinese aid allowed Giap to build units up to the level of battalions and even regiments, the regional forces were incorporated to carry conventional warfare and general offensives. In 1951, a series of debacles at the hands of de Lattre forced Giap to review his strategy and, since then, the regulars troops would carry both guerrillas and conventional warfare.

EMILE BOLLAERT

Bollaert was a high-ranking civil servant. In October 1944, as a de Gaulle representative, he was deported to Germany. After the liberation of France, he was appointed prefect of the Rhone department and later commissioner of the Republic at Strasbourg. His mission in Indochina was scheduled for only six months and consisted of the integration of the Associated States into the French Union.

Bollaert arrived in Saigon on April 1, 1947, with a major preoccupation: to find "the partners" ready to negotiate on the basis of his agenda. He soon found out that, although all parties had not rejected the notion of French Union, the idea was forced upon them, since none had been consulted on the matter. This could hardly grant any legitimacy to future accord. Furthermore, whether the interlocutor represented the people or not was not considered by d'Argenlieu so far.

By contrast with his predecessor, Bollaert chose to be forthright. "We have legitimate interests in Indochina. We had a sowed a lot, and we do not want to be deprived of the harvest."[16]

First of all, on May 12, 1947, he dispatched Paul Mus to meet with Ho Chi Minh. After the December 19 incident, Ho took refuge at Ha Dong, only 10 kilometers from Hanoi. It was not an easy mission, for the French offer was a simple ultimatum for Ho to turn over his weapons, to cease attacks against French troops, to free hostages, and to deliver deserters. Although he held the professor in very high esteem, Ho rejected the French proposals. Later, Mus candidly confessed that failure was inevitable for Ho would be a fool if he had accepted Bollaert's demand.

On May 15, 1947, to destroy any illusion Ho Chi Minh might have nurtured, Bollaert declared in Hanoi: "Let me be clear: France will remain in Indochina and Indochina in the French Union."

Taking a deep look at d'Argenlieu's brainchild, the Republic of Cochinchina, Bollaert was not enthusiastic: they totally lacked popular support. Thus, after the failure of the Mus mission, Bollaert had no other choice than to approach the ex-emperor. He began to dispatch envoys who came back with empty hands, Bao Dai claiming a lack of popular mandate. Hence, on May 17, Bollaert appealed to all parties.

The Bao Dai Solution: A Myth.

In response to Bollaert's call, on May 19, Dr. Truong Dinh Tri, ex-minister of Ho Chi Minh's government during the period 1945–46, declared he accepted unity and independence within the French Union and demanded the formation of a central government. VNQDD Tran Van Tuy followed suit, calling for the return of Bao Dai.

On September 9, 1947, 24 delegates from the three Kys, including high mandarins like Viceroy Nguyen Van Sam, Interior Minister Ngo Dinh Diem, and provincial Judge Dinh Xuan Quang came to join Bao Dai. Later Cao Daist Tran Quang Vinh, Catholic Tran Van Ly, VNQDD Truong Dinh Tri, Dong Minh Hoi Nguyen Hai Than, Dai Viet Nguyen Tuong Tam, social democrat Phan Quang Dan, and United National Fronts (Mat Tran Quoc Gia Thong Nhut) Tran Van Tuyen joined the club. There is no doubt that such a congregation formed an appreciable political force to be reckoned with.

On September 10 in Ha Dong, Bollaert accepted a Vietnam independent within a French Union. In response, on September 14, a demonstration in Saigon demanded the return of Bao Dai. That day, the United National Front dispatched Cao Daist Le Van Hoach as its representative in Hong Kong. At the same time, the Cochinchinese Front (Mat Tran Nam Ky), founded by well-known Saigon personalities Nguyen Tan Cuong, Tran Van Ty, and Nguyen Hoa Hiep, agreed on a Bao Dai platform for the reunification of the three Kys. With the rally of these new parties and the presence of the two ex-presidents of Cochinchina, Le Van Hoach and Nguyen Van Xuan, the "Bao Dai solution" emerged as the only alternative to a Viet Minh bid.

On September 19, Bao Dai declared that he accepted the call of the people and was ready to negotiate with the French either in Hong Kong or in Indochina. Yet, he was still wavering, for the question of Cochinchina remained an overwhelming obstacle to further negotiations.

On October 7, 1947, the French army began a huge offensive against the Viet Minh "to facilitate negotiations with Bao Dai." On October 9, 1947, to give more impetus to the Bao Dai solution, Nguyen Van Sam and Truong Dinh Tri launched the Allied National Front (Mat Tran Quoc Gia Lien Hiep) to support a Constitutional monarchy. Cao Daist Superior Pham Cong Tac also gave his agreement to the Allied National Front agenda. It seemed that Sam and Tri were considered dangerous enough to be summarily executed on October 10 by Viet Minh squads. As for Pham Cong Tac, he remained unharmed. Perhaps his opportunistic policy backed by a Cao Daist army was a sufficient deterrent.

Finally, on September 18, 1947, Bao Dai proclaimed he accepted the mission to obtain unity and independence for Vietnam. Hence, Bollaert sent Major Raynaud, a personal friend of the emperor, to ask for a rendezvous.

On December 6, 1947, Bao Dai flew to meet Bollaert in the Bay of Ha Long. The discussions lasted for two days. At the end, after having Bollaert's assurance that it would not engage him in any way, Bao Dai prudently placed his initials on a protocol: "France recognizes the independence of Vietnam as an Associated State within the French Union. Vietnam is now free to realize its unity."

Satisfied, Bao Dai flew back to Hong Kong. The protocol was a disaster. Ngo Dinh Diem adamantly rejected the text as ambiguous and insufficient. Prince Buu Hoi, the emperor's cousin, seriously declared "in the name of the imperial family," that the French should instead deal with Ho Chi Minh. To add insult to injury, Buu Hoi's father, Prince Ung Uy, a great-grandson of Emperor Ming Mang and formerly head of the imperial family council, went to stay with Ho

Chi Minh in the North. Why he had waited so long to take this step could only be explained by the fact that the Viet Minh, which were all along acting behind the scenes, had succeeded in infiltrating the imperial circles as well as the administration itself.

To get off the hook, Bao Dai rationalized that there was no harm done since he was acting as a private citizen on his own behalf. But Bollaert would cling to the document as a basis for further negotiations.

Profoundly hurt, Bao Dai went to seek refuge in Geneva. There he informed Bollaert that the protocol was only a tool for further negotiations, which could not take place until a Vietnamese government was formed. Bollaert reacted typically: He sent SFIO Louis Caput to deal with the Viet Minh in Hong Kong. Caput failed to produce any significant results, but it was intended to be a warning for Bao Dai to refrain from building more stakes.

On April 24, Nguyen Van Xuan, Tran Van Huu, and Le Van Hoach were appointed by Bao Dai to create a Central Government. This decision showed Bao Dai's determination to deal with the Cochinchinese since they were mainly interested in the problem of reunification. On May 27, Xuan presented his cabinet with an oath of allegiance. "We solemnly declare that we shall loyally follow Your Majesty's instructions and directives." On May 31, Bao Dai explained that the new government was only a step in negotiating with France and could become official only when France recognized a Vietnamese government for which the emperor would negotiate. The message was clear enough for Bollaert to ask Paris to comply. Hence, the French government "took note" of the constitution of the new government but any treaty would have to be signed not only by Premier Xuan but also by Bao Dai.

On June 5, on board the warship *Duguay Trouin*, the so-called Ha Long Agreement was signed between General Xuan and Bollaert and countersigned by Bao Dai. In fact, it was the same protocol once rejected by Bao Dai's entourage. That night, the emperor declared: "I leave definitively Hong Kong. For me as well as for Vietnam, it is now the past." And he flew to France.

Anyway, as the word independence was clearly spelled out, optimist observers applauded Bao Dai for "having during two years of negotiations obtained what Ho Chi Minh was not able to acquire during four years of war." Nevertheless, in France, opposition arose from all sides. To begin with, de Gaulle typically declared: "Pretty soon we will just keep the right to visit the Angkor ruins."[17] As for Coste Floret, the minister of colonies, he opened another debate by stating that the "three regions Thai, Annam, and Tonkin" could be united but Cochinchina would remain French territory. Yet, premier Jean Marie ratified the Ha Long accord, not only by political conviction but also to support fellow radical Bollaert.

The problem with the French was that they were unable to detect the similarity of goals between North and South: Both wanted unity and independence. But the colonial administration spent most of its time pitting Bao Dai against Ho, and by so doing, they underestimated Bao Dai's political forte. Finally, on the one hand, new French Premier Schuman declared that the status of Cochinchina could only be changed by a vote of the French National Assembly and on the other, Bollaert imprudently proclaimed that France would act "as the arbiter between the different governments of the three Kys," Bao Dai and Ho Chi Minh no longer doubted French opposition to Vietnam unity. Both reacted quite differently. Ho Chi Minh ordered Nguyen Binh to step up his attacks on the French in Cochinchina. As for Bao Dai, he publicly denounced Xuan's agreement, claiming that without the union of the three Kys, independence only had a hollow ring. On August 25, Bao Dai informed Bollaert that he would not go back to Vietnam until he had a sufficient guarantee in regard to unity and independence.

By the end of 1948, China increased aid to Ho Chi Minh. In 1949, when the communist victory in China confirmed the fears of the rightists, France decided to jettison her political cargo. As for Bollaert, faced with these mounting problems, he would not extend his stay and left Saigon on November 10, 1948, replaced by Leon Pignon.

Pignon had been a man of d'Argenlieu and would rather follow his steps for an independent Cochinchina. But the presence of Chinese communist troops at the Tonkin border led him to realize that, unsolved, the Vietnamese problem could be a good excuse for China to interfere. Thus, on March 8, 1949, President Vincent Auriol exchanged letters with the emperor, which would later be called the Elysees agreement. This time France agreed to a procedure to achieve unity and independence for Vietnam. Yet keeping under French control the Montagnard tribes in the South and the Thai minorities in the North could hardly be seen as a step toward unification and independence. If in view of a possible conflict with China the choice of the Thai region as a buffer zone was strategically justified, nothing explained the exclusion of the Montagnard tribes from Vietnamese communities. Under these conditions, it was difficult for Bao Dai to return to Vietnam.

BAO DAI RETURNS

Bao Dai's stubborness forced France to create on March 14, 1949, the Territorial Assembly of Cochinchina, composed of 16 French and 48 Viet, to find a procedure for reunification. On April 24, the French National Assembly accepted the unification of the three Kys. The very next day Bao Dai flew back to Vietnam.

On June 4, 1949, France officially recognized the state of Vietnam under Chief of State (Quoc Truong) Bao Dai. The United States and Great Britain followed suit in 1950. On May 1, President Truman approved military aid of $15 million to the French. A U.S. economic mission would stay in Saigon.

But Bao Dai was too shrewd to take France's word at face value. Indeed, upon his arrival in Saigon, Bao Dai showed little surprise when the French refused to turn over the Norodom Palace, arguing it was not the symbol of

Vietnam sovereignty, but that of entire Indochina. Thus, Bao Dai quietly settled in his Dalat mountain resort, which, after all, would keep him far away from French pressure and close enough to his hunting passion.

On January 1, 1950, Cao Daist bishop Nguyen Phan Long became prime minister. Owner of the influential *Echo Annamite* newspaper, Long was "highly literate, with a touch of something like genius . . . For years he savaged the colonialists in his newspaper, spoiling their breakfast."[18]

His first move was to offer peace to Nguyen Binh, who responded by threatening to destroy all French and their collaborators. Then to show that he really meant business, in broad daylight, he sent his killers to gun down Marcel Bazin, the redoubtable chief of French security.

In a second move, Nguyen Phan Long insisted on having the U.S. military and economic aid delivered directly to the Vietnamese government. He affirmed that with $146 million, he could defeat Ho Chi Minh in six months.[19] The French were outraged. And since the Viet Minh continued to spread havoc in the entire south, they had a good reason to ask for Long's removal.

On May 6, 1950, Nguyen Phan Long was replaced by French citizen Tran Van Huu, a debonair agronomist. It is difficult to explain Huu's role except he had been playing backstage politics and had held the key post as minister of finances in the Hoach and Xuan governments. Yet he made a major contribution by organizing, in June 1950, the Pau Conference in the southwest of France.

The purpose of the meeting was to materialize the Elysees agreement by building a common structure for the Indochinese Union. Vietnam was exclusively represented by premier Tran Van Huu and the absence of the Viet Minh was certainly a cause of satisfaction for Bao Dai. But what Huu wanted was the transfer of powers first. He declared that it was not necessary that young men die so that a French engineer could be director of the port of Saigon. Many people were dying because Vietnam was not given independence. Minister of Colonies Letourneau assured the delegation that France would not attempt to reestablish control over the states. In fact, what France wanted now was the control of foreign trade and wealth distribution between the states. Everyone agreed that no modification of the parity between Indochinese and French currency[20] could take a place without consultation between the parties. We shall see later that France would bring the franc down from 17 to 10 in a blatant violation of the agreement and that the U.S. aid to Vietnam had to proceed through French channels.

After the passing of de lattre in January 1952, Minister Letourneau took over as high commissioner while retaining his ministerial function. This double title—minister and commissioner—gave him unlimited power, which he used to corrupt the entire system. He helped Bao Dai cast off his national ambitions for personal advantages. Indeed, Bao Dai was no longer the Hong Kong poor devil. His pension incidentally increased with each new cabinet. By 1950, his annuity amounted to 7 million piastres (119 million francs) per month; under Nguyen Phan Long, he received $200,000 per month; under Tran Van Huu $350,000.

His association with Bay Vien, chief of the Binh Xuyen gang, who concurrently ran the Grand Monde casinos, the huge Binh Khang prostitution park, and the Saigon city police, enabled him to collect a monthly 1.2 million piastres. He also pocketed from Bay Vien 40 million piastres for the control of the Saigon police. This led some Western observers to declare that Bay Vien was a unique politician to concurrently run police administration and con game management in the history of Vietnam. As for General Xuan, after one year as president of the Central Government, he had 10,600,000 piastres in his BIC account.[21] In 1952, as rumors circulated around cabinet turnover, U.S. Ambassador Heath, after some investigation, reported to his government. All ended up with a parliamentarian inquiry from the French government and the subsequent recall of Letourneau.

On June 2, 1952, Tran Van Huu was replaced by the Doc Phu Su Nguyen Van Tam. Tam was extremely unpopular because during his tenure as a province chief, he had carried out savage repressions against Cochinchinese rebels. In the process, he earned the title of "Tiger of Cai Lay." Thus, because of Tam, Bao Dai began to lose support among the southern people who were, of course, not aware of his financial deeds.

Tam's son Nguyen Van Hinh was promoted to chief of staff of the new Vietnamese army. It was easy, for he was a lieutenant colonel in the French Air Force. But Bao Dai had not been so lucky in his staff selection. At the outset de Lattre had opposed the nomination of ex-Tonkin governor Nguyen Huu Tri as minister of defense and exgovernor of Central Vietnam Phan Van Giao as Chief of staff, for none of them had any military background. Air force and navy were nonexistent. The only naval officer was the captain of Bao Dai's yacht, the *Huong Giang*, and he was holding a merchant marine license.

After de Lattre's death, there were only 36 infantry battalions, one of them being a gift from witty Cao Daist Pham Cong Tac. To offset that calculated loss, Tac let his chief of staff, Trinh Minh The, build up in the Rung Trau (Tay Ninh), a powerful maquis with 2,000 partisans.

In 1953, the problem of independence was still lingering on the Vietnamese political agenda. To explain the delay, on July 3, 1953, Premier Joseph Laniel declared that it was necessary to "perfect" the independence and the sovereignty of the associated states. To which the future president François Mitterrand retorted: "We have granted total independence to Vietnam 18 times since 1949. It is time to do so once more but for good," for the Bao Dai solution was losing steam.

"Perfecting independence" was an excuse for dilatory tactics, advised by de Gaullle. Indeed, in a press conference on November 17, 1948, he had declared: "The correct rule to observe presently in Indochina is to avoid taking action. We must know how to gain time."

On January 11, 1954, abstention of prominent politicians led Bao Dai to name his own cousin Prince Buu Loc prime minister. Buu Loc lasted only six months. On March 3, he led a delegation to Paris for the purpose of obtaining a "real independence." But it was too late. Given the Dien Bien Phu situation, he would not come back. As for Bao Dai, under the same pretext, he flew to France on April 10.

REALITIES OF WAR

From 1946 to 1954, the years of Dien Bien Phu, the French military command in Indochina changed hands almost every year as a result of political games in Paris. In 1949, a series of scandals erupted that discredited the Fourth Republic and eventually brought France to her knees. After the traffic of piastres was denounced by the two writers Arthur Laurent and Jacques Despuech as an immense financial scheme of the Banque de l'Indochine, the "affaire des Generaux" dealt a fatal blow to French prosecution of the war. Although the authors were later convicted of libel, the exchange was later corrected to 10 francs, and two generals were sent into retirement.

The Banque de l'Indochine

Created in 1875 in France, 13 years after the treaty of 1862, the Banque de l'Indochine (BIC), well known around the world as the "French Bank," was gratuitously granted the lucrative privilege of currency emission and, thus, became the brain trust of the colonial machinery. It had among its shareholders celebrities in the world of finance (Rothchild and Reynolds), politics (Boncour, Baudoin, and Giscard d'Estaing), and academics (François Mauriac) to cite a few. At the outset, the BIC, in 1922, by authorization of Indochina's interim Governor General Baudoin, who was also a BIC director, the emission volume reached 15 times the cash on hand.

Baudoin was on the board of more than ten important organizations, including the Banque de l'Indochine, Plantation d'heveas de l'Indochine, Societe de Draggages et de Travaux Publics, and Air France, to cite a few. As Petain's minister of foreign affairs, he was a personal friend of Mussolini and the Mikado. He also obtained the post of governor general in Indochina for Admiral Decoux, his protégé. This gives us some insight into how, during World War II, the Japanese and French were able to cohabit in Indochina. But more than Baudoin or anyone else, Jean Laurent led the BIC to financial prominence.

Jean Laurent

Laurent[22] was the epitome of the unique breed of "inspecteurs des finances" who included, with the notorious Réné Bousquet, chief of the pro-German Laval's police, Andre Diethelm, de Gaulle's war minister, and, of course, Paul Baudoin, Petain's minister of foreign affairs.

After the "Speciale Financiere" scandal when he was on the BIC board, he was temporarily transferred to Saigon "pour se faire oublier."

During World War II, instead of following de Gaulle abroad, Laurent decided to stay behind to do business with Germany. After the liberation of Paris, following his business philosophy, he imprudently ventured into General Bradley's headquarters. Instead of accepting his offer of cooperation, Bradley sent him to the firing squad, and if it were not for the intervention of a British Intelligence service agent, Arnoux,[23] Laurent's life would have ended there.

On November 23, 1944, Laurent was arrested again, this time by the French security. He was released after an intervention of Defense Minister Andre Diethelm.

The following year, 1945, Laurent took over Paul Baudoin's post as director general of the BIC in Indochina. On his way to Saigon, he met with d'Argenlieu and Sainteny in Calcutta to "discuss the future of Indochina." Later, in Hanoi, his refusal to "advance" Chinese occupation outlay led General Lu Han to put him behind bars. In fact, the Chinese were not the first to act against the Bank. After the March 9 coup, the Japanese robbed a BIC director of his personal gold stock.

These vicissitudes led Laurent to chose a "geographical repartition of risks." As a result, the Bank would control some 30 international affiliates and more than 100 industrial complexes, which included 28 mining industries from wolfram to tin, gold, and phosphate and 20 agricultural exploitations (rubber, rice, tea, coffee, and sugar). The BIC also possessed the Yunnan and Djibouti railroads.

At the same time, allegedly to step up economic exchange between France and Indochina, Laurent concocted with Indochina Director of Finances André Diethelm the boldest scheme in Franco-Indochinese economic history: the incredible conversion rate of "la piastre á 17 francs," which allowed a huge traffic that ultimately contributed to French demise.

The Traffic of Piastres

Since 1930, the piastre was the Indochinese monetary unit. By a decree of May 31, it was convertible to 0.655 kilograms of 900/1,000 fine gold, the equivalent of 10 French francs. The privilege of emission was given "free" to the BIC.

On December 25, 1945, on advice from the BIC, the French government fixed the Vietnam piastre at the artificial rate of 17 French francs. At that time, the real value of the piastre was between 7.00 and 8.50 francs, while its purchasing power was situated between 5 and 10 francs.[24] This was the origin of a worldwide traffic of piastres promoted by the BIC. Since there was no jurisdiction over piastre transfers, this traffic was not illegal. High Commissioner Leon Pignon himself had declared that "there was no misdemeanor in the matter of piastres transfers."

The process was organized at three levels. At the bottom, the government post offices handled individual transfers limited to 5,000 francs per month. Yet the daily transaction reached 1.2 million piastres, entailing a daily loss of 8.4 million francs to the French treasury.

At the second level, an Office of Changes (OIC), created with a staff on BIC payroll, proceeded to "repatriate" only windfall incomes, such as sales of properties, war damages payments, retirement benefits, year-end bonuses, or savings. But the true role of OIC related to "political transfers" made by government officials or political parties. In 1949, William Baze sent to the personal account of General de Gaulle the proceeds of RPF stamp sales.[25] As for the Vietnamese government, OIC records showed that in 1949, Emperor Bao Dai and the Empress had transferred 176.5 million francs. In 1951, Bao Dai transferred $2.3 million to France and Geneva, while Madame Didelot, the empress's sister, transmitted 44.7 million francs. Other administrations followed suit: the central government of General Nguyen Van Xuan with 76 million and the governor of South Annam, 6.7 million. These examples show why many politicians supported the concept of "separatism," which gave them such financial advantages. The following year, 1952, Bao Dai had his new prime minister, Nguyen Van Tam, transfer $6 million. Personally, he had transferred 2,350,000 to France and Switzerland. He also invested in real estate in France and Morocco.

On the top, the "operations de haute voltige," or transcendental speculations, were the unique domain of the banks themselves. It involved not only the exchange rate but also all specialities of the banking system: A BIC employee later testified at a hearing of the French National Assembly that "everything is fake, everything is false: the figures, the balance sheet, the capital, the benefits, the bookkeeping."[26]

According to author Arthur Laurent who, as a former associate, had an ax to grind with BIC, the bank was found behind a typical import-export case. A routine complaint about the bad quality of a 500,000 piastre pepper cargo led the Marseilles police to discover that it was a bogus operation. There was no trace of any exporter or importer, but the French government lost 8,500 million francs in reimbursing BIC for the related transfer.

In the commercial sector, those who had an account with "OIC authorized banks" (read BIC and affiliates), benefited twice a year from an automatic transfer of 50,000 piastres. Thus, with accounts in different BIC branches, these individuals were able to make a few million francs profit each year.

There was no record on the acquisitions of foreign firms by BIC. Hence, Arthur Laurent concluded that the BIC had paid these transactions with some concealed funds. Indeed, the Paris police found a quantity of gold bars, U.S. dollars, and jewels in the apartment of two BIC directors, Rolloy and De Flers.

The BIC did not even spare the French government. Since the Great Depression, the state owned 20 percent of BIC capital with one-third of the board of directors seats[27] and Laurent found this cohabitation too close for comfort. On July 10, 1947, he bought back the 60,000 government shares well below their market value. By a single entry in the books, he realized a benefit of 260 million francs on the back of the French republic. It was not to be the last case.

In 1953, Director Jean Laurent had to relinquish the emission rights to the newly created Indochinese Institute of Emission. The BIC was then reimbursed 102 billion francs for the sale of the emission building and equipment plus a stock of currency, which totaled 60 billion francs.[28] And as the new Institute was not ready to operate yet, the BIC kept its emission privileges for three more years.

Because gold and U.S. or Hong Kong dollars cost less abroad than in Vietnam,[29] the entire world rushed to bring them into Saigon for further conversion into francs. Among these speculators was High Commissioner Bollaert's daughter who stuffed diplomatic valises with gold bars, jewelery, and all sorts of foreign currency. Finally, a stroke of fate led a new customs recruit to discover her trade.[30]

If these individual operations endangered the economy of France, international manipulations would prove fatal to her security, for the Viet Minh had no problems collecting piastres either by taxation or by sales of local produces from zones under their control. These proceeds were used by their procurement missions in Hong Kong, Macao, Siam, the Philippines, Malaysia, and, of course, China. Thus, even before the 1949 communist victory in China, the Viet Minh were able to organize a few battalions.

On May 11, 1953, France made the fateful decision to bring the rate of exchange to a more reasonable level by lowering it from 17 francs to 10 francs. Although this move was to suppress the staggering traffic that was bleeding France to death, it was nevertheless a political error for it was against the Pau treaty by which France had promised to refrain from any unilateral action with regard to the Indochinese currency conversion. Moreover, coming after the diversion of the BIC assets to other countries, it appeared as an act of premeditation against the Associated States.

Actually, the government began to look into the problem after the publication of Jacques Despuech's book *Le Trafic de Piastres*. Despuech was an agent of the BTLC (Bureau Technique de Liaison et Coordination)—another French intelligence service. The ensuing general commotion had not yet settled when another book by Arthur Laurent, an exassociate of the BIC, appeared with the title *La Banque de l'Indochine et la Piastre*. Hence, if this decision had triggered protest from associated states, it had a positively deleterious effect on the safe pursuit of the war.

According to the authors, 1947 records showed that the Expeditionary Corps had transferred a total amount higher than its entire pay and that a North African soldier could save enough to buy a farm and to marry when he returned home. Thus, Lancaster affirmed that devaluation of the piastre "aroused the resentment of the Expeditionary Corps, whose rate of pay was adversely affected."[31] To be fair, if some elements of the French expedition were interested in such a profit as professional soldiers, a notable proportion were rather preoccupied cleaning up a record tarnished by two consecutive defeats: World War II and the March 9 Japanese coup. Nevertheless, an event of paramount importance occurred to raise more doubt about military interest in the problem of the piastre.

"Affaire des Generaux"

What was called the "affaire des generaux" erupted after the Viet Minh broadcast a report authored by Chief of Staff Revers after his tour of inspection in Indochina. In this report, Revers outlined the poor prospect of the Bao Dai solution, the weakness of French defense in Tonkin, and advised the abandonment of some outposts including Dong Khe and Cao Bang, two vital positions on the Chinese border.

It all began in September 1949 when in a crowded Parisian bus, a Vietnamese passenger stepped on the toes of a French soldier recently returned from Vietnam. Following an insignificant verbal exchange, the two parties were taken not to a police station but to a railway terminal where they were questioned by SDECE agents. In the process, a copy of Revers's report was found inside the Vietnamese's brief case. What came out of the interrogation was that he had received this report from a man named Hoang Van Co. Further search of Van Co's apartment produced 38 more copies.

Van Co was not known as a Viet Minh sympathizer; on the contrary, he belonged to the entourage of General Xuan and Emperor Bao Dai. Things became worse when Van Co confessed to having obtained the document from Peyre, an agent of the SDECE,[32] who had accompanied General Mast in a recent visit to Saigon. There, with the help of Van Vi, president of the Credit Commercial Bank (a subsidiary of the BIC), both tried to establish contact with the Viet Minh.[33]

Mast's activities in Saigon suggested the existence of a French government plan regarding future administrative changes: Indeed, he had been a resident general in Tunisia and was now scheduled to replace Governor General Pignon in Indochina.

As for Peyre, he had no problem confirming that, by order of General Mast, he had delivered a copy of the Revers report to Van Co. He had also remitted to Mast and Revers 1 million francs. The funds came from a 5 million franc loan made by Van Vi to Van Co.

Notwithstanding the sensitive character of Revers's report, the French government officially declared that the document had no bearing on national security. Yet, the two generals were sacked, while Peyre was put behind bars at Fresne prison. He was freed by the SDECE under the pretext that he had to resume a secret mission. Thus, Peyre disappeared and some time later was found living comfortably in Brazil with $80,000 of unknown origin.

The following year, 1950, with the Chinese communist victory, Revers's prediction became a tragic reality. While Chiang Kai-shek sought refuge in Taiwan, in the process killing some 50,000 natives who opposed the Chinese presence,

Kuo Ming Tang General Pai Chung Hsi, hunted by his communist counterpart the legendary Lin Piao, crossed the Tonkin border with 30,000 Kwang Si troops. On December 11, 1949, General Lin Piao demanded that the French disarm the Nationalist refugees, otherwise he would come and do it himself.

Commander in Chief General Carpentier decided to fight both Lin Piao and Pai Chung Hsi. For this purpose, he would dispatch one single company to reinforce his border outposts.[34] Not long afterward, tragedy broke out on the Route coloniale No. 4, marking the end of French control of Tonkin.

RC4: Street without Hope

Ho Chi Minh had all along denied military help from China, but Chinese sources revealed that he had led a Vietnamese delegation to sign an agreement on January 18, 1950, providing the Viet Minh with 150,000 Japanese rifles and 10,000 American carbines and ammunition. That same year, five divisions—the 304th, 308th, 312th, 316th, and 320th, were formed in the Yunnan-Kwang Si provinces. Before the fall offensive, the Viet Minh army had a combined force of 250,000 regular and guerrillas troops with 30 pieces of heavy artillery, 140 mortars, 230 machine guns, and 100,000 rifles.[35]

After testing the ground in late 1949 against Cao Bang, Dong Khe, and That Khe, 2,000 Viets took Dong Khe on May 25, 1950. It was reoccupied by the French three days later. On September 16, 1950, Dong Khe was again shelled by Viet Minh artillery.

This increased North Vietnamese activity caused much concern to the French high command over the defense of Tonkin outposts. A consensus was reached over the abandonment of Cao Bang as recommended by Revers's report, of which the North Vietnamese possessed many copies.

Then a curious situation developed: If they agreed on the withdrawal principle, Carpentier, the commander in chief, and Alessandri, the Tonkin commander, disagreed on the strategy. In spite of the fact that the limestone mountains and their treacherous gorges were infested by overwhelming Viet Minh forces, Carpentier decided to operate a surprise withdrawal through the RC4, capitalizing on total secrecy and swift maneuver. Alessandri questioned: "Why not use aviation to move the Cao Bang garrison to Lang Son?" And Carpentier replied: "Because it is against the tradition of the French army. No one leaves the battlefield without a baroud d'honneur." As Alessandri still disagreed, insisting on a safer retreat through RC3, which led to the South, far from the reach of Giap troops, both submitted their case in France, and Carpentier won government approval. Back to Hanoi as Alessandri stubbornly opposed, Carpentier barked: "I am the Commander in Chief. I give the orders. You just obey."

Thus, on October 3, 1950, the 4,000 garrison, under Foreign Legion Colonel Charton, left Cao Bang after evacuating by air 3,000 inhabitants. The city power plant was demolished and 300 water buffalo were gunned down to deprive the

Viets of meat supply. But the apocalyptic explosion of 150 tons of munitions became a public festivity for the Viet Minh who were quietly watching. And yet it was supposed to be a secret operation. Then, Charton's column moved eastward on the RC4 in order to meet with Lepage's rescue column at Nam Nang, a small locality (Map 3).

From That Khe, on the RC4, in accordance with Carpentier's orders, Artillery Colonel Lepage moved westward with 2,000 men to secure Dong Khe. Since Carpentier upheld the utmost secrecy, Lepage was not even aware that his true mission was to "collect" Charton's column at Nam Nang and to go back with it to Lang Son. He learned it later in the midst of a North Vietnamese offensive. But it was too late. It was he who called Charton to his rescue.

As anticipated by Alessandri, the fly by the RC4 was a disaster. The Viet Minh were waiting for them on their way out of the cities. Soon, both French columns under Viet pressure found themselves lost in the jungles. It became a hide-and-seek party in a darkness exacerbated by the lack of guides or precise maps on the French side. The Quang Liet trail, by which Charton had planned to escape to Dong Khe, disappeared under dense vegetation. Poor visibility forced the French troops to progress hand in hand, to be destroyed one after the other by an enemy who was close enough to snatch in the dark a submachine gun from the hands of a French soldier.

The tragedy ended 40 days later. Besides the capture of the two colonels, Charton and Lepage, the French had "suffered their greatest colonial defeat since Montcalm had died at Quebec. They had lost 6,000 troops, 13 artillery pieces and 125 mortars, 450 trucks and three armored platoons, 940 machine guns, 1,200 submachine guns, and more than 8,000 rifles. Their abandoned stocks alone sufficed for the equipment of a whole additional Viet Minh division."[36] The loss of the RC4 opened the entire delta to Giap troops.

Evacuation of Lang Son

At Lang Son, the last major outpost, troop demoralization was such that upon a rumor of Viet Minh presence at the gates of the town, the French commander ordered immediate evacuation on October 18, 1950. In fact, Giap's troops were still at Na Chan 30 miles away. He took a few more weeks before entering an empty Lang Son.

This was not the first time that Lang Son was abandoned in panic. Fifty years before, fearing a Chinese offensive, Colonel Herbinger ordered total evacuation and had all arms and munitions thrown into the river. Preferring life to wealth, he even dumped the regimental cash.

This time at Lang Son, to avoid repetition of Cao Bang's blaring withdrawal, no destruction was ordered. Yet Carpentier would say later that a time device had been set to explode after the retreat. But no explosion occurred, the garrison remained intact, and the supplies and munitions were used by Giap's troops for an entire year.

The only bright note was, according to Air Force General Chassin, a night air raid over Cao Bang on 24 October, which surprised the Viet Minh in the midst of their victory celebration. But that attack had more to do with petty vengeance than military strategy.

By January 1, 1951, the French had lost control of all of North Vietnam.[37] After the successive abandonment of Cao Bang, Lang Son, Dong Khe, That Khe, and Thai Nguyen, two more posts, Hoa Binh and Lao Kay, fell into Giap's hands. In retrospect, the RC4 drama was the harbinger of Dien Bien Phu's ultimate defeat.

In a last ditch effort, on December 7, 1950, the French government appointed General de Lattre de Tassigny as Indochina's high commissioner with full civil and military powers. For almost one year he was able to turn the tide in favor of the French, but his premature death put an end to any hope for an honorable end.

De Lattre de Tassigny

Hero of World War II, de Lattre was a controversial figure. In December 1946, when the Allied forces arrived at a point some 20 kilometers from the capital of Alsace-Lorraine Colmar, de Lattre's First Army was ordered to join Leclerc's division for a common offensive, which would only take three days. But de Lattre declared that since Leclerc alone had liberated both Paris and Strasbourg, it was now his first Army's turn to have its share of glory. Thus, against the orders of his superior U.S. General Devers, de Lattre alone moved his troops through the Vosges massifs. After two months of bloody battles, costing him almost his entire army, de Lattre finally entered Colmar in triumph. An incensed Eisenhower ordered his removal, but de Gaulle and Juin opposed.[38]

De Lattre arrived in Saigon on December 17, 1950, preceded by his reputation as the "roi Jean," given his love for military decorum. Upon his first review of his troops, he fired many officers just for their shabby appearance. "Le bateau! Le bateau!" he shouted. Because at that time French families were sailing back to France to seek refuge, to stop the mounting panic, de Lattre interdicted boarding on departing ships. To set an example, he refused to recall to Hanoi his only son Bernard, who was in command of an isolated outpost. The young lieutenant would later succumb under a Viet assault.

De Lattre fully realized that his soldiers were fighting to preserve civilian interests. Thus, he declared bluntly that businessmen should share the burden of the war with his own soldiers. For the "Noel des combattants," he forced all French firms to send in fat checks and big presents. French ladies were invited to give their leisure time to military clinics while their husbands picked up the tab for the improvements of military hospitals. Indeed, morale was so low that this arm-twisting technique, instead of triggering protest, was unanimously greeted as a sign of superior leadership.

To his soldiers de Lattre repeated: "No matter what, you will be commanded."[39] Calling young Vietnamese to participate in the war, he said: "Be men. If you are communists, go and join the Viet Minh, they are fighting well for a bad cause."

In January 1951, a few days after de Lattre's arrival in Tonkin, an over-confident Vo Nguyen Giap attacked Vinh Yen and, like Nguyen Hue 150 years before, he promised his troops they would celebrate the 1951 Tet in Hanoi. He lost 6,000 men and withdrew. In March, he reiterated at Mao Khe and was again defeated. His Chinese advisors recommended that, following Mao's example, Giap should practice guerilla warfare. Undaunted, Giap tried again in May at Ninh Binh and was beaten lock, stock, and barrel. This time, Giap retreated to Viet-Bac for "a period of rest, ideological remoulding, reorganization and military training."[40]

But such was the fate of France that, after the death of his son, an ailing de Lattre had to go back to Paris where he died on January 11, 1952. Anyway, the war was definitely settled: In spite of his superior competence, all de Lattre would have been able to do was to create a stalemate paving the way to an honorable departure from Indochina. One month after his death, in February 1952, with 160,000 troops, Giap seized Hoa Binh in spite of heavy French bombing.

On April 12, 1952, General Raoul Salan took over the command of the expeditionary corps. His long stay from 1924 to 1937 in the Thai region had brought him two Laotian sons, two degrees in Laotian and Thai linguistics, a profound knowledge of the country, and a mild opium addiction. Known also as the Mandarin for his oriental fancy, he was "adopted" by de Lattre as his chief of staff.

Salan was the promoter of the "herisson" (hedgehogs) strategy, which allegedly had been used with some success during World War II. At Na San he managed to hold against North Vietnamese assaults. But Giap outwitted him by bypassing Na San to take Nghia Lo on October 17, 1952, and occupying Dien Bien Phu without resistance on November 30, 1952.

The fall of Nghia Lo and Dien Bien Phu marked the beginning of the third phase of Giap's strategy, which consisted of coordinating three fronts—Vietnamese, Cambodian, and Laotian—in order to carry out general offensives.

In May 1953, an event of unfathomable consequence occurred: Almost the entire high command, including Salan the commander in chief, de Linares the commander in Tonkin, and Colonel Allard chief of staff, returned to France upon completion of their tour of duty. Hence, in December 1953, Vo Nguyen Giap forces threatened Lai Chau, the capital of the Thai region.

General Navarre

When, on May 28, 1953, General Navarre came to replace Salan in Indochina, one can say that the die was cast. Yet, for some reason, Navarre caught the eye of a *New York Times* reporter who found in him the best French strategist. On

September 29, 1953, he wrote: "A year ago, none of us could see victory. There was not a prayer. Now we can see it clearly—like light at the end of a tunnel."

Yet Navarre himself had admitted that he was in no way capable of succeeding Salan. He had served as Marshall Juin's chief of staff and nothing in his career destined him for a critical combat post. "He had never served in the Far East and he knew about Indochina what the man of the street knew."[41] Indeed, he had spent more time in the intelligence field than in field operations. But he was keen enough to realize that a military victory was not possible and the best bet would be for a stalemate.[42]

The reason for chosing Navarre stemmed from Marshall Juin's pressure: As he had twice refused the nomination, Juin felt responsible to find a replacement. As Navarre was weighing his options, Juin insisted: "Just say yes and tell the government about your misgivings. But someone has to sacrifice." This was how Navarre made himself the scapegoat of French politics.

It was argued that at the outset Navarre made mistakes in recruiting his staff. On the one hand, he took as deputy chief of operation Colonel Berteil who would convince him to choose Dien Bien Phu as the mooring point for the herisson strategy. On the other hand, he hired Colonel Cogny as his chief of staff, even promoting him to brigadier. Indeed, Cogny was the youngest and the brightest French officer at that time. He graduated from the prestigious Ecole Polytechnique and had a degree in political science as well as a doctorate in jurisprudence. Yet, he would only provide lip service with ambiguous advice and dialectical contradictions. Obviously, he had nothing but contempt for Navarre, describing him as an "air conditioned general who froze me. As for his way of thinking, he disconcerted me like an electronic computer, which I do not succeed in feeding the necessary basic data and, which, unperturbed, bases its reasoning on I-don't-know-what."[43]

In 1950, the war in Korea finally awakened Western consciousness, and the United States forgot Roosevelt's opposition to a return of France in Indochina.

Dien Bien Phu

To be fair, one must say that under normal circumstances, Dien Bien Phu (Map 4) would not have been selected. For the French, it had no strategic value, since they had left it to the Viet Minh in 1952 without even firing a single bullet. At that time, the French command judged that the Viet Minh "occupation of this hole-in-the-ground isn't yet the invasion of Laos."[44] But later the Franco-Laotian treaty compelled the French to undertake defense of the Thai region. Thus, on January 10, 1953 Salan had on his agenda the reoccupation of Dien Bien Phu as the first step of regaining the control of the Thai country.

Situated some 160 miles west of Hanoi and 50 miles south of Lai Chau, the capital of the Thai region, the Dien Bien Phu valley is surrounded by 1,000-meter hills. Originally known as Muong Thanh, it was renamed Dien Bien Phu (Border County Prefecture) after French Auguste Pavie signed a treaty of protectorate on April 7, 1889, with the Ho tribe leader Deo Van Tri. Only one road, the RC 41, linked Dien Bien Phu to Lai Chau,

The decision to choose Dien Bien Phu alerted the French government. By a tradition dating from Clemenceau, who found that "war was a too serious matter to be left to the military," at the end of January 1954, Armed Forces Secretary De Chevigne flew to Dien Bien Phu with Air Force Chief of Staff General Fay and Army Chief of Staff General Blanc.

To a question from General Fay concerning the possible flooding of airstrips after heavy rains, Navarre had this startling answer: "I was never made aware of this defect."[45] Yet, the Hedgehog strategy depended entirely on the assistance of the aviation. As for de Chevigne, he found the entire garrison in the highest mood: From the commander to the last artillery man, everyone wished an immediate confrontation with the Viet Minh.

On February 9, 1954, new Defense Minister Réné Pleven arrived with the Chairman of the Joint Chief of Staff General Ely. To Pleven, the artillery commander Colonel Piroth strongly affirmed that the Viet would never be able to scratch a single bit of his installation for they would be identified and destroyed in ten minutes. When Pleven offered him to freely serve himself on the existing weapons reserves, an irritated Piroth retorted: "What? Look at my firing plans. I have more cannons than I need."[46] He had only twenty four 105 guns, one 155 battery, and 16 heavy mortars. Perhaps he was not aware that the Viet Minh had some "twenty-four 105 mm Howitzers, twenty 75-mm Howitzers, twenty 120-mm mortars, forty 82-mm mortars, eighty 37-mm guns, 100 antiaircraft guns, and 16 Katyusha six-tube rocket launchers"[47] well hidden in the surrounding hills. Anyway, in some military cultures, there is no clear line between bravado and bravery.

Later, at a secret meeting in Paris, the three generals, Ely, Fay, and Blanc, ruled out a military victory. Blanc forcefully advocated the immediate evacuation of Dien Bien Phu. It might then have been too late, for Vo Nguyen Giap had assembled 49,000 men in the valley in 4 units: the 308th, the 312th, the 316th and the 351st heavy division.

On March 13, 1954, the battle began by an artillery attack, which came as a complete surprise to the French: As a stroke of fate, the first volley hit Gabrielle's command post and killed the entire staff, including Colonel Gaucher, the commander of the famous 13th armored division of the Foreign Legion. The two outposts, Beatrice and Anne-Marie, succumbed under Viet Minh human waves after the desertion of their Thai units. When French aircraft were sent out to destroy Viet cannons, they were downed by Russian flack manned by Chinese artillerymen, even before they could identify enemy positions. In the evening, the air strip was destroyed together with a large quantity of airplanes; in desperation, Colonel Piroth removed with his teeth the pin of a grenade and holding it against his chest with his remaining hand (he had lost an arm during World War II) let it go. To prevent troop demoralization, his body was secretly buried in a corner of the command post.

On March 15, 1954, French High Commissioner Dejean and Commander in Chief Navarre knew that there was no way out except a U.S. intervention from the air. It was the Vulture operation for which U.S. Admiral Radford dispatched two aircraft carriers to the Gulf of Tonkin. To obtain congressional approval, Secretary Dulles sought a coalition with Great Britain. But Churchill and Eden opposed any hostile action that could jeopardize the forthcoming Geneva conference with the Soviet Union. Indeed, after the death of Stalin on March 5, 1953, the end of the Korean war was made possible by joint Sino-Soviet declarations: the Chinese newspaper *Jen Min Jih Pao* and the Russian organ *Pravda* were for the first time advocating peaceful resolutions to international disputes.

As for Indochina, on September 2, Dulles declared that the West wanted peace in Indochina also—if Red China wanted it. In France, on October 27, 1953, Premier Laniel declared that he was ready to make peace. On November 26 and December 17, Ho Chi Minh also expressed his desire for a peaceful settlement with France.

The Berlin Conference

Thus, the four powers, United States, France, Great Britain, and Russia, met in Berlin on January 25, 1954, to discuss Indochina and Korea. Before the meeting, Molotov offered Bidault Russia's help for an armistice with North Vietnam; in exchange, France would stay away from the European Defense Community (EDC). During the meeting, Molotov insisted on having China participate in peace talks. The Berlin conference ended with a consensus to meet again in Geneva with the presence of China.

As for the United States, it wanted the French to continue fighting. Operation Vulture was set up to include large scale U.S. bombing. The project was rescinded upon British refusal to be involved in the Indochinese conflict. But according to Bernard Fall, Dulles was so concerned that, on April 14, he told French Premier Bidault: "And if we give you two atomic bombs to save Dien Bien Phu?"[48] This version, although not officially confirmed and for a good reason, was also discussed by Jules Roy in his book, *La bataille de Dien Bien Phu.*

On April 23, 1954, the Viet Minh took the Dien Bien Phu airstrip. Then one by one, all positions fell. On May 7, 1954, after 36 days of heroic resistance, Dien Bien Phu surrendered, costing France 20,000 dead and wounded and 6,500 prisoners[49] against an unconfirmed 10,000 Viet killed and 20,000 wounded.

The Geneva Conference: A Farce

The following day, May 8, the Geneva Conference opened. Called by the Allies to take part, Bao Dai reluctantly dispatched his delegates who had lost faith in the Bao Dai solution. They were opposed to the division of Vietnam into North and South of the 17th parallel. Yet, that partition was the only way for them to survive. Apparently, the loser was North Vietnam who, under Chinese pressure, renounced immediate reunification for which they had been fighting so hard.

Probably peace might not be on the minds of the participants. The Chinese, by having North Vietnam accept the partition (with option for a referendum later), intended to demonstrate their leadership in Asia thus, justifying their claim to a seat among the superpowers. Indeed, on October 8, 1953, Chou En-lai had declared that without the participation of the People's Republic of China, it was impossible to settle any international problem, above all the question of Asia. Therefore the United Nations, he said, must first restore the legitimate rights of the People's Republic of China. As for the Russians, by helping the French to prolong their stay in South Vietnam, they expected to win rejection of the EDC. As for the United States, their refusal to sign the accord portended their support for a real anticommunist South Vietnam. As for Great Britain, ANZUS had led to enough trouble with the United States.

As for France, although the defeat affected only 4 percent of her total forces, she had to deal with more crucial problems right in her own backyard: the insurgency in Algeria. Yet, according to Bernard Fall, "the eight years of war had cost the French about $10 billion (in addition to $1.1 billion the United States aid delivered before the cease-fire), and 172,000 dead or missing, including three generals and 2,000 other officers."[50]

The Geneva Conference ended with a "final declaration" which as Devillers and Lacouture said in *End of a War: Indochina 1954* "bore no signatures whatsoever, simply took note of the other texts." Furthermore, by setting a referendum for July 1956, the Conference apparently left the reunification problem to the Vietnamese themselves.

Failure to grasp this implication led the United States to carry out 20 more years of a war that deeply divided the nation at home and challenged American prestige abroad.

On July 20, 1954. the curtain fell on the last scene: As French general Berteil and North Vietnam political commissar Ta Quang Buu together signed the Geneva accords, Buu asked: "And, now I hope that you will take a glass of champagne with us?" And Berteil replied: "You will understand that I cannot accept."[51]

End of the Bao Dai Solution

After Dien Bien Phu, Bao Dai took Ngo Dinh Diem as his prime minister. Given the long-term relationship between them, the fact that he demanded from Diem an oath of absolute obedience might seem ludicrous at best. Actually, it revealed that Diem's appointment was not his own choice but was forced upon him by those powers that had finally realized that the "Bao Dai solution" was not viable. It had become obvious to all parties that a membership in the French Union was not compatible with a true independence. Thus, in spite of his vow of loyalty, Premier Ngo Dinh Diem would oppose such a fallacy. But for him the most urgent task was to reestablish law and order.

Cochinchina had become a chaotic land of unruled warlords. In the provinces, a Eurasian, Leroy, first lieutenent in the French army, held the province of Bentre with his private troops. Chinese priest Father Hoa had his own Catholic legion in another sector. Hoa Hao and Cao Daists held their own territories in Tay Ninh and the west. In Saigon and the suburbs, the notorious Binh Xuyen gang controlled at the same time the city police, casinos, and brothels.

Under pressure from the French and Bao Dai, Diem had to take some of the Hoa Hao, Cao Dai, and Binh Xuyen leaders into his cabinet. Now they wanted government subsidies for their troops and stars for their officers, but adamantly refused to integrate into the national army. To force the issue, the sects provoked a government crisis by withdrawing their representatives from the cabinet, giving Diem an ultimatum to form another cabinet within five days. In response, Diem closed the "Grand Monde" casinos, vital resources of the Binh Xuyen. In a second step, he removed Binh Xuyen Lai Huu Sang from his post of Saigon police chief.

Diem's repressive policy first stumbled over the reluctance of the South Vietnamese army to start a conflict with the sects because a certain proportion of troops were adepts of the Hoa Hao or the Cao Dai. Yet, given their arrogance, the army was quite willing to give them a "good lesson." Thus, with support from Bao Dai, Chief of Staff General Nguyen Van Hinh refused to cooperate and even threatened Diem with a coup d'etat. To keep him away, Lansdale managed to get him invited to the Philippines by President Magsaysay. Later, Hinh claimed to have been duped. But the fact of the matter was that his authority over the regular forces was only nominal: Coming from the French army, he was considered a "French officer" without any close connection with the native officers formed in Vietnam. Thus, there was little chance that he could rally the army against Diem. On November 11, 1954, Diem sacked Hinh. As Bao Dai protested, Diem had President Eisenhower confirm by writing America's support for his government. As inspector General Nguyen Van Vy refused to take over the command, he was put behind bars. Actually, Vy's refusal was not due to his support for Hinh but his repugnance of serving Diem. Only when famous paratrooper Colonel Do Cao Tri threatened to attack his palace did Diem accept to release Vy.

General J. Lawton Collins, extraordinary envoy of President Eisenhower, was not happy with the troubles stirred up by Diem and said so to Washington. A decision was made to replace Diem when news of his victory over the sects came to change all plans. Indeed, with only the help of Lansdale, Diem succeeded in obtaining the allegiance of Hoa Hao and Cao Dai: Hoa Hao General Tran Van Soai (Nam Lua) received $3 million to go into a trouble-free retirement. For $3.6 million—the most expensive acquisition at that moment— Nguyen Thanh Phuong, chief of staff of the Cao Daist army went back to Tay Ninh Holy See to place his superior, Pham Cong Tac, under house arrest. On

February 13, 1955, Cao Daist dissident Trinh Minh The also pocketed $2 million to rally Diem.[52]

Then with Nung[53] mercenaries, Trinh Minh The's troops and the South Vietnam army, General Duong Van Minh (Big Minh) put down the "Binh Xuyen pirates." In the process, the South Vietnamese paratroopers went into a horrible carnage: During an attack on the Lycee Petrus Ky where a Binh Xuyen battalion had taken position, many rebels pleaded for mercy: "Stop! Please stop. I already surrender. Why do you want to kill me?"[54] When this drama unfolded, the emperor watched it on television in his Cannes residence. Urged by his director of cabinet Nguyen De to fly back, he replied: "Go back if you like and take the power if you want. As for me, I have no need to be killed."

On October 23, 1955, after having eliminated the sects, Diem undertook to eliminate his king. In a national referendum, he won 98 percent of votes and became president of the first Republic of South Vietnam. His mystical nature and his close connection with the Catholic Church were not conducive to an "entente" with a communist regime, and hence, to a North Vietnam approach for reunification. Diem rejected the elections provided by the Geneva convention. Hanoi's subsequent creation of a National Liberation Front would draw South Vietnam into a 20-year labyrinth of war and destruction in which Diem and his brother, Nhu, would lose their lives.

As for Bao Dai, now financially secure, he safely retired to his Cannes residence. For him, there were no illusions lost: No later than 1950 he had realized that there was no Bao Dai solution, but a French solution."[55]

In the Aftermath

Ngo Dinh Diem's first move on January 19, 1956, was to advise the French that their presence was incompatible with the concept of a Vietnam independence. On April 10, the French army paraded for the last time in Saigon before boarding a ship named SS *L'Esperance*.

But France was by no means at the end of her misery. The most salient effect of the Dien Bien Phu defeat was the loss of army prestige and the ensuing troops' demoralization. According to Jean Larteguy, those who survived detention in North Vietnam camps went home to become Roman Legions.[56] The Viet Minh reeducation process had opened their eyes on the fallacy of their Republican system. They now realized that they had been the scapegoats of unscrupulous politicians. All commanders from Cogny to Navarre, although both embroiled in a bitter controversy over Dien Bien Phu, unanimously rejected the ultimate responsibility to the government. As for the troops, having lost their pristine loyalty, they wanted nothing more than to throw ministers and politicians into the Seine River.[57] Assigned now to fight in Algeria, they wanted to make sure that no other Dien Bien Phu could happen by the politics of the parties. In August 1954, analyzing the spirit of the army, General Cherriere, commander of French troops in Algeria, noted the "rancour and contempt for all those who shared the responsibility of the Indochina war."[58]

Navarre also gave the signal for rebellion: The true reason of our defeat in Indochina is political . . . It is the end of three centuries of military obedience . . . of this "great mute" that had served the motherland through various governments and regimes." Again in 1957, he repeated, "We had no policy at all. After seven years of fighting, we reached imbroglio and no one from the private to the commander in chief knew why in fact he was fighting."[59]

In October 1954, General Chassin, ex-Air Force commander in Indochina, called for a general awakening: "It is time for the Army to cease being la grande muette (the "great mute"). It is time for the free world . . . to apply some of its adversary methods. And one of these methods, resides in the ideological role which is reserved to the military forces."[60] Thus, back home, Dien Bien Phu paratroopers adopted the Viet Minh doctrine of psychological warfare and had "political officers" trained in special schools.

The Indochinese war was also an unexpected opportunity for soldiers from other colonies to learn for the sake of their own emancipation. Thus the North Africans also rose up to demand independence. While the problem was relatively easy for Tunisia and Morocco, in Algeria the presence of long generations of French rural settlers called "pieds noirs" (black foot), became the stumbling block for political change. Like the Indochinese colons, they did not want independence but a French Algeria.

On May 13, 1958, 100,000 students seized the seat of the governor general in Algiers, demanding the resignation of the French cabinet and the transfer of power to the army. Indochinese old hands Salan, Massu, and Cogny demanded the dissolution of the parlementarian regime and a public salvation government in Paris "to prevent another Dien Bien Phu in North Africa.[61] The gendarmery and the CRS,[62] sent to defend the Republic, refused to intervene. Paratrooper Colonel Trinquier was carried in triumph by the crowd. He said: "You are crazy. How can anyone seize the power alone?" And the crowd chanted: "Yes, yes, you can do everything."

On February 6, while the National Assembly was celebrating the anniversary of the Fourth Republic, a bomb exploded in the toilets of its Palais Bourbon. The following April, a poll of public opinion rated the performance of the Fourth Republic below that of the United States, West Germany, Great Britain, and even the USSR.

On June 2, 1950, upon the news that paratroopers from Algiers were about to land in Paris, a terrified National Assembly remitted its powers to General de Gaulle. The fourth French Republic ceased to exist.

NOTES

1. Ellen Hammer, *Struggle for Indochina*, pp. 42–43.
2. GBT stands for Gordon Laurence (Canadian), a Texaco oil director in Haiphong,

Bernard Harry (British), a tobacco businessman, and Tan Frank (Chinese American), who later went to work for an important Sino-American company in Saigon during the American war.

3. According to Chen King C., "The gold unit (Kuan Chin) was then a new banknote valued at 20 times the old Chinese currency. Both notes were in circulation." See King C. Chen, *Vietnam and China: 1938–1954*, p. 134f.

4. Raoul Salan, *Indochine rouge*, p. 17.

5. Ibid., p. 159.

6. Ibid., p. 25.

7. Phillipe Devillers, *Histoire du Vietnam*, p. 242.

8. Ibid., p. 16.

9. Philippe Devillers, *Histoire du Vietnam*, p. 170.

10. Ibid., p. 367.

11. Joseph Buttinger, *Vietnam: A Dragon Embattled*, p. 1015.

12. The author was at the meeting.

13. King C. Chen, *Vietnam and China*, p. 158 n.6.

14. Salan, *Indochine Rouge*, p. 17.

15. Ibid., pp. 17–18.

16. Arthur Laurent, *La Banque de l'Indochine et la piastre*, p. 25.

17. Roger Delpey, *Dien Bien Phu l'affaire*, p. 79.

18. Lucien Bodard, *The Quicksand War: Prelude to Vietnam*, pp. 169–70.

19. Hammer, *The Struggle for Indochina*, p. 273.

20. It was 17 francs to 1 piastre.

21. Arthur Laurent, *La Banque de l'Indochine*, p. 206.

22. Not to be confused with author Arthur Laurent.

23. According to Laurent, his real name was Olivier Serge, a BIC finance director.

24. Jacques Despuech, *Le trafic de la piastre,* pp. 47–48.

25. Ibid., p. 156. RPF was the Gaullist "Rassemblement du peuple Français" party.

26. Arthur Laurent, *La Banque de l'Indochine*, p. 135.

27. Ibid., p. 74.

28. Ibid., p. 78.

29. Gold cost 500,000 francs in Paris and 1,275,000 in Saigon. The U.S. dollar cost 35 francs in Paris or 850 francs in Saigon.

30. At that time, a brother-in-law of the author was an agent of that powerful Indochina Customs Fraud Service having jurisdiction all over the Indochinese Federation.

31. Donald Lancaster, *The Emancipation of French Indochina*, p. 270.

32. Service d'espionnage et de contre espionnage.

33. Jacques Despuech, *Le trafic*, pp. 89–96.

34. Lucien Bodard, *L'illusion*, p. 273.

35. King C. Chen, *Vietnam and China*, pp. 261–263.

36. Bernard Fall, *Street Without Joy*, p. 33.

37. Ibid., p. 139.

38. Jean Larteguy, *La guerre nue*, p. 139.

39. Robert Shaplen, *The Lost Revolution*, p. 79.

40. King C. Chen, *Vietnam and China*, pp. 267–268, citing Vietnamese studies No. 7, p. 111.

41. Roger Delpey, *Dien Bien Phu l'affaire*, p. 21.

42. Bernard Fall, *The Two Vietnams*, p. 147.

43. Bernard Fall, *Hell in a Very Small Place*, p. 27.

44. Ibid., p. 25.

45. Philippe Devillers and Jean Lacouture, *Vietnam; De la guerre française á la guerre americaine*, p. 74.

46. Jules Roy, *La bataille de Dien Bien Phu*, pp. 209–210.

47. Ibid.

48. Bernard Fall, *Hell in a Very Small Place*, pp. 306–307.

49. Ibid., pp. 483–484.

50. Bernard Fall, *Vietnam Witness*, pp. 38–39.

51. Philippe Devillers and Jean Lacouture, *End of a War*, pp. 299–300.

52. Bernard Fall, *The Two Vietnams*, p. 282.

53. North Vietnam tribe.

54. This author was an eyewitness.

55. Robert Shaplen, *The Lost Revolution*, p. 64.

56. Jean Larteguy, *La guerre nue*, pp. 310–312.

57. Jean Ferniot, *De Gaulle et le 13 Mai*, p. 141.

58. Ibid., p. 60.

59. Ibid., p. 22.

60. Ibid., p. 21.

61. Ibid., p. 31.

62. Equivalent of the American SWAT teams.

BIBLIOGRAPHY

Bain, Chester. *Vietnam: Roots of Conflicts*. Englewood Cliffs, N.J.: Prentice-Hall, 1967.

Bernard, Paul. *Le probleme economique indochinois*. Paris: Nouvelles Editions Latines, 1934.

Blythe, Wilfred. *Impact of Chinese Secret Societies*. London: Oxford University Press, 1969.

Bodard, Lucien. *The Quicksand War: Prelude to Vietnam*. Boston: Little, Brown & Co., 1967.

Bowles, Gordon. *People of Asia*. New York: Charles Scribner's Sons, 1977.

Browne, Malcolm W. *New Face of War*. New York: Bobbs-Merrill Co., 1968.

Bui Dac Hum. *Outline of Cao Daism*. Redlands, Calif.: Chan Tam, 1994.

Burchett, Wilfred. *The Furtive War*. New York: International Publishers, 1963.

———. *Vietnam Inside Story*. New York: International Publishers, 1965.

Buttinger, Joseph, *Vietnam: A Dragon Embattled*. New York: Praeger, 1967.

Cadiere, Leopold. *Croyances et pratiques religieuses des Vietnamiens*. Paris: EFEO, 1992.

Cady, John F. *Roots of French Imperialism*. Ithaca, N.Y.: Cornell University Press, 1954.

———. *Southeast Asia: Its historical development*. New York: McGraw-Hill Book Co., 1964.

Cao Huy Thuan. *Dao Thien Chua va Chu Nghia Thuc dan tai Vietnam*. Los Angeles: Huong Que, 1988.

Chan, Hok Lam. *White Lotus-Maitreya, and Popular Uprisings*. Sinologica X, 4.

Chapuis, Oscar. *A History of Vietnam: From Hong Bang to Tu Duc*. Westport, Conn.: Greenwood Publishing Group, 1995.

Chen, King C. *Vietnam and China 1938–1954*. Princeton, N.J.: Princeton University, 1969.

Chesneaux, J. *Popular Movements and Secret Societies*. Stanford, Calif.: Stanford University Press, 1932.

———. *Peasant Revolts in China*. Ann Arbor: University of Michigan Press, 1971.

———. *Secret Societies in China in the Nineteenth and Twentieth Centuries*. Ann Arbor: University of Michigan, Press, 1971.

Chinh Dao. *Vietnam Nien Bieu Nhan Vat Chi*. Houston, Tex.: Van Hoa, 1997.

Collins, John J., *Primitive Religion*. Lanham, Md.: Rowman & Littlefield, 1978.
Corson, William. *The Betrayal*. New York: W. W. Norton & Co., 1968.
Cotterel, Arthur. *China: A Cultural History*. New York: Penguin Group, 1988.
Coulet, Georges. *Les Societes secretes en terre d'Annam*. Saigon: Imprimerie Ardin, 1926.
Dalloz, Jacques. *The War in Indochina*. Savage, Md.: Barnes and Noble, 1990.
Darcourt, Pierre. *Bay Vien the Master of Cho Lon*. Paris: Hachette, 1977.
Dat Si and Nguyen Van Hau. *That Son Mau Nhiem*. Los Angeles: Dai Nam, 1955.
Davidson, Phillip B. *Vietnam at War. The History: 1946–1975*. New York: Oxford University Press, 1988.
Delpey, Roger. *Dien Bien Phu l'affaire*. Paris: Ed. Pensee moderne, 1974.
Despuech, Jacques. *Le trafic de la piastre*. Paris: Ed. des deux rives, 1963.
Devillers, Philippe. *Histoire du Vietnam de 1940 á 1952*. Paris: Editions du Seuil, 1952.
Devillers, Philippe and Jean Lacouture. *Vietnam: De la guerre francaise á la guerre americaine*. Paris: Editions du Seuil, 1969.
Diem Bui, and D. Chanoff. *In the Jaws of History*. Boston: Houghton Mifflin Co., 1987.
Do Mau. *Vietnam: Mau Lua Que Huong Toi*. Mission Hills, Calif.: Que Huong, 1986.
Do Van Ly. *Tim Hieu Dao Cao Dai*. Perris, Calif.: Cao Dai Giao Vietnam Hai Ngoai, 1989.
Dong Tan. *Su-luoc Dao Cao-Dai*. Saigon: Cao Hien Xuat Ban, 1972.
Du Berrier, Hilaire. *Background to Betrayal*. Boston: Western Islands, 1965.
Duby, Georges. *Histoire de la France des origines á nos jours*. Paris: Larousse, 1995.
Duncanson, Dennis J. *Government and Revolution in Vietnam*. New York: Oxford University Press, 1968.
Duong, Quang Ham. *Vietnam van-Hoc Su-yeu*. Los Angeles: Dai Nam Reprint, n.d.
Fall, Bernard. *Political and Religious Sects in Vietnam*. Richmond, Va.: Pacific Affairs, September 1955.
————. *Street Without Joy*. New York: Schocken Books, 1967.
————. *The Two Vietnams*. New York: Frederick A. Praeger, 1967.
————. *Hell in a Very Small Place*. New York: Vintage Books, 1968.
Favier, Jean. *Histoire de France*. Paris: Moliere, 1993.
Fitzgerald, Frances. *Fire in the Lake*. New York: Random House, 1972.
Gelb, Leslie. *Irony of Vietnam*. Washington, D.C.: Brookings Institution, 1979.
Gettleman, Marvin E. *Vietnam*. New York: Penguin Books, 1967.
Gobron, Gabriel. *History and Philosophy of Caodaism*. Saigon: Le Van Tan, 1950.
Groslier, Bernard. *Indochina*. New York: World Publishing Co., 1966.
Gruening, Ernest, and Beaser H. Wilston. *Vietnam Folly*. Washington D.C.: National Press Inc., 1968.
Halberstam, David. *The Making of a Quagmire*. New York: Random House, 1964.
Hall, D. G. E. *A History of Southeast Asia*. New York: St. Martin's Press, 1964.
Hammer, Ellen J. *The Struggle for Indochina*. Stanford, Calif.: Stanford University Press, 1954.
Hastedt, Glenn P. *American Foreign Policy*. Englewood Cliffs, N.J.: Prentice-Hall, 1988.
Hendry, James Bausch. *Small World of Khanh Hau*. Glenside, Pa.: Aldine Publications, 1964.
Hickey, Gerald C. *Village in Vietnam*. New Haven, Conn.: Yale University Press, 1964.
Hirth, Friedrich. *The Ancient History of China to the End of the Chou Dynasty*. Freeport, NY: Books for Libraries Press, 1969.
Hobsbaum, Eric. *Primitive Rebels*. Manchester, N.H.: University Press, 1959.

Ho Tai Hue Tam. *Millenarianism and Peasant Politics in Vietnam*. Cambridge, Mass.: Harvard University Press, 1983.

———. *Radicalism and the Origins of the Vietnam Revolution*. Cambridge, Mass.: Harvard University Press, 1992.

Huong Hieu. *Dao Su Xay Ban*. Washington D.C.: Reprint, 1994.

Hutin, Serge. *Les societes secretes en Chine*. Paris: Robert Laffont, 1976.

Kahler, Miles. *Decolonization in Britain and France*. Princeton, N.J.: Princeton University Press, 1984.

Karnow, Stanley. *Vietnam: A History*. New York: Penguin Books, 1983.

Kim Nhat. *Ve R*. Los Angeles: Dai Nam, 1967.

Lamb, Helen. *Vietnam Will to Live*. New York: Monthly Review Press, 1972.

Lancaster, Donald. *The Emancipation of French Indochina*. New York: Oxford University Press, 1961.

Larteguy, Jean. *Les pretoriens*. Paris: Presses Pocket, 1961.

———. *Les centurions*. Paris: Presses Pocket, 1961.

———. *La guerre nue*. Paris: Stock, 1976.

Laurent, Arthur. *La Banque de l'Indochine et la piastre*. Paris: Edition des Deux Rives, 1954.

Le Thanh Khoi. *Histoire du Vietnam*. Paris: Sudestasie, 1992.

Le Van Sieu. *Vietnam Van Minh Su Cuong*. Saigon: Song Moi, 1983.

Li Tana and Anthony Reed. *Southern Vietnam under the Nguyen*. Singapore: SEA studies, 1993

Louis, Henard Nicole. *Une épisode ignorée de l'historie d'Annam*. Paris: BEFEO, 1986.

Lyle, E. R., II. *China's Resources*. Washington, D.C.: University Press of America, 1977.

Manich, Jumsai M. L. *History of Thailand and Cambodia*. Bangkok: Chalermit, 1970.

Marr, David G. *Vietnamese Anticolonialism*. Berkeley: University of California Press, 1971.

———. *Vietnam 1945, Quest for Power*. Los Angeles: University of California Press, 1995.

Maspero, Henri. *Etudes d'histoire d'Annam*. Hanoi: Imprimerie Extreme Orient, 1917.

McAleavy, Henry. *Black Flags in Vietnam: The Story of a Chinese Intervention*. New York: Macmillan Co., n.d.

McAllister, and Paul Mus. *The Vietnamese and Their Revolution*. New York: Harper & Row, 1970.

McLeod, Marc W. *Vietnamese Response to French Intervention*. Westport, Conn.: Praeger, 1991.

Melling, Phil, and Jon Roper. *America, France and Vietnam. Cultural History and Ideas of Conflict*. Brookfield, Mass.: Gover, 1991.

Miquel, Pierre. *Histoire de la France de Vercingetorix á de Gaulle*. St. Amand (Cher): Bussiere, 1997.

Mus, Paul. *The Role of the Village in Vietnam Politics*. Richmond, Va.: Pacific Affairs, September 1949.

———. *Ho Chi Minh, le Vietnam, l'Asie*. Paris: Editions du Seuil, 1971.

Ngo Si Lien. *Dai Viet Su Ky Toan Thu*. Los Angeles: Dai Nam Reprint, n.d.

Nguyen Chanh Thi. *Vietnam: Mot troi tam su*. Los Alamitos, Calif: Xuan Thua, 1987.

Nguyen Khac Ngu and Nguyen Dinh Tieu. *Dia ly Viet-nam*. Saigon: Co So xuat ban Su Dia, Reprint, n.d.

———. *Ky Dong nha cach mang*. Montreal: Tu Sach Nghien cuu Su Dia, 1990.

————. *Lien Lac Viet Phap XVII, XVIII*. Montreal: Tu Sach Nghien cuu Su Dia, 1990.

Nguyen Khac Vien. *Histoire du Vietnam*. Paris: Editions sociales, 1974.

Nguyen The Anh. *Nationalism Vietnamien au debut 20 siécle*. Paris: BEFEO, 1978.

Nguyen Tien Hung and Jerrold L. Schecter. *The Palace file*. New York: Harper & Row, 1986.

Nguyen Van Trung. *Chu Nghia Thuc Dan Phap*. Saigon: Nam Son, 1963.

Osborne, Milton. *River Road to China*. London: George Allen & Unwin, 1975.

Overmayer, Daniel. *Folk Buddhist Religion*. Cambridge, Mass.: Harvard University Press, 1976.

Patti, Archimede. *Why Vietnam?* Berkeley: University of California Press, 1980.

Pham Cao Duong. *Vietnamese Peasants under French Domination*. Berkeley: University of California Press, 1985.

Pham Van Son. *Viet Su Tan Bien*. Los Angeles: Dai Nam reprint, 1958.

Phan Boi Chau. *Vietnam Vong Quoc Su*. Houston, Tex.: Xuan Thu Reprint, n.d.

Phan Khoang. *Lich Su Dang Trong*. Houston, Tex.: Xuan Thu reprint, n.d.

Melling, Phil, and Jon Roper. *America, France and Vietnam. Cultural History and Ideas of Conflict*. Brookfield, Mass.: Gover, 1991.

Pym, Christopher. *Henri Mouhot: Diary*. Kuala Lumpur: Oxford University Press, 1966.

Roy, Jules. *La Bataille de Dien Bien Phu*. Paris: Union generale d'éditions, 1963.

Salan, Raoul. *Indochine rouge*. Paris: Presse de la Cité, 1945.

Sar, Desai D.R *Vietnamese Trials and Tribulations*. Long Beach, Calif.: Long Beach Publication, 1988.

Shaplen, Robert. *The Lost Revolution*. New York: Harper & Row, 1965.

Smith, Ralph. *Vietnam and the West*. Ithaca, N.Y.: Cornell University Press, 1968.

Tanham, George K. *Communist Revolutionary Warfare*. New York: Frederick A. Praeger, 1961.

Thanh Ngon Hiep Tuyen. New Orleans, La.: Hoi Tin Huu Cao Dai, 1992.

Thich Nhat Hanh. *Vietnam: Lotus in a Sea of Fire*. New York: Hill and Wang, 1967.

Thompson, Virginia. *French Indochina*. New York: Octagon Books, 1968.

Toa Thanh Tay Ninh. *Tieu Su Pham Cong Tac*, n.d.

Toan Anh. *Phong Tuc Viet Nam*. Los Angeles: Dai Nam Reprint, n.d.

Topley, Marjorie. *Great Way of Former Heaven*. BSOAS, 1963.

Toye, Hugh. *Laos Buffer State*. London: Oxford University Press, 1968.

Tran Trong Kim. *Vietnam Su Luoc*. Los Angeles: Dai Nam Reprint, n.d.

Tran Van Don. *Vietnam nhan chung*. Los Alamitos: Xuan Thu, 1989.

Tran Van Giap. *Le Bouddhisme en Annam*. Hanoi: BEFEO, 1932–33.

Tran Van Rang. *Dai Dao Su Cuong*. Tay Ninh: Toa Thanh Tay Ninh, 1970.

Trinh Van Thanh, *Thanh Ngu Dien Tich danh Nhan Tu-Dien* (Dictionary of Vietnamese Celebrities). Vol. 2. Glendale, Calif.: Dai Nam Reprint, 1966.

Truong Buu Lam. *Patterns of Vietnamese Response to Foreign Intervention, 1858–1900*. New Haven, Conn.: Yale University SEA Studies, 1967.

Truong Nhu Tang. *A Viet Cong Memoir*. New York: Random House, 1986.

Vo Nguyen Giap. *Guerre du peuple, Armee du peuple*. Hanoi: Langues étrangères, 1961.

Wallace, Anthony F. C. *Religion: An Anthropological View*. New York: Random House, 1966.

Werner, Jayne Susan. *Peasant politics*. New Haven, Conn: Yale University SEA Studies 1981.

INDEX

About the Author

OSCAR CHAPUIS is a former French Merchant Marine Captain who served as maritime inspector for the French High Commissioner in Indochina and as a maritime expert at the Saigon Court of Appeals. He was Professor at the Vietnam Maritime College, and he acted as a speaker on Vietnamese culture at the Multi-cultural Mental Health Training Program (MMHTP) at the University of South Florida. His other books include *A History of Vietnam* (Greenwood, 1995).

ISBN 0-313-31170-6

EAN

9 780313 311703

90000>

HARDCOVER BAR CODE